The Matrix of Christian Ethics provides a comprehensive, readable, and up-to-date overview of Christian ethical thought. Interacting with classical and contemporary theologians and philosophers, Nullens and Michener find a balanced approach that integrates Scripture, theology, and history for addressing the issues of our time. An ideal textbook for the classroom.

DENNIS P. HOLLINGER, Ph.D.
President & Colman M. Mockler Distinguished Professor of Christian Ethics
Gordon-Conwell Theological Seminary, South Hamilton, MA

Eminently readable and theologically nuanced, *The Matrix of Christian Ethics* serves as an excellent primer in Christian ethics. The evangelical approach of Nullens and Michener does justice to the often complex situations that we face by advocating an integrative approach that takes the best from each of the main ethical models. The result is a charitable and insightful book that takes seriously the values, norms, virtues, and purposes at stake in the Christian life.

HANS BOERSMA
J. I. Packer Professor of Theology
Regent College, Vancouver, BC

This is one of the few introductions in Christian ethical thinking that offers both moral philosophy and theological ethics. *The Matrix of Christian Ethics* is written with evangelical passion, intellectual honesty, and a sensitive awareness of the moral perplexities of our postmodern, global era in a clear and attractive style that surely will seduce our students!

FRITS DE LANGE
Professor of Ethics
Protestant Theological University, Kampen, The Netherlands

W9-CYC-201

The Matrix

of

Christian Ethics

Integrating Philosophy and
Moral Theology in a Postmodern Context

Patrick Nullens & Ronald T. Michener

Paternoster:
thinking faith

Paternoster Publishing
A Ministry of Biblica
We welcome your questions and comments.

USA   1820 Jet Stream Drive, Colorado Springs, CO 80921
        www.authenticbooks.com
India   Logos Bhavan, Medchal Road, Jeedimetla Village, Secunderabad
        500 055, A.P.

The Matrix of Christian Ethics
ISBN-13: 978-1-60657-042-5

12 11 10 / 6 5 4 3 2 1

Published in 2010 by Paternoster

A catalog record for this book is available through the Library of Congress.

Printed in the United States of America

Contents

Preface

Christian ethics is one of those topics that many believe to be a simple truism. A Christian is seen as one who has been handed his or her values "down from above," as it were. After all, there is a direct connection between the values of a Christian and the values of the Bible. With deeper reflection, however, we understand such notions to be sheer naiveté. The hermeneutical distance between us and the text of the Bible combined with the complexities of today's multicultural, postmodern world plainly demands a loss of innocence.

Christian ethics today must be about the business of charitable bridge building across cultures, races, languages, and continents; between the ancient world and contemporary life; and between philosophy and theology. A relevant Christian ethics must reflect the "matrix" of influences coloring everyday life. Massive amounts of information and correspondence can be sent and received from multiple continents in multiple languages via a variety of media. We can be on a business trip in Brussels today, leave for Tokyo tomorrow, then relax on a beach in Florida with our family and friends the following week. Moreover, the evangelical Christian church has become increasingly diversified in its expression, from fundamentalism to postconservatism, and from paleo-orthodoxy to emerging-church communities. Many are asking what it means to be Christian or evangelical in a pluralistic world racing along the uncontrollable information highway, where there are competing worldviews. More than ever, as committed Christ followers we must demonstrate intellectual honesty with theological and international hospitality in the quest to manifest the reality of Jesus' love in our conversations, commitments, and moral decisions. In this book we attempt a modest step in this direction.

As for the authors, we were raised in different lands, cultures, and languages. Patrick Nullens is a Flemish, Dutch-speaking Belgian. Ron Michener is a Northwestern U.S.A., English-speaking, American resident of Belgium. Both are professors at the Evangelische Theologische Faculteit in Leuven, Belgium. Nullens brings his rich European heritage and training, along with his service as a pastor and his years of writing and teaching in the field of moral theology. Michener brings his background of many years in church ministry and missions work and several years of writing and teaching in the area of postmodernism and theology. We have learned from each other through the years in a spirit of mutual respect, through both our friendship and our professional work. We also have the experience of building cross-cultural bridges with international students from thirty different nations. With this in mind, we believe we can offer an integrated American-Continental perspective that will provide a unique approach to Christian ethical reflection today.

Christian ethics ultimately probes our deepest sensibilities as humans and how we, as followers of Christ, go about seeking "the good" for others as well as for ourselves. We will provide an introduction to this relevant and contemporary subject through methodological reflection, not only on the norms and purposes but also on the values and virtues of Christian life in today's context.

The postmodern climate allows a radical questioning of the moral foundation often assumed in Western society. We submit that moral behavior is governed and shaped by one's interpretive context in reading the Bible, by the tradition(s) of the church, and by society itself. To address these factors, we seek an integrative approach to ethics, borrowing from classical ethical models such as consequential ethics, principle ethics, virtue ethics, and value ethics. This approach is what we are calling the "matrix of Christian ethics." This matrix theme will be played out in a variety of ways throughout the book, from a discussion of the postmodern situation of ethics and values to a proposal for the ongoing development of Christian ethics today. We will conclude with some practically oriented guidelines to help the reader work through (but not exhaust) contemporary ethical questions and conflicts. We will do this within a framework of biblical wisdom and in view of the ongoing work of the Holy Spirit in the lives of followers of Christ. It is our goal to provide a book that offers scholarly methodological reflection yet remains accessible as a textbook for university and seminary students.

A couple of years ago, Nullens approached Michener with the idea of a complete critical rewriting and reworking of a book Nullens had published in Dutch: *Verlangen naar het goede: Bouwstenen voor een christelijke ethiek* (Zoetermeer, The Netherlands: Boekencentrum, 2006). This is a Christian ethics textbook used at various seminaries and universities in Belgium and the Netherlands. Nullens desired to rewrite the original book for a wider English-speaking audience in both Europe and North America, taking into consideration interpretive challenges for ethics presented by the postmodern critique of rationalism and empiricism. As a result, this book was born in coauthorship. Although we used the basic framework of the original work, *Verlangen naar het Goede*, we have made deletions, additions, and adjustments in such as way that it clearly presents a new English book.

We owe much gratitude to those involved in helping bring this book from its inception to its completion. We thank the *Via Via* café for providing a great ambiance on that rare sunny day in Leuven, when, over a good plate of spaghetti, we decided to do this book together. We express our gratitude to Raymond Volgers and Sarah Bogaers for numerous hours of tedious translation of the original Dutch book into English, which provided a background script for this current work. We are very grateful for our student assistant Michiel DeWolf and for his hours of chasing footnotes and helping with editorial comments, formatting, and indexing the book. We are also grateful for Maaike De Jong for her help with the tedious work of index pagination. Many thanks to Bette Smyth for her careful editing work that has helped make this book more readable, as well as to John Dunham and the rest of the Paternoster staff that have helped bring this book to completion. We also express our appreciation to our faithful colleagues at the Evangelische Theologische Faculteit in Leuven for their encouragement and support of our efforts. Finally (but certainly not in order of importance!), we thank our wives, Jo Nullens and Sandra Michener, for their enduring support and care.

Chapter 1

Introduction

Ethics and Morals

Values and Everyday Choices

Making decisions is something we do every day. Most of these choices we make without much thought. What color of socks will I wear today? Will I eat bran flakes or oatmeal? Most decisions simply happen because they are habits in our daily lives. But in some way or another they do reflect our priorities and are silent witnesses to our worldview. We choose to study for an exam or "wing it," accept one job and refuse another, choose to marry or remain single, drive lawfully or exceed the speed limit, and the list goes on. Some of these choices stem from principles and values we inherited from our parents. They always did it this way, so it becomes natural for us to follow in their footsteps. In other cases we take on values that our parents did not have and purposefully make decisions that reflect a different set of principles than those we were raised with. Regardless, our personal backgrounds and cultures strongly shape the way that we make our decisions—either negatively or positively.

The climate of postmodernity has allowed a radical questioning of those values that once provided the footing to moral worldviews. Values that seemed stable to our parents and grandparents are now scrutinized. This postmodern scrutiny does not necessarily imply that values themselves are pernicious, but it challenges the self-made foundations of Western society that have been used to bolster the value systems of modernity. But, as we all know, life must go on. We continue to pass on our values and principles to our children. "There are rules in this house!" we say with authority. As Christians, of course, we believe that our rules stem from the Bible—in one way or another. The world also has house rules, but sometimes they are not so clear. Slogans such as "Show mutual respect," "Be tolerant of other perspectives," or "Be concerned for the environment" may ring hollow in our ears, but they have, nevertheless, contributed to making society what it is today.

Values and Ethical Crises

Peter is the chairman of his church council and a devout Christian. His wife Christine is the worship leader. They are considered pillars of their local church. One day their sixteen-year-old daughter Emily comes home with shocking news—she is pregnant. Her friends tell her to have an abortion. Her boyfriend wants her to keep the baby. After all, he argues, "It's half my baby too!" He says he will quit school and get a job at the local supermarket to support his girlfriend and the baby. But he says marriage is out of the question. If she keeps the baby, it appears that she will be condemned to live as an unwed mother dependent on an irresponsible father. Her devastated parents urge adoption as the best option. What is the best choice? Even more, what is right? What is ethical?

Charles is a Christian working as a software engineer for an airplane design company. He is struggling to maintain his job in the midst of a difficult market situation and a plummeting economy in the region where he lives. He is the sole breadwinner for his family of six. His wife Elizabeth has a chronic illness preventing her from employment. All she can do is care for the children during the day until Charles returns home from work. One day at work, Charles notices on the desk of his boss some confidential plans from one of the company's minor competitors. Charles is asked, under false pretenses, to modify the plans a little so that they appear new and original. If Charles protests or submits an ethical challenge, he may be fired. If he is fired, he knows that finances would be so tight that his family would suffer. Understanding the lean prospects for another job in today's economy, he faces sleepless nights under the cloud of his dilemma. What is ethical? What is right?

Of course, there are many everyday examples that are much less complex. A father receives a new tie from his ten-year-old daughter for his birthday. As soon as he sees the tie, he loathes the color and the design. The daughter looks up at her father and says, "Do you like the tie, Papa?" The father, desiring to be truthful, spends the next several seconds agonizing about what to say and how to say it without crushing his daughter's feelings. The father wonders if it is ever right to lie. What is a lie, anyway? Are all deceptions lies?

The choices people make in these scenarios speak to the values and principles they hold dear. It is a grave misunderstanding of ethics to believe that it is only concerned with crisis-focused moral decision making or developing practical answers to an array of controversial case studies. Certainly, careful study in Christian ethics should help us think through issues such as war and pacifism, abortion, in vitro fertilization, euthanasia, capital punishment, and a host of other difficult moral questions. But the discipline of ethics is much broader, richer, and more complex than this. In this book we desire to go behind the actual choices themselves and examine the latent values, thoughts, and outlooks on life that precede specific choices made when people are faced with ethical dilemmas.

In specifically Christian-centered ethics there is a constant cycle and interplay between society, the church, and our inherited religious values. As we have noted, there is also an ongoing transfer of values and value evaluation as these are handed down from generation to generation. Values do not remain static but are dynamic. We do not get our values simply by following the Bible and the church; culture and society influence our interpretation of values stemming from these sources. There is a vast network of factors at work that shapes and governs our moral decisions and behavior. This is what we are calling the *matrix of Christian ethics*.[1]

Is Etymology Helpful?

Etymology is often overrated. Good hermeneuticians remind us that etymology does not determine the contemporary meaning or understanding of a word. Simple reflection on words such as *gay, cool,* and *bad,* among countless others, will easily demonstrate this. Yet some etymological reflection may be helpful as we think through the background development of the discipline of ethics and the divergent use of the word *ethics* today.

---

1. This "matrix" theme will be played out in a variety of ways in this book, from the postmodern situation of "ethics" and values, to our proposal for the ongoing development of a Christian ethic itself.

In Greek there are two similar words. The first is ἔθος (*ethos*), which refers to what a person is accustomed to, or regular habits. Jesus went to the Mount of Olives "as usual," or "as was his custom" (Luke 22:39). The second word is ἦθος (*ēthos*), which may be used in the more abstract sense of morality or character. For example, it is used in the plural form in 1 Corinthians 15:33: "Do not be misled: 'Bad company corrupts good character.'" Here the word for *character* or *morals* is *ēthos*. We cannot make generalizations or define necessary distinctions between these words, however, for both have similar etymological roots and are often used synonymously.

The English word *moral* is derived from the Latin *mos* (pl., *mores*), which stems from the verb *metiri,* or "measure." The Latin translation for the subject or discipline of ethics is *moralis*. Cicero used this as a technical term for that aspect of philosophy that addressed the virtuous and good life (*philosophiae pars moralis*).

Dating back to Aristotle, ethics has always included more than simply theoretical reflection, involving also customary patterns of life and practical conduct.[2] In Aristotle's *Nicomachean Ethics,* he argued, "Every art or supplied science and every systematic investigation, and similarly every action and choice, seem to aim at some good; the good, therefore, has been well defined as that at which all things aim."[3] For Aristotle, nature is saturated with purpose, and the job of the philosopher, and all human beings for that matter, is to see this. The overarching goal of humanity in all affairs, conduct, and interaction is goodness, and the highest good is happiness (*eudaimonia*). Aristotle attempted to articulate a coherent vision of this good life in his ethics. For Aristotle, knowledge of the virtues and the practice of the virtuous life ultimately lead to this happiness.

Certainly, the study of ethics has evolved and matured through the years since Aristotle, but it remains a theoretical academic discipline with practical consequences for the patterns of daily life.

---

2. See Kelly James Clark, Richard Lints, and James K. A. Smith, "Aristotle," *101 Key Terms in Philosophy and Their Importance for Theology* (Louisville: Westminster John Knox, 2004), 8–9.

3. Aristotle, *Nicomachean Ethics*, trans. Martin Ostwald (Indianapolis: Bobbs-Merrill, 1975), 3.

Distinguishing between Morality and Ethics Today

Morality, morals, and *mores* refer to principles and values accepted either individually or within a specific culture. *Ethics* is essentially scholarly reflection on morality as a whole, subjecting all of the above to systematic and critical evaluation. In common English vernacular, references to *ethics* usually indicate moral behavior. For heuristic purposes, in this book we will make a distinction between the terms. *Ethics* will be a broad term emphasizing the methodical thinking of morality rather than morality itself. A person may be a skilled academic in the field of ethical reflection yet still lead an immoral lifestyle. Similarly, a very competent dentist may use chewing tobacco, or a hairstylist may have unkempt hair.

There are three levels of reflection we wish to consider when it comes to the study of ethics. The first level involves customs or mores, the second morality, and the third ethics proper. Customs or mores point descriptively to life as it is lived in a particular context or culture. For example, we may choose to address the moral customs and traditions of the people of the Netherlands, Ghana, or the South Pacific islands, and the moral climate of the youth in each distinct culture. The goal here is generally scientific and objectively descriptive.

The second level, morality, speaks to normative issues claimed by specific cultures or individuals. Morality points beyond description to latent ideals. If we take a survey among a particular people group and discover that they all believe stealing from neighbors is wrong, it tells us what they think is right to say, according to their customs and mores, but it does not tell us what they actually practice. The study of morality is precritical or prescientific in this sense, but not unscientific or nonacademic. People often hold to certain values, norms, and moral behaviors without being able to substantiate or explain why they hold such values and norms.

The third level is ethics proper. As mentioned before, this pertains to critical reflection on mores, customs, and morality. To return to a previous example, if a person believes stealing is always wrong, we may now ask the reasons why stealing is always wrong and, more specifically, what it means to steal. If someone steals something from me and I discover this object in his or her possession two years later, is it right to steal it back? Would this be stealing or simply a retrieval of what is properly mine? Does stealing relate simply to material possessions or also to ideas? Contemporary Christian ethical reflection must take into account the issues of the day. We doubt that plagiarism was specifically in the minds of the Hebrew people when they heard and read the injunction "Do not steal," but in today's world plagiarism is definitely considered stealing—not in terms of durable goods, but in terms of the ideas and writings of others. The study of ethics must interact with these types of contemporary issues.

Biblical Ethics?

Naturally, each level of inquiry discussed above is relevant for Christian theological ethics, and we suggest making a distinction between biblical moral behaviors and customs, biblical morality, and biblical ethics. Biblical moral behaviors are concrete lifestyle patterns encountered in the stories of the Bible. Human beings are described in the earthiness of life. We read about lying, stealing, exploitation, hate, and murder, as well as love, joy, and compassion. We see the lows and highs, the struggles and triumphs of everyday life. The Bible narrative provides a literary reflection of human ugliness and corruption as well as the beauty of those created in the *imago Dei*. Yet in the midst of these descriptions of life as it is stands the revealed law of the Holy God incarnated in Scripture. God works through his people and their stories, providing them with moral directives. Some actions and attitudes are praised; others are condemned.

Is it proper to speak of *biblical* ethics as such? We know that the Bible is not an ethical textbook, nor does it scientifically analyze human psychology, sociology, philosophy, or the natural sciences. This is not the intention of the language of Scripture. The principle of accommodation becomes a challenge in the field of ethics, just as it does for other areas within the corpus of systematic theology. God has revealed himself by incarnating truth for us using the weaknesses of human language, writing, and culture. Biblical ethics must look at the stories, accounts, commands, and promises of Scripture in their historical contexts. Biblical ethics must discover, apply, reappropriate, recontextualize, and adapt such matters to the contemporary world. The notion of biblical ethics becomes confusing and controversial because that which is claimed as biblical is always a second-order interpretation of the Bible. This is perhaps why some choose to speak instead of biblical morality.

We will suggest an evangelical approach to Christian ethics that takes into account these controversies as well as the plurality of contemporary thought, while still affirming a view of Scripture as the *norming norm* for both theological expression and moral behavior.[4] With this intent, we will continue to use the term *biblical ethics* in this book, but we acknowledge that Christian ethics from the Bible is always in dialogue with our "situatedness" within a matrix of shifting cultures and contexts. Biblical or Christian ethics must not be equated with direct, immediate access to the full revelation of God. We do not have an unbiased connection to absolute truth. We are limited by our sinfulness and finiteness. Yet we continue the interpretive process of discerning the will of God for our actions as far as we are able, willing, and free to do so. Our point of departure lies in our confession and proclamation of the triune God of the Bible, his special revelation manifested to us through Scripture, and the Holy Spirit, who manifests the presence of the incarnate, resurrected Jesus Christ in the life of the church. This confession precedes our methodological reflection. Christian ethics is a discipline that occurs *a posteriori* to our confession of faith. It is a disciplined reflection, processing what we believe we have received from God's commands and guidance through the Spirit, in Scripture, and in the context of the church community.

Various definitions of Christian ethics have been proposed. Definitions often confine, enclose, and stifle rich ideas rather than allowing them breathing room to develop and expand, but they may help us reflect on how others see key themes of the discipline. Baptist theologian James McClendon suggests that Christian ethics refers to "theories of Christian way of life."[5] Reformed ethicist Jochem Douma describes Christian ethics as "the contemplation of moral acts from the perspective which is presented to us in the Holy Scripture."[6] Douma desires to place the task of Christian ethics in the realm of contemplation but seems to have recoiled before appropriating the notion of Christian ethics as *scholarly* reflection, stating rather that it is a reflection from the perspective of Holy Scripture. W. H. Velema defines ethics more generously as "the scholarly contemplation of the acts committed by human beings, acts made normative through the

---

4. See Stanley J. Grenz and John R. Franke, *Beyond Foundationalism: Shaping Theology in a Postmodern Context* (Louisville: Westminster John Knox, 2001), 64.

5. James William McClendon, *Systematic Theology, Vol. 1: Ethics* (Nashville: Abingdon, 1986), 47.

6. Jochem Douma, *Grondslagen christelijke ethiek* (Kampen, Neth.: Kok, 1999), 51 (translation mine).

commandments of God, human beings as those who bear the image of God in relation to the neighbor."[7]

Douma's definition seems to be limited to "moral acts" and Velema's to "acts made normative through the commandments of God." In our estimation, these definitions are too restrictive. As previously mentioned, Christian ethics must also address character issues, ideals, and life values in the broadest sense. Stanley J. Grenz proposes that "ethics is the study of how humans ought to live as informed by the Bible and Christian convictions," yet he admits that the study of ethics itself is "a broader concept."[8] Grenz does provide a fuller definition of ethics that includes life as a whole, but it still does not sufficiently address root values or character issues.

In view of the above, we suggest the following working definition: *Christian ethics is methodological reflection on the values, norms, virtues, and purposes of Christian life in one's contemporary context, drawing on Scripture and the tradition of faith.* We will look at various aspects of this definition in the course of this book. A quadrilateral matrix of values, norms, virtues, and purposes will be of particular importance for the development of our specific approach to Christian ethics. Ethics is not simply a string of arbitrary and incoherent commands and duties, nor is it simply the art of beautiful prose with a moral dimension. Ethics may include both commands and prose, but this does not negate the need for responsible methodology and systematic reflection.

Subdivisions of Ethics

Ethics, like other academic disciplines, may be divided into various subcategories, each with its own areas of research. We may express these subcategories as follows: descriptive ethics, normative ethics, special ethics, and metaethics.

---

7. W. H. Velema, *Oriëntatie in de Christelijke Ethiek* (The Hague: Boekencentrum, 1990), 17, in and translated from Patrick Nullens, *Verlangen naar het goede: Bouwstenen Voor een Christelijke Ethiek* (Zoetermeer, Neth.: Boekencentrum, 2006), 22.

8. Stanley J. Grenz, *The Moral Quest: Foundations of Christian Ethics* (Downers Grove, IL: InterVarsity Press, 1997), 23.

Descriptive or Comparative Ethics

This aspect of ethical research seeks to describe rather than evaluate moral values and conditions. The ethicist working in this arena must borrow from the toolbox of scientific disciplines such as sociology, cultural anthropology, psychology, and history. For instance, descriptive ethics may examine the history of sexuality and family in a particular cultural group. A European ethicist might analyze the research publications of the European Value System Study Group (EVSSG) that began in 1981. Over a nine-year period, surveys were conducted in various countries regarding religious convictions, norms, and values. Looking at the findings of this research would provide insight into shifts in morality in these countries.

The descriptive or comparative ethicist looks for causes of and connections between moral perspectives, with the goal of remaining as objectively detached as possible so that personal perspectives do not influence the results. The postmodern turn has unmasked the myth of total, impartial objectivity, rendering questionable a full-scale or exclusive commitment to this aspect of ethical research. This is not to deny, however, the significant value of scientific research, as long as presuppositions and cultural and religious biases are acknowledged. Such acknowledgment does not guarantee unbiased objectivity (nor should it), but at least it creates a space of humility that allows continuation of dialogue in the face of a trumpeted neutrality.[9]

Normative Ethics

As descriptive ethics seeks to declare the "is," normative or prescriptive ethics declares the "ought." It moves from mere observation of moral happenings and circumstances to making behavioral judgments and recommendations as to what should and should not be. Where descriptive ethics presents the cartography, normative ethics is the compass. This is not to say

---

9. It is impossible to be completely unbiased or neutral in one's scientific research. Our research is always governed to some degree by our preconceptions, our own personal criteria, and our expectations or hopes for certain outcomes. In this regard, Thomas S. Kuhn is known for pointing out paradigm shifts in scientific discovery. Kuhn's work helps us understand that science itself, often in the name of "objectivity," cannot be some overarching neutral discipline for discovering reality "as it is" apart from sociological factors. See Thomas S. Kuhn, *The Structure of Scientific Revolutions*, 2nd ed. (Chicago: University of Chicago Press, 1970).

that there is only one compass. Various magnetic fields arising from different worldviews, cultures, and philosophical or religious backgrounds may
cause competing readings of north, but the goal of normative ethics is still
to make prescriptions and to defend values in light of a specific worldview
or religious understanding. J. de Graaf defines it this way: "Normative ethics
sets itself as a goal to formulate the fundamental ethical principles, which
are reasonably responsible and can be tested as hypotheses in practice, and
through practice can be nuanced."[10] We are in agreement with de Graaf
that normative ethics not only seeks to provide direction but also helps us
think critically about an ethical framework. In this regard, normative ethics
is also called general ethics, insofar as it considers the broad framework of
norms and values.

Applied or Special Ethics

Applied ethics sharpens the focus of normative ethics. By way of
example, specific areas considered include bioethical issues, ethics and
technology, moral aspects of politics, ethical issues in the media, ecological
or environmental ethics, sexual ethics, and business ethics. In each of these
arenas, specific fields of activity and decision making are scrutinized as to
their ethical underpinnings and implications.

Applied ethics always stems from normative or general ethics. Usually
a broad area of ethical concern is identified; then a specific area of application is noted. It may also work in the opposite direction. We may draw
out a principle for normative ethics from a specific field of application.
For example, love as a central theme in a normative Christian ethic would
seem to be immediately relevant to the health care sector. But to apply the
love principle to an international political conflict requires broadening the
scope of what is meant by *love*, in a personal context, to that of a global
context in view of the principle of justice. In this sense a person's normative
ethical principles work in an interconnected manner with applied ethics.

Applied or special ethics requires interdisciplinary dialogue. As we
wander in and out of various areas of philosophy, theology, biblical studies,
and biomedical issues, teamwork among multiple experts becomes essential. In the medical sector the concept of an ethics commission is used.
This commission consists of diverse medical personnel, including doctors,

---

10. J. de Graaf, *Elementair Begrip van de Ethiek* (Utrecht, Neth.: Bohn, Scheltema & Holkema, 1986), 3, cited in and translated from Nullens, *Verlangen*, 12.

nurses, psychologists, managers, and ethicists. All must work together to develop the moral policy of a given health institution.

Metaethics

The research field of metaethics is not concerned with moral norms, but with the analysis of moral language. It examines the logic of ethical reasoning and the way ethical concepts are described. It considers the meaning of such words as *good, duty,* and *virtue.* Are moral pronouncements verifiable or demonstrable, or are they simply emotional expressions?

Moral assertions such as "Honesty is good" and "Violence is bad" are probed beneath the surface. Even with such simple assertions, metaethics might ask, In what sense is the word *is* used? In the expressions "Two plus two is four," "The flower is beautiful," and "Stealing is wrong," we notice that *is* refers respectively to the mathematical/factual, the aesthetic, and the ethical. Metaethics is concerned with analyzing such abstract yet necessary linguistic expressions.

Personal and Social Ethics

In addition to the classic four-branch classification of ethical research as descriptive, normative, applied (or special), and metaethics, we may also consider the divisions of personal and social ethics. Personal ethics (or microethics) considers individual responsibility, conscience, freedom, and neighborly love. Social ethics (or macroethics) looks at large structures, institutions, and political entities where personal relationships remain in the background. Of course, there is often overlap between personal and social ethics.

Evangelicalism often leans strongly toward personal ethics, as seen in its emphasis on personal conversion, regeneration, and the personal devotional life. Although trends are changing, social justice themes have often remained distant from mainstream evangelical thought, perhaps because of their association with theological liberalism. It is perhaps presumed by evangelicals that the world will improve through personal virtuous actions in everyday affairs. Some may not presume to improve the world in the least; they may be committed simply to living pious lives in a depraved culture, awaiting its certain condemnation. With such a perspective, sin and evil would be interpreted individually and personally rather than corporately or socially. A social ethical approach, on the other hand, would see sin as the greatest cause of evil. It would not emphasize privatization of sin but would stress the effects of sin on depraved institutions and oppressive political structures that oppress and exploit others.

Various theological perspectives have embraced these approaches, in different degrees. The Reformed ethical position has traditionally sought a balance between personal and social ethics by emphasizing tradition and proclamation of Scripture to the individual, while providing influence on and calling to redemption culture and society. In the political theology of Latin America, there is almost an exclusive emphasis on social ethics. Liberation theology defines sin in terms of oppressive social and political structures occurring within an unjust society. Jesus is seen as the liberator of the poor more than as a personal redeemer. The elimination of sin is tantamount to the elimination of oppressive or suppressive structures. This is not necessarily limited to overt oppression or violence. Such oppression may occur through capitalistic habits that have become ingrained within a society. An unbridled passion for affluence and material goods may inadvertently oppress and exploit the poor in an international economy.

In a similar vein, this also relates to environmental ethics. Desire for affluence, control, and luxury goods often conflicts with the need to care for natural resources, thus harming the general welfare of other human beings and the world we share. When we think of future generations— including our own sons, daughters, and grandchildren—things become more complex in our ethical ponderings. Our personal vision and ethical concerns easily flow into social-structural concerns.

It is not an easy matter simply to draw up a chart with clear-cut divisions for the discipline of ethics as a whole. There are too many overlaps and interrelated connections. This is why we prefer to speak of a *matrix* of ethics rather than of a *foundation* of ethics in which one stone of thought is built on another.

Incentives for Studying Ethics

In general, the study and contemplation of ethics is necessary for everyone. Any school of higher education must consider how the study of ethics fits into its curriculum. Whether your field is technology, business, management, caregiving, or education, ethical questions are unavoidable. Decisions must be made regarding technical competencies, and policies must be drafted that promote fairness in the workplace. We will suggest three primary incentives for everyone to consider ethics an essential discipline.

Anthropological Incentive

One perspective argues that humans are moral creatures. Morality flows spontaneously from our existence as human beings. Although values differ, all human societies strive to promote fairness and goodness. Animals consistently react instinctively, responding immediately to the environment around them without moral reflection or argument in favor of particular moral values. The adder bites the outstretched hand because of its instinct of self-preservation. It does not try to justify or excuse its behavior in view of some higher order of reflection. Although we could argue that a scolded dog may *appear* ashamed and guilty, shame in animals is significantly different from that in humans, with respect to emotional complexity.

Some have used this observation as an argument in favor of the existence of a personal God. After all, how could personal morality stem from something impersonal? C. S. Lewis is known for his use of the moral argument as a strong reason to believe in God. But for many religious philosophers, attempting to provide a religious anchor for morality is going too far. The ability to make moral judgments does not lead us to the origin of that moral capacity. Yet to deny the moral dimension of humanity altogether is simply to deny humanity itself.

This is not to say that everyone acts in a morally responsible manner. If this were the case, we would wonder why we have such things as overloaded prisons, genocide, and political corruption. Morals are often compromised and ignored. Sometimes morality is repressed and ignored—through active or passive conditioning—to such a degree that moral consciousness is severely damaged or lost. Some specialized forms of military training attempt to train soldiers to use conditioned rather than reflective responses in critical combat situations. By conditioning soldiers for rapid and blind obedience, in combination with an innate survival instinct, the delay of conscience is eliminated. Granted, this is an extreme example, but it illustrates that when self-alienation and self-respect are ignored in a community context, personal moral responsibility may decline. The discipline of rigorous ethical reflection is basic for the development of how we interact with each other as human beings.

Existential Incentive

The existential incentive is closely related to the anthropological incentive, but here we refer less to a general moral consciousness and more to the need to make individual moral choices. Throughout life we are constantly confronted with ethical challenges. It is commonly presupposed that we all have the freedom to make particular choices and that we take individual responsibility for our actions. No one can step in and make decisions for us; we must decide for ourselves. The way that we perceive the value and function of personal decisions depends on our culture and background. Those from a more community-centered culture will tend not to make personal choices that are fundamentally different from the choices traditionally made in their community. Furthermore, in this context an individual may not actually make an individual moral decision apart from the endorsement (either passive or active) of the shared community. Regardless, the point remains that human beings make ethical decisions and must accept responsibility for those decisions.

What if you were offered a bribe of $100 from a fellow employee to keep quiet about his calling in sick for his job when he really was going to interview for another job? Would it make a difference if the amount were $10,000? Or what if you and your wife were childless and the doctor recommended a fertility therapy involving drugs that would destroy embryos? What would you do? What if your aging mother were suffering due to cancer and the doctor suggested delivering her from her misery by "letting her go" to die peacefully? How would you respond? Compassion is important, but is compassion more important than values? In situations of intense emotion, decisions are much more difficult than textbook answers. The complex problems we face existentially in the crucible of our lives will often challenge traditional values. This is why it is so important to develop a practice of profound ethical reflection in the classroom and in personal study before we face an emotional onslaught near a hospital bed.

Cultural Incentive

The anthropological and existential incentives for ethical reflection tend to be centered on the individual, but the cultural incentive is focused on the role of society. Wherever humans live together in communities, there are moral codes of some sort. In democratic societies a juridical framework stems from a moral/social consensus. Since we find stealing, deceit, and murder reprehensible and impractical for order in society, such things are translated into laws involving penalties and prosecution.

Through an ongoing process of secularization, morals have often become detached from religion, and ethics from theology. Modernism, radical individualism, and the eroding values of Western culture have resulted in either a relativism of ethical opinion or a radical objectification of morality. Postmodern critics have launched a full-scale attack on the notion of *objective* moral judgments. Judgments, by their nature, are based on cultural, environmental, psychological, and spiritual considerations. We must be cautious, however, not to confuse objectivity with reality or with what is reasonable to believe. Simply because moral judgments are contextually driven does not negate their truthfulness or goodness. Christians may readily agree that human moral codes are often contextually driven. But, despite variance of expression, a Christian ethicist would still reason that moral codes ought to be derived from the biblical-theological *sapientia* latent in God's moral order.

The first line of the preamble of the *Universal Declaration of Human Rights* of the United Nations recognizes that the "inherent dignity and . . . the equal and inalienable rights of all members of the human family is the foundation of freedom, justice and peace in the world."[11] Often the moral basis of a culture is naively presupposed. Cultural sentiments come and go; cultures define and redefine their identities, and laws are changed to adapt to these shifts. It is ultimately the morals of a given society that determine the laws of that society. Laws are functionally shortsighted with regard to moral problems. A law restricting alcohol intake while driving refers to a maximum blood-alcohol content and demands a penalty for exceeding that limit. But the law does not address the moral issue of drinking responsibly in view of personal health or in relationship to fellow human beings. If moral issues are ignored completely, the deterrent for a particular unjust or morally reprehensible action becomes threat of punishment rather than moral responsibility. If a culture is unsuccessful in passing along the value of moral reflection, it may end up as a police state where power and control, rather than human dignity and charity, become the regulative norms for society. Ethical reflection contributes to the moral backbone (or lack thereof) of a society. It helps us see the inextricable relationships between the worldviews, values, and norms of a given culture.

---

11. United Nations, *Universal Declaration of Human Rights* (1948), http://www.ohchr.org/EN/UDHR/Pages/Introduction.aspx.

Christian Ethics Reflecting the Imago Dei

Humans are moral beings created in the image of God. The redeeming work of the gospel restores and fulfills the purpose of humanity—to reflect God's goodness. As we strive to live in honesty and integrity and to work toward social justice with others created in his image, this itself *images* our Creator. The Christian seeks to manifest Christ to the poor, the oppressed, and the weak in society through the gospel's good news and good works. The gospel of Jesus changes lives and provides healing liberation. Christian ethics is so much more than simply following a list of rules that you can check off from day to day. It is careful, hard thinking about what it means to be a follower of Jesus in daily decisions, with ultimate respect for God and others. As Dennis Hollinger notes, "The heart of the Christian story that guides our moral life is the story of Jesus. . . . The church is a people of virtue by remembering and living the story of the crucified Savior, which entails not an attempt to control the world by power but a challenge to the powers of the world by the very life of Christ embodied in the church."[12] This is a difficult call. Christians are asked to relinquish personal preferences and conveniences and take up the cross, to follow Jesus (Luke 9:23), and to do all for his name's sake (Colossians 3:17). Following Jesus means that, at all costs, we must stand contrary to a world that has rejected him. Despite such complexities and anticipated hardships, there is still the ironic invitation and promise of peace from Jesus in Matthew 11:28–30: "Come to me, all you who are weary and burdened, and I will give you rest. Take my yoke upon you and learn from me, for I am gentle and humble in heart, and you will find rest for your souls. For my yoke is easy and my burden is light." The peace Jesus offers is a peace that comes from living out our humanity the way it was intended to be lived—in harmony with God, with others, and with our environment.

Christian Ethics in Faith and Life

We are reminded from the book of James that faith without action is dead (James 2:14–17). Living Christianly means that our actions display the grace, love, and charity of Christ to others. Christian faith produces visible, tangible fruit. As we love God, so we love others; as we love others,

---

12. Dennis P. Hollinger, *Choosing the Good: Christian Ethics in a Complex World* (Grand Rapids: Baker Academic, 2002), 55.

so we show we truly love God. Theology and faith are integral to and inseparable from the Christian life. Theology is critical reflection on the content of our faith (*credenda*). Christian ethics helps place this theological reflection into the context of human activity that visibly demonstrates the charitable graces of the Christian life (*agenda* or *facienda*).[13] Christian morality is about showing the authenticity of our faith commitment.[14]

This is nothing new; it has been basic to the mission-centered church from its early beginnings. Yet we recall that the new morality and ethical zeal of the early church was at odds with both the legalistic zeal of Judaism and the utter lawlessness of the Gentiles. The *Didache* (*The Teaching of the Twelve*), an early Christian treatise written at the end of the first century, gives us an impression of the moral instruction of the early church. Its first chapter begins by providing a choice between two paths: the way of life and the way of death. The way of life is the ethic of the double-edged love command of Jesus found in Luke 10:27: "'Love the Lord your God with all your heart and with all your soul and with all your strength and with all your mind'; and, 'Love your neighbor as yourself.'" The next chapter of the *Didache* gives stern injunctions against grave sins such as murder, abortion, adultery, and witchcraft. These are specific rules stemming from the reality that Christians were guided by a new moral order in the person of Jesus. Christians were (and are) to be characterized by a community of love and care, not debauchery.

The early Christians began caring for and sharing with each other with deep compassion, in ways completely unknown in the classical world. The poor were given food, drink, and clothing. The sick were cared for instead of being shunned. Christians attended to prisoners, widows, and orphans. During plague epidemics in Alexandria and Carthage, followers of Christ risked their lives to care for the sick and bury the dead. This was an upside-down revolution in a society with a low regard for the value of human worth. Contrary to the horrible oppression of *Pax Romana*, the early church led its own quiet revolution of gospel peace. The early church made no distinction between theology and ethical practice; teaching and life went hand in hand. These early Christians shook the classical foundations on

---

13. Ethics, however, is not simply concerned with conduct but also with moral orientation in general. See Johannes Fischer, *Theologische Ethik: Grundwissen und Orientierung* (Stuttgart: Kohlhammer, 2002), 52.

14. See G. Th. Rothuizen, *Wat is ethiek?* (Kampen, Neth.: Kok, 1973), 81.

which Rome had been built. Instead of such virtues as courage, power, and pride, Christians emphasized humility, simplicity, and love. All men and women were seen as created in the image of God and as those Christ came to redeem and liberate. Without a concrete political program, Christians began to transform society, from the trenches of the oppressed commoner all the way up to the imperial throne. Despite Christian imperialist abuses of power throughout history, emancipation from sinful bondage has been the heart of the gospel ethic from the beginning.[15]

Helmut Thielicke, a Lutheran ethicist and theologian, writes that Christian ethics is particularly characterized by a tension between life in the here and now and the Christian future. Christian ethics focuses on how we need to live in our current secularized world. We live in a world scarred by sin, often succumbing to its pressures ourselves, but we also hold to the hope of righteousness and complete justice.[16] However, the evangelical focus on eschatological justice and doctrinal orthodoxy has often overshadowed an emphasis on *orthopraxy*. The social relevance of the gospel has been overlooked in a desire to win souls for the future kingdom. But Christians can and must make contributions to the structuring of the ethical convictions shaping today's society. This may happen not through grandiose social programs and political influence (although we are not discouraging this), but through well-prepared pastors and church leaders who learn how effectively to engage with and respond to formative ethical issues in contemporary societies.

This is not about the socialization of the gospel, but about the authentication of the gospel and its outworking, as it flows from our transformed lives in Christ. Without this, the gospel lacks authenticity, and it remains abstract and purely theoretical. This is what Dietrich Bonhoeffer calls "cheap grace." Cheap grace is the mortal enemy of the church. Grace without discipleship is like consuming without paying the price. For Bonhoeffer,

---

15. "Sinful bondage" stems from spiritual bondage because of sin and may have multiple expressions: physical, social, or political. Redemption is about freedom from oppressive structures inhibiting or suppressing the *imago Dei*. Of course this begins with God's reconciling work, reconciling humanity to God and to each other. Christians are to be God's ambassadors, carrying this message and participating as instruments of redemptive activity in all spheres of life.

16. Helmut Thielicke, *Theological Ethics* (Philadelphia: Fortress, 1996), 43–44.

Luther's message of justification by faith is no pretext for cheap grace. Faith means actively living out a life of gospel service to Jesus, in the world.[17]

The Instability of Ethics:
Responsive and Contextual

The study of ethics is not like reading a fantasy novel on a summer day in an idyllic pastoral countryside. It is rather like moving through heavy traffic during rush hour. It is not a neat and tidy discipline safely nestled in the comforts of the ivory tower. Ethical reflection must be done in a turbulent world with an eroding *terra firma*. As steadfast and determined as we may be, our culture is rapidly changing. John D. Caputo, in *Against Ethics*, remarks on a modernist picture of ethics as a "wholesome" discipline that provides "solid" answers:

> It throws a net of safety under the judgments we are forced to make, the daily, hourly decisions that make up the texture of our lives. Ethics lays the foundations for principles that force people to be good; it clarifies concepts, secures judgments, provides firm guardrails along slippery slopes of factical life. It provides principles and criteria and adjudicates hard cases. Ethics is altogether wholesome, constructive work, which is why it enjoys a good name.[18]

Caputo points out, however, that ethics is not safe and uncluttered in an academic box; it is, rather, dangerous business. It is difficult to keep our hands clean and our eyes clear. When face to face with others, tough decisions often escape theoretical categories. Modernist academic cartography is inadequate to map even one clear highway when the road ahead warns of falling rocks and potholes.[19] Theoretical abstractions have their place in many academic disciplines, but ethical reflection demands social action and difficult decisions in real time and in real places. Honest ethical thinking occurs in a matrix of complicated and interconnecting passages, not in the

---

17. Dietrich Bonhoeffer, *The Cost of Discipleship* (London: SCM Press, 2001), 3–14.
18. John D. Caputo, *Against Ethics: Contributions to a Poetics of Obligation with Constant Reference to Deconstruction* (Bloomington and Indianapolis: Indiana University Press, 1993), 4.
19. Ibid.

center of a well-paved superhighway. It often demands action and response in unsafe territory, into unfinished roads and contextual outlets.

To illustrate the responsive, contextual nature of this discipline, we will briefly consider two key historical figures who have greatly influenced philosophical and theological reflection today: Socrates and Jesus.

Socrates and the Rational Human

Socrates (469–399 BC) is known as the father of philosophical ethics. His moral philosophy was a response to a crisis in Athenian democracy. People had been deceived by the subtlety of Sophists, political and religious leaders who had only self-interest in mind. Language and rhetoric had become manipulative devices rather than tools by which to discover the truth. Athens had become so democratic that even generals were chosen by lot rather than leadership skill.[20] But Socrates believed that only competent leaders should take positions of authority. Each discipline requires particular knowledge: farmers must take care of crops and cows, not steer ships; and captains must steer ships, not drive cattle. The same applies to those desiring to command the state. State leaders must have insight into goodness, in order to distinguish right from wrong. Socrates was perhaps the first thinker who clearly pointed out a connection between knowledge and morality. He argued that true morality and real goodness can only be gained by rational insight, not through vague ideas passed down from generation to generation. Customs and tradition do not provide sufficient grounds for morality. The philosopher's task and vocation is to seek such grounding in an all-embracing truth that gives direction to life.

According to Socrates, knowledge functions as a neutral referee, an unbiased guide that can lead us to the good. He believed in an objective and universal truth that can effectively ground moral and public life. Insight brings morality. Immorality represents lack of insight or ignorance. Therefore, ignorance itself is immorality. If we learn that stealing is wrong, we will not steal. If we do steal, it is due to insufficient insight into the principle of lawful property and the consequences of theft. Knowledge is rooted in knowing ourselves, not in knowing the environment. Self-

20. See Bertrand Russell, *A History of Western Philosophy* (New York: Simon and Schuster, 1945), 83. Russell provides a short discussion of Socrates in the sociopolitical context of Athens.

knowledge, then, reveals individual ignorance and the consequent challenge of wisdom.

Socrates raised difficult questions about the nature of righteousness and the good. Through a process of dialogue and rigorous questioning, often in a public arena, Socrates believed truth could be discovered. This dialectical method still plays an important role in philosophy today. The more questions we raise and work through, the closer we get to the essence of truth and goodness. The philosopher must ask probing questions that radically challenge a student's basic ideas. Words such as *bravery, happiness,* and *goodness* cannot simply be thrown around without analysis as to their exact meanings. When we say someone is brave, we must ask what we mean, precisely, by *brave*.

Through this method of constant cross-examination, it became impossible to give final answers (*aporia*), often to the embarrassment of Socrates' students. But Socrates believed this painstaking process was a method by which to reach the truth hidden in the soul of the human being. The philosopher's job was to uncover and give birth to knowledge otherwise hidden, like a midwife (the profession of Socrates' mother) helping to deliver a child. Knowledge was always local and accessible, within the soul of the human being rather than outside in an obscure reality beyond.

Socrates confronted the superficiality of his social and political context. He neither bowed to the structures of power nor whined with the crowds but challenged the stupidity of leaders and their gullible, infatuated followers. His methods unmasked the superficial knowledge of the sovereigns and put them to shame—so he was not well liked. Socrates was aware of his own ignorance, but those in authority were not so enlightened as to their own insufficiencies. Ultimately, Socrates was sentenced to death on charges of impiety and spoiling the minds of youths. He perished by drinking hemlock, believing that his rational, immortal soul would live on. Even today he is still considered a patron saint of humanistic moral philosophy.

In Socrates' quest we find the responsive and the contextual character of ethics. He was in search of a solid point of orientation for social life in the midst of political exploitation. He discovered this in the rational soul. His pupil Plato (427–347 bc) continued this rational philosophical quest in the development of his social ethics. Plato pleaded for insightful, wise, educated leaders (philosopher-kings), who would not be swayed by the simple worldly lusts of the crowd. With the unjust death of his mentor clearly in mind, Plato renounced democracy. If a democratic state had allowed the people to murder the wisest man in the land, then for Plato this proved that the foundation of ethics needed to be sought through the wisdom of the few rather than the ignorance of the many.

Jesus and the Will of the Father

Although Christians can learn a great deal from Socrates and Plato, the central person for our dialogue in this book is Jesus, and the primary goal is not anthropocentric but theocentric. Rigorous philosophical reflection on the nature of the human being is helpful, but, in our view, it must be accompanied by a grid for understanding. Faith in Jesus, the incarnate second person of the triune God, is our point of departure for knowledge of ourselves as created in God's image. Jesus came to herald the message of the kingdom of the triune God of the Bible. Not knowledge but faith and conversion are the primary ingredients for life orientation and ethics.

We also notice the responsive and contextual character of ethics in Jesus' teaching. His moral guidelines do not read like disconnected oracles or a dictionary of codes of conduct. He did not come with a black book full of rules from heaven. He incarnated among us—the Son of God became fully human and lived in the crucible of earthly life. He is Messiah and the son of David, the son of Abraham, and the Son of Man. He came as a rabbi different from other rabbis and teachers of the day. His life and teaching together were in complete accord with the will of the Father. We see this exemplified in Jesus' Sermon on the Mount, especially in the six antitheses reacting against the letter-of-the-law, legalistic moral education of his day (Matthew 5:21–48).[21] Jesus' righteousness surpassed that of the teachers of the law; he was concerned more with motives than with rules. At the same time, his revolutionary focus on the heart astonished the crowds that saw him as teaching with authority (Matthew 7:28–29). Often Jesus was blunt in his confrontational style, dismantling the manipulative legalism of the religious leaders: "Woe to you, teachers of the law and Pharisees, you hypocrites! You are like whitewashed tombs, which look beautiful on the outside but on the inside are full of dead men's bones and everything unclean" (Matthew 23:27).

Jesus was clear about why he incarnated. It was not for the sake of those who perceived themselves righteous or for those who were strong and self-assured. He came for sinners in need of rescue (Matthew 9:13), for the

---

21. Richard B. Hays, *The Moral Vision of the New Testament: A Contemporary Introduction to New Testament Ethics* (San Francisco: HarperSanFrancisco, 1996), 95–96.

weak and the lame. He came to forgive and to enable forgiveness through his own mercy and love. He was a physician among the sick, cleansing the wounds of the people with his own hands. He overturned the ethics of the prevailing religious caste. He deconstructed and *reconstructed* the filter of the law so that everything would be filtered through the eyes of God's compassion.[22]

Both Socrates and Jesus ventured into unsafe territory. Like Socrates, Jesus was despised by the prevailing class of knowledge brokers. He also was condemned because of his threatening claims, suffering a disgraceful death on a Roman cross. Of course, there are some critical differences between Jesus and Socrates as well. Jesus' death was prophesied and is replete with theological implications for atonement from sin. He willingly chose a path of suffering in full knowledge that he would be rejected. Jesus chose his path sacrificially, knowing it was the only path that would provide the healing needed for humanity and the only healing that would allow humanity the opportunity to live with moral fortitude. Jesus' bodily resurrection also provided an eternal healing that overturns the spiritual and the physical consequences of death, which entered the world through sin.

Jesus' resurrection was not simply an event in time, affirming his divinity or assuring our immortality, but it has tremendous ethical implications that dwarf the moral values we learn from the death of Socrates. Jesus' death and resurrection conquered the power of condemnation, enabling freedom from the power of the flesh and participation in the community of Christ as adopted sons and daughters. As Christians we share a positional relationship with Christ in his sufferings (Romans 8:17) that also allows us to share with and minister to those who are suffering (2 Corinthians 1:3–7). This ministry is motivated by a vision of eschatological and glorious fulfillment, when all suffering will end and all believers will enjoy perfect Christian community.[23]

The Prophetic Task of Jesus' Disciples

Before his ascension Jesus gave a mandate to his disciples to continue his teaching to all nations (Matthew 28:19). This prophetic task continues

---

22. Ibid., 100.
23. Ibid., 25–27. For a thorough analysis of Christian ethics based on the resurrection of Jesus, see Oliver O'Donovan, *Resurrection and Moral Order: An Outline for Evangelical Ethics*, 2nd ed. (Grand Rapids: Eerdmans, 1994).

through his church. The risen Christ, through the Holy Spirit, is present among his followers. The church is the visible manifestation, the body of Christ (1 Corinthians 12:12). As Jesus' prophetic task continues, so the responsive task of Christian ethics continues, confronting today's challenges. To be a Christian is to be a Christ follower in a world largely committed to not following Christ. Christians live in the world but do not want to be absorbed by it. They are called to be nonconformists, set apart to proclaim and display the radical love of Jesus. Christian ethics acknowledges the reality that Jesus' followers are outsiders, strangers, and pilgrims in this world, sometimes subject to persecution for their perspectives and values.

But this is not a call to a ghetto mentality with a sectarian ethic. Ironically, Jesus' criticisms within the religious sphere were more severe than they were against the pagan Roman world outside. His radical indictments were often directed against the theological and spiritual elite caught up in ungracious legalistic literalism. As followers of Jesus, the Christian community is called to grace, charity, and hospitality. Christian ethics must not lose the responsive and contextual character of life in the church. Christian ethics must be inwardly and externally focused. The earliest church communities mentioned in the book of Acts demonstrated this brilliantly as they shared together in goods, food, prayer, and even persecution. The internal love of the community was contagious. Indeed, we are called to be salt and light in the world around us (Matthew 5:13–16). But perhaps the primary means by which we can be salt and light is through the love that characterizes the church internally. The Christian community displays its ethic of love externally by consistently demonstrating that love among its own people (John 17:20–26). At the same time, the love from Christ we show is missionally focused on those outside the circle of faith, as we are humbly driven by Christ's challenge to love our neighbor despite our own imperfections and struggles to love each other. In our view, only an ethics of grace stemming from a gracious response to Jesus Christ crucified, buried, and risen (1 Corinthians 15:3–4) can offer an answer for renewal in the contemporary landscape of our polemically driven world.

Signals of a Moral Crisis

Simply by picking up a daily newspaper or scanning the headlines on Google News, we easily see the decadence and corruption of modern society. Our moral fiber seems to be disintegrating, and we are losing the capacity for peace both among our nations and in our families. We are often shocked by the moral degradation before us. Divorce rates are on the increase, and we hear increasing reports of child abuse. Traditional family households are being replaced with alternative lifestyle structures. Ecologically, despite the recycling efforts of the few, our natural world is subject to increasing pollution and various forms of environmental destruction. Terrorism and the fight against terrorism through war have diminished our value for human life. Suspicion of differences reigns, whether in airports, supermarkets, or neighborhoods. The dream of multicultural hospitality seems lost in the nightmarish brutality of reality.

For years we have heard of the moral decomposition of Europe. A post-Christian mentality has diminished the moral structure on which its nation-states were built. But some believe that the modern abandonment of Christianity is a step forward, attributing the wars through the ages to religious conflict. Today North America is certainly no exception to this, even with a significant evangelical, fundamentalist population. Moral crises within and without the church are prolific. The gap between authentic Christian worldviews and practices and those of modern Western culture seems to be widening.

German ethicist Georg Huntemann writes in apocalyptic terms of the process by which traditional values have eroded with the removal of formerly perceived taboos. We live in a culture of shamelessness, and we worship our own personal fulfillment. Immediate personal gratification is more important than the norms of a holy God. According to Huntemann this has created a destabilized European society. He supports this notion by pointing out the contrast between the extreme expansion of Islam in Europe and the dramatic decline of Christianity.[24]

Pope John Paul II spoke of a "culture of death." When humanity rejects God, humanity disappears into the void: "A culture which no longer has a point of reference in God loses its soul and loses its way, becoming a culture of death. This was amply demonstrated by the tragic events of the twentieth century and is now apparent in the nihilism present in some prominent circles in the Western world."[25] Each year some forty-six million women choose abortion, ending the lives of more than a hundred thousand babies

---

24. Georg Huntemann, *Biblisches Ethos im Zeitalter der Moralrevolution* (Neuhausen, Switz.: Hänssler, 1999), 15–33.
25. Pope John Paul II, *Dialogue Between Cultures for a Civilization of Love and Peace*, Message for the Celebration of the XXXIV World Day of Peace 2001 (Vatican, December 8, 2000), § 9. Cf. his encyclical *Evangelium Vitae* (March 25, 1995).

every day.[26] Anti-AIDS campaigns in the media often outweigh instruction on preventative measures or abstinence. Teens are directly confronted and enticed with graphic sexual content in advertisements, television programs, and movies. They are encouraged by culture to be sexually active, yet young girls are scorned when they become pregnant. "Personal choice" and "individual freedom" have become the politically correct buzzwords regulating moral behavior. Sadly, in a world of addictions and lack of self-control, most people are completely incapable of managing these personal freedoms.

Much is also changing in the legislative arena. The democratic judicial system is perhaps a delayed mirror of culture. When the moral mindset slackens in the minds of the majority, laws are changed to reflect the changed values. The prevailing character of politics in a parliamentary democracy is, therefore, relative to those values that predominate in culture. In many cases legislative decisions and changes are the result of what has already been a primary part of the mindset of the people for a long time. By way of example, in our country of residence, Belgium, nearly 90 percent of the people consider themselves Roman Catholic. Yet new laws were launched permitting abortion in 1991, euthanasia in 2002, and homosexual marriage in 2003. Such legislation represents a stark contrast to traditional Catholic Christian moral values.

We see similar tendencies in other European countries, particularly in the countries of the former Soviet Union. Under the reign of communism, there was a precise framework of values. The notion of a collective morality was stressed so much that individual freedom was suppressed and personal moral behavior was irrelevant. Since the fall of the Berlin Wall, these countries have struggled to find their way within the new value system delivered by Western capitalism. The multitude of newly found freedoms has resulted in uncritical acceptance of liberties. We read of a horrendous increase in alcoholism, drug abuse, prostitution, and human sex trafficking in these regions. An insatiable craving for money and wealth, along with an unbridled freedom, has led to corruption. The scenario in Eastern Europe seems to present an ironic return to the moral climate of brute feudalism that existed before the communist revolution.

---

26. Exact numbers are uncertain. The rate varies widely among countries where legal abortion is available. It has declined in many countries since the mid-1900s. In the Russian Federation, China, and the United States, the legal abortion rate is extremely high. See Gilda Sedgh et al., "Legal Abortion Worldwide: Incidence and Recent Trends," *International Family Planning Perspectives* 33, no. 3 (2007): 106–116.

Technology and Moral Confusion

It is surprising how many contemporary moral crises are aggravated by recent technological developments in science and medicine. Moral questions arise frequently regarding prenatal diagnosis and abortion, euthanasia and therapeutic obstinacy, gene therapy, environmental ethics, animal rights and industrial stockbreeding, just war and the use of nuclear weapons, and the list goes on. The gap between rapid technological growth and slower ethical reflection on the consequences of that growth is startling. In the sciences the human being is often viewed simply as an animal. The stark, modern dogma of scientific naturalism often prevails in our high-tech world, where morality is reduced to the practical and expedient.

American philosopher Francis Fukuyama recognizes the challenge of the current biotechnological revolution. Biotechnology improves human quality of life, but it may also be used unwisely in the hands of those wielding its powers. The same technology that grants freedom may also take it away by creating a new elitism. According to Fukuyama the unequal division of talents now determined by genetic fate may eventually become determined by human decision. Instead, human rights should be determined by human nature, that is, by species-specific structures and capacities. *Contra* John Locke, the human being is no *tabula rasa* but possesses innate ideas or species-specific forms of cognition and emotional reaction. Morality does not begin with acquired behavior but is rooted in human nature itself. Fukuyama uses a "natural rights" argument to suggest that there must be something basic, which he calls "Factor X," that makes us human, that gives us dignity, and that provides a basis for our morality. But this Factor X cannot simply "be reduced to the possession of moral choice, or reason, or language, or sociability, or sentience, or emotions, or consciousness, or any other quality that has been put forth as a ground for human dignity. It is all these qualities coming together in a human whole that make up Factor X."[27] Fukuyama's words highlight the need for a nonreductionist approach to moral direction, in view of the contemporary technological revolution, that mandates certain choices for political policy and legislation.

---

27. Francis Fukuyama, *Our Posthuman Future: Consequences of the Biotechnology Revolution* (New York: Farrar, Straus and Giroux, 2002), 171, as cited by Mike Lepore in his book review of Fukuyama, *Our Posthuman Future,* for crimsonbird.com in Athenaeum Reading Room, http://evans-experientialism.freewebspace.com/fukujama03.htm.

Ecological troubles throughout the world also point to a collective moral crisis.[28] Especially in the West, we witness humanity's ongoing excessive consumption of natural resources. Population growth and industrial pollution together create a menacing state of affairs. Both the economy and the environment often mirror our values. Unfortunately, values usually stem more from societal affirmation than from spiritual reflection in concert with our Creator. In today's complex world, opinions on ethical conundrums are as diverse as the myriad of websites that give them a voice.

Tracing the Moral Climate of Today

Although we cannot, nor should we attempt to, provide a complete analysis of the intellectual development leading to the complex moral climate of today, it may be helpful for us to trace broadly the intellectual/ historical landscape that has colored and shaped its terrain. We will briefly discuss three overarching paradigms of history to help us chart this background: premodernity, modernity, and postmodernity. We readily admit we run the risk of oversimplification and superficiality by attempting such a task in the scope of one chapter. Many important figures in this development of ideas must be omitted. Nevertheless, it is our desire to present an overview of how these key historical intellectual climates have left their marks on the moral thought of today.

Premodernity

Kevin Vanhoozer suggests that one "rough-and-ready way to distinguish among premodern, modern and postmodern eras is precisely on the basis of what each considers its first philosophy."[29] That is, what is it about an era that is considered of primary importance for living and understanding? The first philosophy for the premodern ancient world was the nature of reality. For Aristotle this was the entire notion of being. The categories of thought Aristotle described were extremely influential on medieval theologians in the twelfth and thirteenth centuries. Christian metaphysics and the question of the being of God became the first theology inherited from

---

28. See Patrick A. P. Nullens, "Leven volgens Gaia's normen?: de verhouding tussen God, mens en aarde en de implicaties voor ecologische ethiek" (Ph.D. diss., Evangelische Theologische Faculteit, Leuven, Belgium, 1995), 17ff.

29. Kevin J. Vanhoozer, *First Theology: God, Scripture and Hermeneutics* (Downers Grove, IL: InterVarsity Press, 2002), 16.

first philosophy. Thomas Aquinas, highly influenced by Aristotle, sought to demonstrate how we could derive knowledge of God's being from the use of natural reason.[30] From such thinking, foundations of ethical thought would flow. Natural order was seen as the expression of divine will and goodness. The world was God's sacred and symbolic reflection of his heavenly order. Consequently, for the premodern Christian West, the church became the omnipresent guard and gatekeeper of the natural ethical order. This was extremely evident in Europe, where villages and towns were built entirely around spires and steeples. The empire of the church was the guarantor of universal morality.

Moral theology manifested the beauty of God's order (*splendor ordinis*), offering the believer a means by which, through spiritual exercises, to climb to the highest good. According to Augustine the highest good, the greatest purpose, was divine love:

> But if the Creator is truly loved, that is, if He Himself is loved and not another thing in His stead, He cannot be evilly loved; for love itself is to be ordinately loved, because we do well to love that which, when we love it, makes us live well and virtuously. So that it seems to me that it is a brief but true definition of virtue to say, it is the order of love; and on this account, in the Canticles, the bride of Christ, the city of God, sings, "Order love within me" (*Cant. 2:4*).[31]

Conversely, immorality was the distortion of the divine order of love, choosing worldly values over heavenly ones.

With this in mind, specific ethical decisions became fairly clear. Adultery was sin, homosexuality was sin, stealing was sin, and on the list went. The application of ethical rules was simply the application of the innate moral law already stamped on the human heart and conscience. This was a culture of moral consensus. The church was the moral authority that, through priests, evaluated and assigned penance requirements for particular sins.

But should we regard such days of presupposed moral unanimity with spiritual nostalgia? Perhaps not. Unfortunately, moral consensus often bred moral hypocrisy. It was one thing to make moral demands and quite

---

30. Ibid.
31. Augustine, *The City of God*, ed. Philip Schaff, trans. Marcus Dods, vol. 2 of *Nicene and Post-Nicene Fathers: First Series* (Peabody, MA: Hendrickson, 1994), 303.

another thing to live by those demands consistently, especially for those holding the power to enforce such demands. John D. Caputo makes an interesting observation pertaining to this premodern order:

> It was a time in which people were all willing to sign on to the idea that there is a deep hierarchical, top-down order inscribed in things, the heavens and God up above and earth and us down below—notice how these ideas of God are related to a pre-Copernican imagination—with kings and queens above and everyday ordinary people down below, priests up, laypeople down, men up, women down. And finally theology above and philosophy below, as a "handmaiden" to the queen. Now it is a sad but true point, almost an unbroken principle in human affairs, that whoever has the power abuses it, and if someone has absolute power he or she abuses it absolutely.[32]

Corruption invaded the church. We simply need to look at the major historical scars the church left on history, such as the Crusades and the Inquisition, to broach this topic. At times it seems that the greater the moral consensus of a culture, the greater the pretense. Moral consensus stresses moral conformity, the demand of moral conformity creates social pressure, and failure to meet social pressure has often resulted in hypocrisy.

This *premodern* ethical situation can be illustrated with a scenario possible today. Suppose a pastor preaches on Jesus' words in Matthew 22:21 about giving Caesar what he is due and argues from the text that Christians need to live honestly and pay their income taxes. Some folks begin to squirm, sensing a personal conflict between what they know is right and what they actually practice. Paul described this well in Galatians 5:17: "For the sinful nature desires what is contrary to the Spirit, and the Spirit what is contrary to the sinful nature. They are in conflict with each other, so that you do not do what you want."

Premodern Christian ethics did not call for personal knowledge and understanding of right and wrong, because it was entirely based in the authority of the church. The church had the power and made the demands; the people simply needed to submit to its demands. In this regard premodern ethics did not lack perceived understanding of the right course of moral action, but it struggled to realize this action with personal integrity. As we

---

32. John D. Caputo, *Philosophy and Theology* (Nashville: Abingdon, 2006), 11–12.

will see, there came a radical shift in this way of thinking with the onset of modernity.

Modernity

With modernity the accent of moral crisis shifted from action to knowledge. The scientific revolution, stemming from the work of people such as Francis Bacon and Isaac Newton, along with the philosophical revolution of René Descartes, ushered in the vital principles that characterized Enlightenment thought, which in turn became the gateway to modernity. This thinking came to full expression in Kant's affirmation of the all-encompassing self and the universality of human experience. Kant called humanity to take up the mantle of *sapere aude*—to have the courage to use our own reason.[33] Modernity is characterized by the use of human reason, rationality, and intellectual progress.[34] For modernity, the human intellect has the innate ability properly to discern truth in ethical matters.

The Reformation played a decisive role as a precursor of modernity. The value of the individual was reinforced, and the power of a person's faith experience became central. Luther and Calvin placed less emphasis on the grand cosmic order, stressing rather a personal relationship with God as the basis for ethical reflection. The main characters in the modern scene shifted from being God and the church to being God and me. The subjective conscience of premodernity became the conscious thinking subject of modernity. Moral consensus was publicly removed. The individual self became capable on its own terms of thinking rationally about ethical matters and living righteously through faith, apart from collective participation in the sacraments of Mother Church.[35] Rome's moral power lost its edge as the absolute sovereign of human conscience. This decline of ecclesiastical consensus created a climate of incertitude. Reason trumped the church and formed the basis for a new consensus.

---

33. See Kant's famous article "An Answer to the Question: What is Enlightenment?" (September 1784).

34. See Ronald T. Michener, *Engaging Deconstructive Theology* (Aldershot, UK: Ashgate, 2007), 23–4. We will refer to the notion of modernity more as an intellectual movement than as a carefully defined historical period.

35. What happens here is more than simply a Protestant-Catholic "divide." What eventually became Protestant liberal theology (Schleiermacher, von Harnack, et al.) was presumed to emancipate the individual from the authority of a written, myth-laden Scripture into the central *kerygma* of the faith message of human authenticity.

Methodist theologian Thomas Oden describes modernity as an enchantment "characterized by technological messianism, enlightenment idealism, quantifying empiricism, and the smug fantasy of inevitable progress."[36] In this sense one religious perspective replaced another. The culmination of the Enlightenment project can be seen in the French Revolution of 1789. The revolt of the people displayed a protest against the power of the medieval social order with its universal norms and values. The new framework called for *freedom, equality,* and *fraternity,* where sovereignty was vested in the common people, not in the nobility or the clergy.

Could ethics stand on reason alone? Was this simply a return to the ancient Greek philosophy from which Hellenized Christianity had drawn its ethical reflection? No. Things were different now. A blank check appeal to the authority of the past clashed with the free mind of modernity. Nature was not simply God's mysterious order but a world to be discovered and explored by reason.[37] It became a "functional rationality" in which "all spheres of human existence" were "governed by calculation and scrutiny."[38] Unfortunately, the ideals of human freedom, equality, and fraternity replaced theological incentives to discover God's creative order.[39] This ambitious human autonomy paved the way for the Industrial Revolution. Then another new consensus emerged through Marxist socialism.

Karl Marx (1818–1883) astutely recognized the tension between freedom and equality. The political and juridical equality of reason stemming from the French Revolution did not produce economic equality. Marx's model attempted to rectify this, using a new morality with changes to social and economic structures. As a historical materialist, Marx observed history through the lens of a continual and inevitable class struggle. Fate was in our own hands, so personal freedom had to be worked out in the struggle for emancipation. With this in mind, Marx provided a social expression

---

36. See Thomas C. Oden, *After Modernity . . . What?: Agenda for Theology* (Grand Rapids: Zondervan, 1990), 44–47, 50; and Thomas C. Oden, "The Death of Modernity and Postmodern Evangelical Spirituality," in *The Challenge of Postmodernism: An Evangelical Engagement,* ed. David S. Dockery (Grand Rapids: Baker, 1997), 24, as cited in Michener, *Engaging,* 23.

37. Michener, *Engaging,* 19.

38. Hollinger, *Choosing the Good,* 94.

39. Such theological motivation is aptly characterized in the popular epitaph written by poet Alexander Pope:
Nature and Nature's laws lay hid in night:
God said, Let Newton be! and all was Light.

to the ideas of equality, progress, and the natural order, the pillars of Enlightenment thought.

Marxism aimed at being a scientific model of social expression, providing a new consensus through reason. Religion was rooted in superstition, so it was unable to provide a true basis for ethics. Marx famously said that religion was the "opium of the people."[40] Religion put people to sleep, so that they resigned to the fate they had been given in life and nothing changed, whereas, Marxist rationalism would liberate the human being. In 1989, two hundred years after the French Revolution, this Marxist "spiritual" child of the Enlightenment collapsed. As the Soviet Union dissolved, so did its accompanying modernistic idealism with its all-embracing economic ethical system.[41]

Postmodernity

It is not an easy task to define postmodernity. The word *postmodern* is slippery, elusive, and controversial. It has multiple meanings and contexts, with applications in politics, philosophy, literature, science, architecture, popular culture, and media. It has driven discussions in the halls of academia and has also left its mark on the tattooed teens in the pool hall down the street. In addition to the diversity of expression of postmodernism, it also defies strict definition because we are situated in the midst of its outworking. Nonetheless, in this book we will attempt to outline some broad strokes of meaning that will help us understand how postmodern thought influences Christian ethics. Primarily, we will be using the term *postmodernism* to refer to an intellectual movement challenging modernism and Enlightenment ideals. The extreme rationalism and empiricism that dominated Enlightenment thought, along with its fixed truths and certain knowledge, have been effectively challenged. The notion of a rational unity is now fragmented. Legal, bioscientific, and moral borders have become obscure.[42] Instead, there is a matrix of interconnecting and overlapping

---

40. Karl Marx, "Introduction to a Contribution of the Critique of Hegel's Philosophy of Right," *Deutsch-Französische Jahrbücher* (February 1844).
41. A symbol of this collapse is readily seen in the ruins of residential blocks where the individual was simply absorbed in the modernistic concrete.
42. Margrit Shildrik and Roxanne Mykitiuk, eds., *Ethics of the Body: Postconventional Challenges* (Cambridge, MA, and London: MIT Press, 2005), 5–6.

categories, "a mutual dependence that belies the traditional insistence on clear and distinct divisions."[43]

However, we are not suggesting that modernist sentiments have simply faded into the past. Modernism is still alive and well in various contexts, but its underpinnings have been radically challenged and questioned. In the midst of this radical questioning we are faced with opportunities to respond. If we cling to modernistic ideals in our epistemology and theological methodology, postmodernism may seem a threat. If we see the postmodern assault on modernism as a prophetic voice beckoning us to forsake conceptual idols of the past and appreciate and appropriate new ways of understanding, then we may welcome many of its insights.[44]

We must be careful to avoid hasty caricatures and generalizations of postmodern thought, speaking of *the* postmodern position or approach, or making sweeping statements about what postmodernists argue for or deny.[45] Postmodernism is multifaceted and divergent in its expressions. It is not about relativism or absolute skepticism, but about showing sensitivity to details, complexities, and close readings that have often been ignored or suppressed.[46] Postmodernists come in all shapes, sizes, and belief backgrounds including devout Christians, atheists, and agnostics. Even among Christians with postmodern sensitivities, there are quite divergent perspectives. As James K. A. Smith puts it, "To some, postmodernity is the bane of Christian faith, the new enemy taking over the role of secular humanism as object of fear and primary target of demonization. Others see postmodernism as a fresh wind of the Spirit sent to revitalize the dry bones of the church."[47] Acknowledging the multiple voices of postmodernism (outside and within Christianity) is not to say, however, that we cannot point out several intellectual tendencies.

Postmodernism underscores the deficiencies of modernism. Over a century ago Friedrich Nietzsche was already staking his claim against the foundations of modernistic morality. Considered by some the "grandfather

---

43. Ibid., 6.
44. Michener, *Engaging*, 1–7.
45. For an example, see Craig A. Boyd, *A Shared Morality: A Narrative Defense of Natural Law Ethics* (Grand Rapids: Brazos, 2007), 25–26.
46. Caputo, *Philosophy and Theology*, 50. Postmodernism is not "inherently relativistic," as some mistakenly argue. See, for example, Hollinger, *Choosing the Good*, 112.
47. James K. A. Smith, *Who's Afraid of Postmodernism? Taking Derrida, Lyotard, and Foucault to Church* (Grand Rapids: Baker Academic, 2006), 18.

of postmodernism,"[48] Nietzsche may be credited with the first major assault on the notion of truth. He saw human rationality and the supposition of truth as both arbitrary and illusory.[49] Of course, this affected his view of morality and moral conventions, leading to this bold claim: "There is an old delusion that is called good and evil."[50] The entire idea of moral convention, whether religious or secular, is ludicrous for Nietzsche. Real freedom only comes through human beings' creating their own values. For Nietzsche the underlying "will to power" (*Der Wille Zur Macht*) is behind everyone's existence. But this will to power must be understood in light of the *Übermensch* (*overman*), a figure that emerges after the death of God and yet is beyond mere humanity. The *Übermensch* uses the will to power not for the oppression of others, but for self-mastery and the discipline to face life despite the death of God and the consequent absence of a justification for morality.[51] Morality is not obtained through some ideal consensus but through the disciplined use of the will to power. Nietzsche replaced reason with the heroic act of the will. The *overman* is not guided by faith or reason but by personal courage. Morality is courage, not mind or belief. As modernity disconnected ethics from religion, Nietzsche's move, becoming also the postmodern move, disconnected ethics from human reason.

Modernism suffered from the delusion of foundationalism, attempting to build systems on absolute truths. Reason was king. The postmodern critique points out the limits of reason and its totalizing nature to attempt forcefully to bring everything under an all-encompassing system, suppressing or ignoring differences.[52] Modernity's hope was that new insights from reason would lead to more virtuous action. But this knowledge and an ideological faith in prosperity were accompanied by an illegitimate, creepy desire for evil.[53] The madness of reason manifested its insanity in the concentration camps of Hitler and Stalin, modeling heartless technological

---

48. See Lawrence Cahoone's introduction to Nietzsche in *From Modernism to Postmodernism*, ed. Lawrence Cahoone (Cambridge, MA: Blackwell, 1996), 102.

49. Michener, *Engaging*, 31.

50. Friedrich Nietzsche, *Thus Spake Zarathustra*, trans. R. J. Hollingdale (London: Penguin Books, 1961), 139.

51. See Michener, *Engaging*, 33.

52. This applies to the class struggle of Karl Marx as well as the presumptuous scientific positivism of the natural sciences today. Science can be oppressive because of its tendency to reduce and abstract reality.

53. Jos Decorte, *De Waazin van het intellect: Twee modellen van de eeuwige strijd tussen goed en kwaad* (Kapellen, Belgium: Pelckmans, 1989), 10–11.

efficiency and management. Modernity did not bring ethical resolution. The postmodern move has consequently placed ethics *prior* to reason, rather than assuming it as a logical outcome.[54]

An important and contemporary representative of postmodern ethics is Michel Foucault (1926–1984). Foucault's doctoral work, *Madness and Civilization* (1960), focused on uncovering the mechanism of oppressive structures in psychiatric institutions. Foucault submitted that real madness is not the absence of reason or order, but a kind of mad reasonableness (*déraison*). In line with Nietzsche, the will for truth is the will for power: it is self-legitimizing. Power produces truth, not the reverse. Truth is not about propositions that correspond to reality but is determined by historical-political factors. Similarly, the medium of moral language is the result of coincidental historical processes.

In the name of reason, people operate various mechanisms of exclusion, justifying the locking up of certain individuals in institutions as the lepers of a modern society. Foucault expanded Nietzsche's critique of the totalitarianism of Christianity as the preserver of a moral consensus in Western human sciences. For Foucault, notions of good and evil were nothing more than the socially accepted ideals of a particular culture. Truth could not be discovered, but only invented as tentative truth practices.[55] The critical task of the philosopher was to examine how the effects of truth competed with each other, not to claim what was or was not true. So our job was not to change the consciousness of others but to change the regimes of power and to detach "the power of truth from the forms of hegemony, social, economic, and cultural, within which it operate[d]."[56]

Plurality and the Loss of the Self

Some will see the postmodern dethronement of reason as an opportunity for radical individual freedom and all the moral abuses stemming from

---

54. In John Rawls' social ethics, *A Theory of Justice* (1971), he still maintains a close connection between morality and rationality.

55. Michel Foucault, *The Order of Things: An Archaeology of the Human Sciences*, 2nd ed. (London: Routledge, 2002), 330–374.

56. Michel Foucault, *Power/Knowledge: Selected Interviews and Other Writings, 1972–1977*, ed. Colin Gordon, trans. Colin Gordon et al. (New York: Pantheon Books, 1980), 133. See also Miroslav Volf's comments in his *Exclusion and Embrace: A Theological Exploration of Identity, Otherness, and Reconciliation* (Nashville: Abingdon, 1996), 249, and also Michener, *Engaging*, 88.

such a notion. But embracing the postmodern critique does not require this at all. The real culprit in this regard is not postmodernism, but modern liberalism with its strong appeal to the rational, autonomous self, which stems clearly from the Enlightenment project.[57] In fact, postmodernism questions the entire idea of the self as individual and autonomous. The absolute "I" of modernism is thrown into the community that shapes us. Our "situationality" as human beings in community shapes who we are.[58] The modern notion of the self as autonomous in thought and action is naive and arrogant, failing to understand the dynamic, influencing factors of culture and community on the person. The self is not an island, but is part of a matrix of interconnecting relationships. The human being must be understood from the perspective of the social web, not as a detached self.[59] We will not learn more of ourselves by introspection but by self-interpretation within our community.

Postmodern thought is often characterized by plurality. As modernism honored universality, postmodernism honors diversity. For ethics, postmodernism "entails an acceptance of provisionality, instability, multiplicity, and an awareness that the task of ethics is never finally done, that the critique must be interminable."[60] Empiricism and rationalism cannot remove plurality and diversity. This is not to say that anything goes, but it is calling for different models of ethical reflection in view of the postmodern critique. We will continue to address this challenge for Christian ethical reflection throughout the course of this book.

This postmodern emphasis on the plurality, yet primacy, of ethics is notable in the Jewish philosopher Emmanuel Levinas (1906–1995). Levinas was not concerned with some vague concept of ontological unity that bound us together, but with the diversity that called us to responsibility toward the other. Levinas questioned modern ethical totalizations and universal appeals to good conscience. Ethics was not about the conscious subject but about a sensible subject living among and vulnerable to the

---

57. Hollinger, *Choosing the Good*, 51. Hollinger refers to Alasdair MacIntyre, *After Virtue: A Study in Moral Theory* (Notre Dame: University of Notre Dame Press, 1981).
58. See James K. A. Smith, *The Fall of Interpretation: Philosophical Foundations for a Creational Hermeneutic* (Downers Grove, IL: InterVarsity Press, 2000), 90–91.
59. Charles Taylor criticizes the liberal concept of the individual as the ultimate foundation in his *Sources of the Self: The Making of the Modern Identity* (Cambridge, MA: Harvard University Press, 1989), 111ff.
60. Shildrik and Mykitiuk, eds., *Ethics of the Body*, 9.

pains and sufferings of the other in the concreteness of life here and now.[61] Levinas reversed the direction of metaphysics by focusing on the human being rather than the abstract ontological question of being. Social interactions had to be supported by ethical relationships with other persons. But acknowledging other persons did not mean reducing them to our knowledge and supposed comprehension. We needed also to acknowledge the separateness and distinctness of the other, respectfully.[62] As Levinas put it, "The face resists possession, resists my powers."[63]

Deconstructionism and the Problem of Interpretation

In view of the complexities and plurivocal fragmentation of postmodernism, we are confronted with the problem of language as the bearer of meaning between human beings. Perhaps the most well-known, most misunderstood and misrepresented postmodern philosopher in this regard is Jacques Derrida. Derrida is known for introducing perhaps the most radical notion of postmodernity: deconstructionism. Deconstructionism seeks to "question and dismantle the entire Western philosophical enterprise that is commonly viewed as unbiased, pure foundational inquiry."[64] This is illustrated by one of Derrida's most famous statements in French: "*Il n'y a pas de hors-texte*," that is, "There is nothing outside the text."[65] In saying this he was not advocating some sort of atheistic linguistic idealism. He was not saying that only texts are real and things like streets, houses, and toothbrushes are mere illusions. Instead, he was making a point about reading and interpretation.

For Derrida, people simply cannot escape the process of interpretation, whether it is the interpretation of books, of culture, or of anything

---

61. Simon Critchley, "Introduction," in *The Cambridge Companion to Levinas*, ed. Simon Critchley and Robert Bernasconi (Cambridge, MA.: Cambridge University Press, 2002), 21.

62. Simon Critchley, *The Ethics of Deconstruction: Derrida and Levinas*, 2nd ed. (Edinburgh: Edinburgh University Press, 1999), 284–86.

63. Emmanuel Levinas, *Totality and Infinity: An Essay on Exteriority*, trans. Alphonso Lingis (Pittsburgh: Duquesne University Press, 1969), 197. See also Emmanuel Levinas, "Is Ontology Fundamental?" in *Emmanuel Levinas: Basic Philosophical Writings*, ed. Adriaan T. Peperzak, Simon Critchley, and Robert Bernasconi (Bloomington and Indianapolis: Indiana University Press, 1996), 9.

64. Michener, *Engaging*, 65.

65. Jacques Derrida, *Of Grammatology*, trans. Gayatri Chakravorty Spivak (Baltimore: Johns Hopkins University Press, 1976), 158.

about the world around them. Interpretation is an inevitable part of being human. Everything we encounter inescapably demands interpretation. In saying this, however, he was not denying truth, reality, or the possibility of good or bad interpretations.[66] Derrida's deconstruction was not about a free-for-all relativism for interpretation and denial of reality. Instead, it was affirming the ubiquity of interpretation. All human understanding is filtered through interpretive schemes, biases, cultures, and backgrounds. Deconstruction seeks to bring these issues to light, to help recognize the latent prejudices causing the suppression of ideas and, often, the oppression of people and the prevention of justice.

Undeniably, justice and ethics work in close collaboration. But in view of Derrida's deconstructionist critique, is there still a place for ethics? If our resolutions are always filtered through interpretive grids, how can we meaningfully discuss ethical responsibility? Rather than abandoning ethics altogether, as Margrit Shildrik points out, "Derrida takes up the notion of the undecidable as precisely the mark of a highly responsive and responsible ethics." Shildrik continues, remarking that it forces us to engage with the "undecidable" and have a "real encounter with the ethical issues at hand," rather than simply "retreat to the security of the known."[67]

There is in Derrida's deconstruction a clear ethical demand for justice, a justice beyond status quo readings and modern complacency.[68] Deconstruction seeks the hidden places where justice has been put aside or rendered unimportant. It seeks ethical reflection in areas that often are ignored. It does not provide a decision-making procedure to test the validity of ethical maxims, but it consistently interrupts the prevailing arguments that result in consensus.[69] It incessantly seeks justice. Derrida claimed that everything could be deconstructed *except* justice; in fact, deconstruction *was* justice. It was deconstruction that actually made justice possible.[70]

This idea of the undeconstructibility of justice is extremely important for moral philosophy. Laws can and should be deconstructed, but not justice, not righteousness. Justice is the *a priori* behind the interpretation of laws. The law is written text, influenced by economic and political

---

66. Smith, *Who's Afraid of Postmodernism?* 38–39, 44.
67. Shildrik and Mykitiuk, eds., *Ethics of the Body*, 11.
68. Simon Critchley has insightfully argued this in his book *The Ethics of Deconstruction*.
69. Critchley, *Ethics of Deconstruction*, 254.
70. John D. Caputo, ed., *Deconstruction in a Nutshell: A Conversation with Jacques Derrida* (New York: Fordham University Press, 1997), 131–32.

powers, altered by compromise and calculation. A judge must interpret the law within a particular context, applying it again and again.[71] We cannot comprehend justice through the rigors of reason and empirical analysis. Justice is more personal, existential, and value centered than laws expressed in propositions.

So the concept of what it means to be human is broadened in view of the deconstructionist critique. Humans are not simply rational creatures subject to their own legal discourses; they are creative beings with feelings, imaginations, and wills. To be human involves a rich matrix of attributes. Along with a more full-orbed view of humanity, personal sincerity and authenticity become invaluable qualities for the postmodern. Postmodernism challenges us to look beyond mere objective goodness as expressed through norms and laws and calls us to a subjective goodness (contra hypocrisy) drawn from a heart for justice before the face of others in the everyday world and, ultimately, we believe, before the face of God. It is our desire to engage these perspectives in our matrix approach to Christian ethics developed in subsequent chapters.

The postmodern critique helps us dismantle the latent structures of power by which we manipulate and oppress in the name of truth. We often forget how our choice of words and our style of language may be used to control others and fight against the Christian call to community. In community we must develop space for internal plurality and dialogue. It is precisely this openness to internal dialogue that makes the church a genuine moral community.[72] The community is not simply a sum of faceless individuals; it is a dynamic collective intended to reflect the triune community of God. This notion pleads against dictatorial church models in which moral consensus is forced on the faith community in all details of life. This is not to say that the community will not exemplify a countercultural cohesiveness, humbly living out the kingdom call of Jesus. Nor is this to say that we have understood it all correctly, for we live in the margins, knowing we often act out the sinfulness of Adam while daily striving after and participating in the narrative of the new life of redemption in the resurrected Jesus.

---

71. Millard J. Erickson, *Truth or Consequences: The Promises and Perils of Postmodernism* (Downers Grove, IL: InterVarsity Press, 2001), 124–25.

72. See Stanley J. Grenz's community-based ethic in his book *The Moral Quest: Foundations of Christian Ethics* (Downers Grove, IL: InterVarsity Press, 1997), 207–39.

The vainglorious, broken promises of modernism, the postmodern critique, and the technological revolution all confront us with the limits of human reason and the myth of scientific and epistemological neutrality. Knowledge is always situated, biased, and filtered through our interpretive grids. But rather than conceding to the temptation of despair, we believe this presents us with some unique opportunities for Christian ethical reflection today. In view of these challenges, we are promoting in this book an embrace of responsible postmodern thought with a deep concern for justice and the well-being of the other. We desire to engage in a deeply Christian ethical reflection that moves beyond a modernist ideal of individual rights due to our sameness as human beings to an acknowledgment of the wonder of our diversity and complexity.[73]

---

73. See Kelly James Clark, Richard Lints, and James K. A. Smith, *101 Key Terms in Philosophy and Their Importance for Theology* (Louisville: Westminster John Knox, 2004), 74.

Chapter 2

Moral Argumentation

As observed in the previous chapter, we all have angles from which we interpret reality. Angles are not bad things to be avoided, because our angles are the lenses by which we access the world around us.[1] But when our angles are unacknowledged, used to control or manipulate others, or our own angles are assumed to be everybody's angles, conflicts arise and conversations grind to an uncomfortable halt. Differences of perspective and opinion should be expected and appreciated. But differences immersed in worldviews routinely turn to a discourse on truth claims, and truth claims often turn into billy clubs. This is especially true when it comes to ethical debates about what is deemed right and what is deemed wrong. In this chapter we will provide a brief overview of four basic approaches used in ethical discourse and reasoning. Rather than positioning these angles against each other as conflicting paradigms, we are suggesting that they complement each other, providing a well-rounded Christian ethic. To illustrate each approach, we will use a hypothetical case study addressing the use of bribery.[2] Our purpose will not be to solve the posed dilemma(s), but simply to use the case study to stimulate our integrative or *matrix* approach to ethical reasoning.

---

1. See John D. Caputo, *Philosophy and Theology* (Nashville: Abingdon, 2006), 45.
2. On the subject of bribery and business ethics, see Bernard T. Adney, "Ethical Theory and Bribery," in *Beyond Integrity: A Judeo-Christian Approach to Business Ethics*, ed. Scott B. Rae and Kenman L. Wong (Grand Rapids: Zondervan, 2004), 223–38.

A Case Study in Bribery

Following a long period of unemployment, John finds a job working as a sales representative for a well-known pharmaceutical company. Enjoying his new job, John is glad finally to provide his family with some financial stability. However, after several weeks he discovers that one of his senior colleagues is engaging in bribery. Several major clients—pharmacists and hospital directors—are being given gifts and vacation trips unrelated to their work. As an accounting ploy, the bribes are declared marketing expenses and so are tax deductible. In one instance the wife of a hospital executive is given a new car. For several years this colleague has used bribes with his major clients to eliminate competitors and ensure the pharmaceuticals will be sold at full price. As the weeks pass, John realizes several other experienced colleagues are also using bribes to increase their sales figures. John is under a lot of pressure, understanding his performance will be compared with that of his corrupt colleagues. He has determined not to compromise his values by bribing his clients. But should he report the illegal practices of his colleagues to his boss? What if the boss is also guilty of the same practices? Then what? Would it not be more sensible and practical for him to keep his head down and his eyes closed to these affairs and simply prove that he can perform just as well by honest means?

Four Approaches

In practice, our chief concern tends to be about the *consequences* of a certain act or course of action. Even when we focus on principles, our minds are drawn to future implications. If John reports the bribery, his colleagues may be punished. As a newcomer, he will be branded a whistle-blower and subjected to harassment. It may get him on the boss's good side, but at what price? And if the boss is one of the culprits as well, he will be less than delighted to discover that his new employee is a moral crusader. If fraud is practiced on a large scale, the issue may go to the managing board or even to court. If the press learns of it, John may be publicly stigmatized. Ultimately, it could cost him his job and prevent him from getting work elsewhere. He must think about his responsibilities as the breadwinner of his family. Should he put aside his personal convictions for the sake of his wife and children? On the other hand, his family and many others may ultimately be burdened by inflated medication prices as a result of these ongoing dishonest practices. If he addresses the problem now, he may be making a contribution toward honesty in medical practices and the long-run well-being not only of his family but also of society at large.

When the ethical dimension comes to the fore, we cannot help but think of the *principles* involved. From the perspective of business ethics and trade laws, bribery is deemed an illegal practice. It entails giving secret gifts to others for which a favor is demanded in return (either explicitly or implicitly), negating the assumed neutrality of the buyer. The exchange is made based on the self-interest of the negotiating parties, rather than the interests of the representative employers. The offering of bribes also creates a context for the proliferation of lies and secret unwritten contracts. This flies in the face of the basic economic principles of mutual trust and honest competition. Such legislation was put into place for reasons of providing justice and fairness to all. Simply from the perspective of principles, the consequences for John are significant. John's duty is to report the illegal actions of his colleagues to his employer and, if necessary, to his disadvantaged customers.

From the aspect of *virtues* or *character*, John faces a situation that demands courage and honesty. If John has invested in personal character development throughout his life, his automatic response will be one of outrage. Ultimately, he must be faithful to his background and upbringing. The requirements of the law and the consequences involved are of secondary importance. It is precisely in difficult situations like this where it is important for John to maintain good character and be who he intends to be, regardless of what his colleagues, boss, or company may decide to do. With this in mind, it appears that the most virtuous route for John is simply to conduct himself honestly and not to worry about responding to the others.

A fourth perspective centers on *values*. John sees the problem as a conflict of values more than as a conflict of principles. After going through a period of unemployment, John appreciates the value of having a job. Losing his job at this point would be a disaster for his family. Yet his appreciation of the value of work also creates an awareness of the value of enjoying work in the context of honest relationships. Bribery detracts from the value of work in and of itself; it elevates greed and selfish gain. And what about the value of friendship with his colleagues? Would this or should this prevent him from reporting their illegal activities? On the other hand, what if John values status and money more highly than honesty and job satisfaction?

In a fairly simple manner this scenario demonstrates that we can evaluate an ethical dilemma from a number of angles and that not every angle will lead to the same conclusion. At this juncture we will only briefly consider the framework of each of these approaches, understanding that we will provide a more detailed discussion and evaluation in later chapters.[3]

Consequential Ethics

The ultimate criteria for determining good and evil according to consequential ethics are, of course, the *consequences* of a deed rather than the deed itself. A given deed may be considered good in one situation and bad in another, depending on the result. For example, speaking the truth is not a moral obligation in itself; its status depends on the consequences. This does not mean, however, that it is acceptable to lie. However, lying is generally deemed to be wrong not because of an isolated act of a lie but because persistent lying disrupts human communication and threatens our general well-being. In consequential ethics, standards or precepts by themselves do not dictate a basis for moral judgment; rather, the effects or consequences of particular acts do. Consequential ethics is also known as *consequentialism* or *teleological ethics.*

An exclusive focus on consequences to the exclusion of all else makes relative the motivations behind the deeds. So it would be possible to act in a morally correct manner while being prompted by reprehensible motives. For example, a dictator motivated by a desire for personal glory may be deemed an exemplary leader as long as the outcome is considered beneficial for his subjects. In our previous example, large-scale bribery may be justified on the grounds that jobs have been saved. Furthermore, landing huge contracts even through bribery may improve the prosperity of an entire region or nation. When compared to such gain, a few million dollars spent on bribes may seem insignificant to the overall results for society.[4] Positive

---

3. For the sake of scope and space, we have chosen not to provide an extensive historical introduction to moral philosophy in our discussion. We would recommend the following capable works in this regard: Robert L. Arrington, *Western Ethics: An Historical Introduction* (Oxford: Blackwell, 1998); Alasdair C. MacIntyre, *A Short History of Ethics: A History of Moral Philosophy from the Homeric Age to the Twentieth Century* (London: Routledge, 1998); and R. E. O. White, *The Changing Continuity of Christian Ethics* (Exeter, NH: Paternoster Press, 1981).

4. One example from Europe is the Lockheed bribery scandal of the 1970s. Prince Bernard of the Netherlands, Premier Aldo Moro of Italy, and Premier Tanaka of Japan, among others, were all involved in this scandal. Several million dollars in bribes were exchanged. Lockheed's primary argument in its own defense was that it was trying to save jobs and avoid

consequences may assume precedence over particular motives or specific laws.

Consequential ethics may be divided into at least two major tendencies: *hedonism* and *utilitarianism*. Philosophical hedonism may be traced back as far as classical antiquity to the Epicureans. Broadly, hedonism is the pursuit of sensual pleasure with a view to avoiding all sense of pain. Although it never enjoyed a large following as a system, there was a resurgence of interest during the Enlightenment, which tended to view humanity in mechano-biological terms. According to hedonism, an act is good if it creates pleasure and lessens pain and bad if it causes or increases pain. Hedonism is based purely on sensory perception of the consequences of an act. In everyday practice many people adhere to a hedonistic ethic in that they perceive life as a sum of seeking pleasurable moments and employing pain-avoidance strategies. We notice this in the struggle between the enjoyment of food and keeping fit to prevent heart disease and obesity. The fast-food market contrasts with the morass of health clubs and slimming products available.

Another tendency in consequentialism is *utilitarianism*, the aim of which is to achieve the highest degree of pleasure and the lowest degree of pain, for the largest possible number of people. This view is commonly attributed to philosophers Jeremy Bentham and John Stuart Mill, often considered prototypes of British moral philosophy. Utilitarianism represents a departure from the typical individual egoism at the heart of hedonism. Applying this to our case study, we would see John shifting from simply considering his personal consequences to thinking also of the social consequences of his actions. His emphasis would shift to the vast array of patients and society at large that would suffer the consequences of medication prices inflated because of the dishonest practices of his colleagues.

Philosophical utilitarianism was developed in conjunction with political theories prevalent in the nineteenth century. When modernism was at its height, an attempt was made to establish a society that could function without resorting to religious authority or a presupposed natural order. Given that people were seen as hedonistic by nature, it was the task of utilitarianism to restructure what came naturally into a culture of social hedonism. In this sense there is a direct link between hedonism and utilitarianism.

---

social drama. See Jef Van Gerwen et al., *Business en ethiek: spelregels voor het ethisch ondernemen* (Tielt, Belgium: Lannoo, 2002), 72–73.

Within utilitarianism a further distinction can be made between *act utilitarianism* and *rule utilitarianism*. With act utilitarianism moral consideration is given to specific moral acts. At each stage a question is posed: What will be the consequences of this act? Rule utilitarianism takes specific moral considerations into account at the first stage and then formulates these considerations into a set of rules to be followed. The strong influence of rule utilitarianism is evident in pluralistic democratic societies. Before a legislative decision is made, moral debate takes place that focuses on the social consequences of the proposal in question. Take for example the discussion surrounding the legalization of soft drugs. Some of the arguments are not about the particular health effects of the drugs themselves but about the influence the drugs will have on young people in society, or about the addictive power of a particular drug, or about the potential for its use to lead to the use of more damaging drugs. Once a discussion reaches this level and some form of consensus is reached, legislation is introduced.

In the Anglo-Saxon world utilitarianism has many adherents.[5] The underlying assumption behind utilitarianism is that pleasure and pain as experienced by a group of people can in some sense be measured. Although consequences have played a major part in shaping the current evaluation of moral issues facing us today, the measurements and calculations involved are extremely complex. The postmodern critique rightly questions the adequacy and sufficiency of our ability correctly to play out the scenarios involved in measuring such consequences. The evaluation of consequences prior to a moral act often assumes a judicious understanding of outcomes based on the twin pillars of experience and rationality. Since these pillars have lost their *terra firma* in the face of postmodernity, utilitarianism itself is at least subject to question.

Principle Ethics

The natural opposite of consequential ethics is *principle* or *deontological* ethics, often associated with the philosopher Immanuel Kant. The term *deontological* is derived from the Greek *deontos*, meaning "obligation." An obligation appeals to our will and demands obedience. According to principle ethics a moral act is good if it conforms to a certain principle (precept or norm), irrespective of the consequences. What is good can only

---

5. Arrington, *Western Ethics*, 318.

be understood in light of particular laws and our unconditional obedience to them. Lying is always wrong, even if in certain cases the consequences appear beneficial. The task of ethics is thus seen as the discovery of principles with a view to applying these principles in everyday moral acts. For example, the rules we have dictating speed restrictions while driving in part relate to the principle of keeping others from harm. This principle is obeyed via obedience to a series of minor injunctions.

There are two forms of principle ethics distinguishable by the source from which we derive our norms: *theonomous* ethics and *autonomous* ethics. Theonomous ethics (from Greek *theos* meaning "God" and *nomos* meaning "law") takes God to be the changeless source of all moral laws. All that is good is ultimately founded on God's will, and it is up to humans to obey God's precepts. The medieval theologian and philosopher Thomas Aquinas, the model for Roman Catholic moral theology, placed natural moral law theory alongside divine command ethics. Both, for Thomas, were based on God's universal and timeless laws. The reformer John Calvin focused primarily on Scripture, seeing the Ten Commandments as a summary of Christian ethics. The neoorthodox theologian Karl Barth presented a modern theonomous Protestant ethic, with the Totally Other God as his starting point. In Barth's view a Christian ethic would not attempt acceptance of or association with universal principle ethics.

Autonomous principle ethics (Greek *autos* means "self") is based on the concept that moral laws are not derived from God but from humanity itself. The motivation for morality lies in rationally recognizable reality, not in the metaphysical or transcendental as is the case in theonomous ethics. Humanity does not need God, for we are a law unto ourselves. A religiously based ethic cannot be universally applied because not everyone believes it, whereas autonomous principle ethics is universal by nature in that it is founded on reason. In a later chapter we will illustrate this perspective with the help of the most important philosopher of the Enlightenment, Immanuel Kant. Kant drew a unique connection between the Enlightenment dogma of freedom and the necessity of moral duty.

Virtue Ethics

The two models discussed above focus primarily on moral acts (principle ethics) and their consequences (consequential ethics). Virtue ethics centers on the person performing the act, the moral subject. It is from this focus that virtue ethics derives its alternate name: character ethics. In contrast to the above two ethical systems, the focus here is not on concrete decisions but on *who we are before* we make moral decisions.

The English word *virtue* is derived from the Latin *virtus*. This term originally referred to manliness. Put in somewhat sexist terms, a virtue was what made a man a "real man." Later the term took on the wider meaning of "excellence" and "competence." Etymologically and historically, virtue was linked to specific goals a human being would try to attain. Virtue was seen as the equivalent of noble and admirable character traits worth emulating. If we had the virtue of generosity, we would spontaneously respond generously when a need arose. The given act of generosity was not motivated by obedience to a precept or by consequences; the person was simply acting according to character. In this sense virtue ethics can be tied to the concept of self-realization of human potential.

Virtue ethics is deeply rooted in classical antiquity and was generally accepted by Plato, Aristotle, and the Stoics. The heroic values of old military Greece were gradually superseded by the more refined virtues of Athenian urban democracy. Socrates in particular raised the deeper question of the necessity and usefulness of a virtuous life. His primary concern was in coming up with the right definition. Plato then developed this definition into a world of ideas deemed more real than the temporal reality around us. Virtue ethics reached its prime with Plato's student Aristotle. According to Aristotle virtue is not as much about theoretical contemplation of the good as it is about living according to practical wisdom—doing what is proportionately right in every situation. By leading a virtuous life, a person can achieve the goal of happiness.

This theme of virtue was also adopted into Christian ethics. The New Testament virtues of faith, hope, and love were integrated into the classical doctrine of virtue. Thomas Aquinas was an important proponent of this Christianized form of virtue ethics.

Virtue ethics is enjoying a renewed popularity among Christian thinkers today. Theologian Stanley Hauerwas has introduced an ethic of Christian character as an alternative to the theonomous principle ethic. Consistent with virtue ethics, he maintains that what matters most is not what you ought to do but who you are.[6] Christian character is developed

---

6. See Stanley Hauerwas, *A Community of Character: Toward a Constructive Christian Social Ethic* (Notre Dame: University of Notre Dame Press, 1981).

in the context of a community within which the authority of Scripture is embraced and applied.

Value Ethics and Personalism

Philosopher Max Scheler (1874–1928) was perhaps the most important contemporary proponent of value ethics. His ethic of the heart was an extension of the tradition of Augustine and Blaise Pascal. To the impoverishment of Protestant ethical reflection, value ethics has remained relatively unknown. The primary focus of value ethics is not on moral decisions, as with virtue ethics, but on our moral being. The essence of morality is not found in laws and obligations or in obedience and rationality but in the perception of values. Through our values we judge some things important and other things superfluous. Values give direction to our lives, including how we view family, culture, friendships, work, beauty, and freedom. A precept tells us what we must do; a value indicates what we cherish. Ethicist Ian Barbour defines a value as "a general characteristic of an object or state of affairs that a person views with favor, believes is beneficial, and is disposed to act to promote."[7] William Schweicker defines a value as "the quality of being good, important or of human concern, or an entity which possesses this quality deserving of care."[8]

A European values study has identified the most important values in Europe as responsibility, good manners, tolerance, and hard work.[9] For many Europeans greater importance is ascribed to these values than to money, material possessions, or independence. This same study has also revealed that money is not seen as the means to happiness. Instead, what people desire the most are good health, positive friendships, and a decent marriage.

A value is not so much *thought* as it is *experienced* within a particular context. Heidegger insightfully argued that we cannot objectify ourselves to get at the notion of being. As John Caputo explains, "As soon as we come to be we find that we are already there. . . . We can never get behind

---

7. Ian Graeme Barbour, *Ethics in an Age of Technology* (San Francisco: HarperSanFrancisco, 1993), 26.

8. William Schweiker, ed., *The Blackwell Companion to Religious Ethics* (Malden, MA: Blackwell, 2005), 582.

9. Loek Halman, Ruud Luijkx, and Marga van Zundert, *Atlas of European Values* (Leiden, Neth.: Brill, 2005), 38.

ourselves and see ourselves come into being, or we can never get out of our skin and look down on ourselves from above. . . . We are in truth shaped by the presuppositions we inherit."[10] In a similar sense, value ethics is primarily anthropological, seeking to gain insight into the inner perceptions and presuppositions of the individual. Values are primarily directive. That is, they form an essential part of our upbringing, passed on from generation to generation. Value ethics allows for emotion and the various complexities out of which we make our moral choices.

Personalism belongs to the tradition of value ethics as well. Here the prime focus is on the absolute value of the other, our neighbor. This value is more than a principle or a precept. It is a direct ethical appeal that precedes the rational. Emmanuel Levinas spoke of the radical otherness of the one I encounter. The face of the other is before me, prompting me to act morally. It is not simply the "I" that is central, but the irreducible value of my fellow human being. Catholic moral theologian Roger Burggraeve reasons along similar lines in his formulation of a Christian ethic of charity and care for the poor. The "radical social care" he advocates is not based on duties, utilitarian motives, or Christian virtues, but based on a direct appeal from a human being in need.[11] It is evident that there may be various overlaps and intersections among these approaches. By way of example, we suggest that a value of charity toward others stems from virtues bestowed by the Holy Spirit into the life of the believer.

Ethics and Worldview

Each of the four models briefly outlined above stems from a worldview that provides its moral sense. Ethics and worldviews gradually blend together. But worldviews can vary tremendously. Some believe in life after death; others say this life is all there is. Some view freedom of expression as a human right to be practiced; others believe personal opinions should not be freely expressed. Ultimately, we try to act in accordance with deeply held beliefs or worldview values in a given situation, whether we are aware of it or not. Often worldviews do not come to the surface in discussions unless we are confronted by an opposing perspective. When tensions arise, implicit worldviews are made explicit. The outrage we feel about a particular

---

10. John Caputo, *Philosophy and Theology* (Nashville: Abingdon, 2006), 45.
11. Roger Burggraeve, *Ethiek & passie: Over de radicaliteit van christelijk engagement* (Tielt, Belgium: Lannoo, 2000), 51ff.

government's supporting the right to euthanasia may readily reveal a suppressed worldview.

If our moral behavior changes or adapts to that of the prevailing culture, our worldview will often be adjusted accordingly. So worldviews are both formative and formed. Consider street gangs, for example. With a worldview centered on conflict and threat from those outside the gang, good is that which means remaining loyal to the gang, regardless of the act. Anything interfering with this basic worldview becomes an enemy; civil laws, police officers, and members of other gangs all represent a hindrance to the gang's identity. What some may consider a criminal act, a gang may consider a virtue for living in the context of a tough street ethos.

Worldviews are not elaborate philosophical systems. They are often prescientific and inconsistent. In fact, depending on our worldview, we may not feel the need for a coherent system in which to articulate it. Christians believe in life after death, yet it is ironic how little impact this belief has on our lives or on how we choose to spend our time. Ideally, our worldview and ethics should work together. Our worldview should govern our lifestyle choices as it does our intellectual values. Worldviews cannot simply be set aside to permit objective discussion of ethical conundrums in society. Our situatedness is always before us as a lens (or series of lenses) through which our vision of reality must pass. We acknowledge our individual lenses, as best as we can, understanding that these acknowledgments are always filtered through the lenses themselves. Dialogue with others both inside and outside our communities is critical for revealing unseen or disregarded presuppositions. When such presuppositions are disclosed, we may choose to make appropriate adjustments to our worldview. For example, if you have been brought up with very conservative ideas on the position of women in society, an ethical confrontation with feminist thinkers regarding the oppression of women may challenge your strongly paternalistic worldview.

If worldviews are seen as the basis for ethics, what are the elements that make up a worldview? From our perspective there are at least three aspects to consider: God, humanity, and nature. How people interpret the relationship between and order of these three will greatly inform their ethics. How people see God (or gods, in some religions) or the absence of God will influence their view of moral accountability. How they see the human person and how humans fit into the natural world or cosmic order will also influence their worldview. If a worldview is rooted in Darwinism, it will affect how adherents see life and its processes and how they fit in with others, in turn influencing their daily relationships.

In view of these considerations, we can see the moral philosophical debate in general terms as an interplay and/or a struggle between anthropological idealism, naturalism, and theism. But these proposed foundations themselves say little about the ethical views that are ultimately held. People will often base different ethical convictions on one affirmed foundation, as clearly evidenced by the frequent moral differences expressed among Christians.[12] For now we will characterize these three perspectives (humanity, nature, God) as anthropocentrism, naturocentrism, and theocentrism. Anthropocentrism sees nature as at humanity's disposal and God as a projection of human desire or fear. Naturocentrism sees humanity as the highest species of animal, with religion as the psychological result of certain evolutionary cerebral processes. Theocentrism sees humanity as created beings subservient to and understood in the context of the Creator. In the following section we will consider each of these more extensively. For heuristic purposes we will concentrate primarily on their differences, but we understand that there may be overlaps and tendencies of all three perspectives expressed in particular worldviews.

Anthropocentrism

The popular sentiment of anthropocentrism is often captured in this famous saying by Protagoras: "Man is the measure of all things." For Protagoras this meant that each individual must decide for himself or herself and that there is, therefore, no objective moral truth. But anthropocentrism does not necessarily imply such arbitrary, radical individualism. An anthropocentric perspective may also focus on humanity collectively, more anthropologically than individually.

Plato (427–347 BC) viewed a person as more than simply a physical being. Humans were unique among all creatures, for they possessed rational souls. Souls would be reincarnated and retained recollections of a higher world of constant ideas. The temporal world in which humans lived was inconstant and therefore of a lower order.

This dualism is clearly seen in the well-known cave allegory of Plato's *Republic*.[13] We live in this world as prisoners chained to a wall inside a dark

---

12. For example, Christians will often claim that the Bible (as the Word of God) is their only foundation for ethics. As noble as this sounds, the claim often neglects the ubiquity of interpretation for understanding and application in particular contexts.

13. See Plato, *The Republic,* trans. R. E. Allen (New Haven, CT: Yale University Press,

cave. On the opposite wall we see shadows of people passing behind us. We suppose the shadows are the real world, but they are merely the reflections of the world of light. We do not know any better because we have spent our entire lives shackled to the wall of the temporal. Philosophers are individuals who have learned, through the rigors of discipline and practice, to see reality. They have gained insight into the world of light and constant ideas and are able to distinguish good from evil. Since philosophical reason is humanity's highest ability, it sets the course for happiness. Ethics must focus on this world of higher ideas as well. When we attain knowledge of these ideas or forms, we will gain understanding of the nature of justice. The highest idea of all is the good, which attracts all other ideas. This attraction that Plato calls love (*eros*) also works in our souls. In Plato's ethics humanity must gain control over the soul, with the higher part of the soul gaining dominance over the lower. Leaders are shaped by this cultivation of self-control and intelligence. As Diogenes Allen puts it, "True morality is thus not the product of convention or arbitrary enactment of human will, but the virtuous individual is a counterpart in miniature of the order and harmony of the cosmos."[14]

Although Plato may seem to have been religious when he spoke of the good, his morality is, rather, based on a reasoning soul that is endowed with the capacity to receive ideas. His ethics is founded on a rational soul that acquires insight into the idea of the good. Capacity to know and freedom to choose are the main elements on which he bases his optimistic anthropocentric approach. For Plato, the reasoning person seeks the fulfillment of his or her destiny and has the ability to discover it.

Naturocentrism

Naturocentrism views humanity as an integral part of nature. Here the basis for ethics is not found within humanity but outside in the cosmic order. Sometimes this approach results in pantheism, where the omnipresent God is fully identified with the natural world. In the classical world we trace naturocentrism to the Stoic ethics of Zeno (333–261 BC); it lasted some five hundred years. Adherents included Seneca (the tutor of Nero) and the philosopher and emperor Marcus Aurelius. In Stoicism, we are

---

2006), 7:227–32, 514–21.
14. Diogenes Allen, *Philosophy for Understanding Theology* (Atlanta: John Knox, 1985), 16.

all part of the cosmic order, as one vast reasoning soul (*Logos*). Ultimately, everything is determined; the course of history is set, and we can do nothing to change it. The universe knows a reasonable order, and we must live according to it. The *Logos*, the universal principle, is like a fire that penetrates and permeates every part of the cosmos. Humanity shares in this divine order by virtue of the divine spark resident within.

By claiming that humans can influence only their inner states, the Stoics internalized ethics. People should not allow themselves to become attached to feelings of happiness or avoid suffering. Humans are by nature rational beings, so it follows that they live according to that nature. So the only reasonable option is numb acceptance of the natural, logical course of events we are faced with.

In the wake of the general acceptance of evolutionary theory, humanity's understanding of the universe faced some dramatic changes. The previous notion of stability in the cosmos made room for the fluctuating and progressive qualities of nature. Nature came to be seen as a subject of continuous change. Friedrich Nietzsche's (1844–1900) philosophical perspectivism reflected this sentiment through his somewhat prophetically styled aphoristic writings. His view of reality was dynamic, in line with ideas propounded by the pre-Socratic philosopher Heraclitus. All is finite. The cosmos is fickle and riddled with conflicting forces, offering no security whatsoever. Life stands alone as a force, and our ethics is merely an expression of power.[15] Only the force of life enables us to carry on. In this regard, Nietzsche's ethics is also referred to as *vitalism*.

The debate between anthropocentrism and naturocentrism continues today. Neo-Darwinism describes humanity as vulnerable and dependent on the natural environment. Some suggest that humans have wrongfully appropriated the throne as the earth's masters—that the difference between people and animals is not essential but merely a question of degree. Australian animal rights philosopher Peter Singer is an exponent of this recent form of naturocentrism. He proposes that science teaches the "capacity to suffer," which is clearly present in higher species and therefore gives rise to a consideration of animal rights and interests. We have never based the

---

15. This theme of power and ethics becomes dominant in the later work of Michel Foucault, who was heavily reliant on Nietzsche. Nietzsche's complex moral perspectivs are played out in a number of his works. For examples see Friedrich Wilhelm Nietzsche, *The Will to Power: An Attempted Transvaluation of All Values* (New York: Gordon Press, 1974); and *On the Genealogy of Morals* (Arlington, VA: Richer Resources Publications, 2008).

rights of humans on their intellectual capacity. If we had, Einstein should have had more rights than the simple laborer. An analogy is drawn here between racism and "speciesism," that is, "a prejudice towards the interests of members of our own species and against those of beings that are not members of our own species."[16]

Theocentrism

For others the basis of morality is not to be found in a particular portrayal of humanity or through a particular perspective on the universe, but in divine revelation from a transcendent God. This revealed ethic may speak of humanity and nature, but humanity and nature are clearly not the starting point. In this model faith and obedience always take precedence over reflection. This theocentric religious ethic is found in Judaism, Christianity, and Islam. Each religion holds to a divine authority providing laws and guidelines for moral living. Ultimately, happiness will be found only as the commandments of that authority are accepted and followed.

The Jewish believer lives by the law, understanding that the law brings happiness through obedience. The law protects and guides life from the cradle to the grave. The focus in Jewish ethics is traditionally placed on family life and moral life in obedience to God—not exclusively through external observance of the commandments, but also through the inner life and motives.[17]

Islam is another example of theocentric ethics. The Arabic word *Islam* means "submission"—complete surrender to the will of God (*Allah*). The word *Muslim* means "obedience to God." The Qur'an provides guidelines for daily living in surrender to Allah. It rules out every form of division between ethics and religion and, by extension, between religion and politics. Islam is practically oriented with much to say regarding civil rights. The Islamic *sharia*

---

16. Peter Singer, *Een ethisch leven* (Utrecht, Neth.: Het Spectrum, 2001), 51 (translation ours). It is interesting to note how the philosopher Fukuyama (an anthropocentrist) attempts to refute the naturocentrism of Singer, taking as his basis a similar neo-Darwinian worldview. See Fukuyama, *The End of History and the Last Man* (New York: Free Press, 1992), 176–81; 189–90.

17. See *Hovot Ha-Levavot*, written by Bahya ben Joseph ibn Pakuda in the 11th century. See Bahya ben Joseph ibn Pakuda, *Duties of the Heart*, trans. Yaakov Feldman (Northvale, NJ: Jason Aronson, 1996). In his introduction, Pakuda draws a distinction between the duties of the heart and of the limbs. This mystical book guides the Jewish believer through ten steps (or doors) leading to spiritual perfection.

(religious law) is largely derived from the Qur'an and from ancient traditions (*hadith*). Islam often tends to emphasize external obedience; a counterbalance is found in *Sufism*, which attaches a spiritual significance to the law and takes a more flexible view of other cultures and customs.

In Islam theocentrism often leans toward theocracy—a society in which Allah holds the highest authority. Human reasoning is not capable of grasping the good and using it as a basis for designing a legal system. A breach of the law is not a contravention of social order but a religious act of disobedience, a sin requiring religious punishment. When negotiations take place in Western diplomatic circles regarding Islamic issues, some underestimate the difference between this understanding and a secularized, anthropocentric model of law. Of course, even within Islam itself there are many differences of opinion about how to relate to modernism. For instance, Muslims in Egypt, Turkey, India, and central Asia have allowed themselves to be influenced more heavily by Western thought than Muslims have elsewhere.

In view of the current moral climate, we have made an effort to give consideration to a variety of elements of morality. Christian ethics often limits itself to command ethics or theonomous principle ethics, while neglecting other facets of moral reflection. In practice there is a continuous interaction between multiple worldviews and moral choices. For example, if we believe in a God who has revealed precepts, then we emphasize ethical principles for action. If we believe in the feasibility of a just society in which each individual can develop and flourish, we place greater emphasis on consequences. In the ethical debate some fail to appreciate that participants are inclined to stress significantly different aspects precisely because of their underlying worldviews.

As mentioned previously, these four methodological approaches (consequences, duties, character, and values) are interactive and also seem to follow a sequence. We begin with values passed on to us as part of our upbringing. These values help shape our moral character, whereby we attribute greater importance to some virtues over others. When faced with a choice, however, we will act not only on the basis of our values and character but also on the basis of certain principles or precepts that reflect our motives. Our actions are followed by consequences, and our values evaluate the consequences. Our values are derived from our worldviews, which are closely related to our values. Our worldviews determine what we deem more important and less important and who or what ascribes validity to our moral choices. In Christian theocentric ethics the claim is that the one ultimately determining our value is the triune God of the Bible.

Moral Philosophy and Moral Theology

We cannot speak of worldviews and methods of ethical argumentation without touching on philosophy. The very word *ethics* may refer to both moral philosophy and moral theology. The former focuses its efforts on reasonable argumentation; the latter takes the supposition of divine revelation and faith as its point of departure. Granted, this is a somewhat simplistic way of putting things. In practice there are areas of overlap between the two. Christian ethics in particular has always shown considerable interest in moral philosophical thought. How we define the relationship between theology and ethics will influence how we interpret Christian ethics. Determining the precise relationship between these two disciplines is a major undertaking and beyond the scope of this book. So we will limit ourselves to a brief description of the ambivalent nature of the relationship between the two, pointing out several practical reasons why philosophical ethics is of value to Christian ethics.

Tertullian's words are well known: "What has Athens to do with Jerusalem?" The apostle Paul warned that we must not allow ourselves to be taken captive by all kinds of "hollow and deceptive" philosophy (Colossians 2:8). In this context, however, Paul was speaking of false teaching and strange superstitions, rather than attacking the discipline we know of as philosophy in general. Regardless, Tertullian's sentiment has reigned true in the minds of many throughout church history. A more recent proponent of the separation between philosophy and theology is Karl Barth (1886–1968), who was particularly opposed to any form of synthesis between the two. For Barth, moral philosophy focuses on the good as an abstract notion, using the tool of reason. According to Barth, Christian theology must take God's gracious act in Christ as its starting point. Theological ethics then addresses our response in faith and obedience. Sanctification is not achieved by cooperation between people and God, but only through the Word of God. For Barth, it is unthinkable for a universal moral creed to serve as the standard by which Christian ethics is to be judged. Moral theology must not allow itself to be seduced into apologetic jousting with philosophical ethics in the hope of gaining scholarly status.[18]

---

18. Karl Barth, *Ethics*, ed. Dietrich Braun, trans. Geoffrey W. Bromiley (New York: Seabury Press, 1981), 19–61; Karl Barth, *The Doctrine of God*, trans. G. W. Bromiley et al., vol. 2, pt. 2 of *Church Dogmatics*, ed. Geoffrey W. Bromiley and Thomas E. Torrance (Edinburgh: T&T Clark, 1957), 521–25; Robert E. Willis, *The Ethics of Karl Barth* (Leiden, Neth.: Brill,

Nevertheless, through the centuries the church has found philosophy essential to its growth and expression.[19] Christianity was increasingly required to give account of itself in a heathen world. The early apologist Justin Martyr (AD 100–165) became an important figure in this regard.[20] Following Justin, the Christian faith tended to be characterized as the new and true philosophy. Valuable pointers to Christian truth were being found in the writings of Socrates and Plato. In medieval Scholasticism the name of Thomas Aquinas became synonymous with the integration of theology with philosophy. He merged the ethics of Aristotle (and, to a lesser extent, Plato) with biblical revelation. Yet revelation maintained the upper hand; he referred to philosophy as the "handmaid" of theology (*filosophia ancilla theologiae*). For Thomas, God is the Creator of the universe and the source of all reason. The order that we perceive with our minds is ultimately God's order.[21]

Philosophy and Theology in Relation to Ethics

There are several reasons why philosophy is important for reflection on Christian ethics. Christian ethics is always practiced within a cultural context. The ability of ethics to respond effectively to a specific cultural challenge is dependent on some understanding of moral philosophy. Moral philosophy delves into the moral arguments of our time. The study of ethical systems provides us with insights to empathize with others wrestling with similar issues. This is necessary if we are to engage in dialogue with people inside and outside our culture who have opposing worldviews, while sharing similar contemporary ethical concerns such as genetic manipulation, overpopulation, poverty, abuse of power, and uncontrolled violence.[22]

1971), 102–13. Karl Barth's brother, Heinrich Barth, was a philosopher. Karl Barth provided a dedication to him in G. Huber, ed., *Philosophie und Christliche Existenz: Festschrift für Heinrich Barth* (Basel, Switz.: Helbing & Lichtenhahn, 1960).

19. See J. P. Moreland and William Lane Craig, *Philosophical Foundations for a Christian Worldview* (Downers Grove, IL: InterVarsity Press, 2003), 14–27.

20. Justin Martyr typifies the transition from an apodictic faith experience to philosophical argumentation, also in the area of morality. At the end of a long journey that took him through various philosophical systems, he came to the conclusion that for him the Christian faith was the "true philosophy." Cf. E. Meijering, *Geschiedenis van het vroege Christendom* (Amsterdam: Balans, 2004), 177–89.

21. Thomas Aquinas, *Summa Theologica* 1.1. article 5.

22. This is not to say we all share such concerns to the same degree.

In today's world more is required than a theological ethics ghetto. Even with Karl Barth's strong stance against philosophy as a means to discern the revelation of God, he appreciated the importance of philosophy as the "advocate of man and the world," with the task of keeping the theologian's feet firmly on the ground. Philosophy reminds the theologian that God is interested in us and our world.[23]

Second, philosophy helps us provide careful descriptions and argumentation for Christian moral education. Ethics is a discipline like any other, making use of its own methods and terminology. Moral philosophy has always had a strong orientation toward moral argumentation and the precise use of terms. For instance, it would consider a question such as "How can we prove that something is good or evil?" Christian ethics, however, has a different point of departure: God's will and biblical revelation. Yet it too is often engaged in the building of arguments from its own vantage point. The power of philosophy lies in in-depth analysis of concepts and an unceasing search for consistency. This is true even of radical postmodern thought with its unrelenting attack on self-proclaimed objective systems. Philosophy need not contradict the presuppositions on which faith is based. Its purpose is to discover how given faith assumptions lead to certain argumentations and truth claims. In terms of ethics, philosophical analysis may help us understand how people support their moral pronouncements. Moral philosophy is therefore a training ground for ethical argumentation, helping us evaluate the various opinions we encounter.

In this manner, philosophy can help us better understand our own Christian moral tradition. Philosophy is not an activity that takes place outside the walls of Christendom. Insight into moral philosophy helps us gain a fuller understanding of great Christian thinkers. Without some understanding of Plato and Aristotle, we cannot make sense of Augustine or Aquinas. These thinkers did not work in isolation but made critical use of classical philosophy. In a similar fashion, we can understand the theological ethics of Karl Barth better if we place it against the background

---

23. As *advocatus hominus et mundi*, cf. Karl Barth, "Philosophie und Theologie" in *Philosophie und christliche Existenz: Festschrift für Heinrich Barth*, ed. G. Huber (Basel, Switz.: Helbing & Lichtenhahn, 1960), 93–106. For a review see Willis, *The Ethics of Karl Barth* (Leiden, Neth.: 1971), 102–13; and Helmut Thielicke, *Theological Ethics*, vol. 1, ed. William H. Lazareth (Grand Rapids: Eerdmans, 1979).

of the existentialist philosophy of Søren Kierkegaard.[24] Bluntly, to ignore philosophy is simply to bury our heads in the sand.

Philosophy also helps us synthesize, contextualize, and integrate our Christian faith with our culture.[25] Christian scholars and those engaged in drawing up and implementing political policies need integrative models to help them with the contextualization of knowledge for church and/or public policy.

One of the greatest threats to the evangelical movement has been its chronic tendency toward anti-intellectualism. Although evangelicals have been deeply propositionally centered in terms of their view of revelation, many have remained relatively unreflective with regard to the application of doctrinal propositions within particular traditions. Consequently, "they tend to gloss over the personal and eventful nature of revelation as well as the revelational power of stories, images and speech acts."[26] Unfortunately, the neglect of philosophical study (as well as of other areas of the liberal arts and sciences) has often led to sectarian attitudes. As Mark Noll notes, "The evangelical ethos is activist, populist, pragmatic and utilitarian. It allows for little space for broader or deeper intellectual effort because it is dominated by the urgencies of the moment."[27] The mentality that Noll identifies fortunately stands in sharp contrast to the openness to the rigors of philosophical thought displayed by evangelical figures such as John Wesley, Jonathan Edwards, C. S. Lewis, Carl F. H. Henry, J. I. Packer, John Stott, and Stanley J. Grenz, just to name a few. Philosophical reflection can train us to be more self-critical within our own context, challenging us to consider perspectives different from or even contrary to our own tradition and stimulating our virtue of hospitality both personally and academically.[28]

---

24. Carl F. H. Henry, *Christian Personal Ethics* (Grand Rapids: Eerdmans, 1957), 132–42.
25. Philosophy is often regarded as a second-order discipline that builds on the insights of a given science. It seeks a common language through which to integrate knowledge. See Moreland and Craig, *Philosophical Foundations*, 16.
26. Roger E. Olson, *Reformed and Always Reforming: The Postconservative Approach to Evangelical Theology* (Grand Rapids: Baker Academic, 2007), 23.
27. Mark A. Noll, *The Scandal of the Evangelical Mind* (Grand Rapids: Eerdmans, 1995), 12.
28. See Moreland and Craig, *Philosophical Foundations*, 16.

With these considerations in mind, we turn in subsequent chapters to consider in greater depth these four basic approaches to ethics: consequentialism, principle ethics, virtue ethics, and value ethics.

Chapter 3

Consequential Ethics

Popular Hedonism

Without question, the most widespread form of consequential ethics is hedonism, the ethics of sensual pleasure. The word *hedonism* is derived from the Greek word *hēdonē*, meaning "pleasure." It is hardly necessary to point out that pleasure is a valued commodity in our consumer society—a commodity for which many are prepared to pay a high price. As the title of Neil Postman's famous book *Amusing Ourselves to Death* (1985) suggests, we will pursue pleasure all the way to the grave.[1] The boundless pursuit of pleasure and the urge to consume are hallmarks of Western society. Parents of young adults complain that their children lack a sense of responsibility and do not take life seriously. Yet many fail to understand that the generation gap often has to do with an unconscious tension between two forms of popular hedonism, which for simplicity's sake we will refer to as *short-term hedonism* and *enduring hedonism*. Short-term hedonists pursue immediate, intense pleasure. Freedom is interpreted as individual freedom to enjoy at whim, often leading to the misuse of alcohol and drugs. After a while the

---

1. Neil Postman, *Amusing Ourselves to Death* (New York: Viking Penguin, 1986). In the first instance, this work is a criticism of American culture. It addresses the role of entertainment and communication via television and the demise of the written word, stating that we live in the age of show business, which has damaged our education and our critical faculties.

intense party life takes its toll, and the short-term hedonist becomes more levelheaded, turning to the pursuit of more enduring pleasure. Of course, this transition is not easy and often takes place against the background of multiple disappointments and painful experiences. However, the more enduring form of pleasure can express itself in a variety of culturally accept-able behaviors: starting a family, buying a home, or taking exotic vacations on sun-soaked beaches. With maturity older adults show a remarkable capacity to forget the wild escapades of their youth and begin lamenting the short-term hedonism of the new youth culture. Different as these two cultures appear at first glance, the reasoning behind both is based on two basic elements: pleasure and pain. The short-term hedonist has his or her sights set on immediate sensual pleasure, the enduring hedonist more on the avoidance of pain.

In this book we will not center our discussion on these expressions of popular hedonism. Rather, we will focus our primary efforts on philo-sophical hedonism, the rational basis of general hedonistic thinking and justification. By nature philosophical hedonism argues that all human beings pursue sensual pleasure and seek to avoid pain. This fundamental motivation behind our actions may be described as *psychological* hedonism. Psychological hedonism is reductionistic in that it reduces *all* human activity to the two elements of pursuit of pleasure and avoidance of pain. It is also deterministic in the sense that humans have no real choice in this pursuit, because it is a motive or rule of human nature to which they naturally must conform.[2]

Ethical hedonism is an extension of psychological hedonism. It argues that not only *is* humankind like this (i.e., hedonistic) but that this is the way humankind is *supposed* to be. Sensual pleasure is our ultimate goal. Hedonism focuses primarily on the sensual and psychological experience of pleasure and pain, rather than on a general state of harmony and well-being. Some interpret pleasure in broader terms, referring to intellectual pleasure or even the pleasure derived from worshiping God. John Piper, for in-stance, titled one of his early books *Desiring God: Meditations of a Christian Hedonist* (1986). Piper claims, "The aim of the Christian Hedonist is to be

---

2. There are many forms of psychological hedonism. One example is "genetic psychologi-cal hedonism," where an infant starts out as purely hedonistic and then morally develops toward a form of "group hedonism." See Jean Claude Wolf, "hédonisme," in *Dictionnaire d'éthique et de philosophie morale*, ed. Monique Canto-Sperber (Paris: Presses Universitaires de France, 2001), 1:816.

happy in God, to delight in God, to cherish and enjoy His fellowship and favor."[3] His logic seems pretty convincing. In Piper's view we were created to worship God, so the worship of God will bring us the most pleasure. Ultimately, we should be *true* pleasure seekers by seeking and worshiping God, because this fulfills our created purpose. This is *Christian* hedonism.

Although we appreciate Piper's direction, we would not embrace his understanding (or reworking) of hedonism. By definition *hedonism* is self-seeking pleasure, with individual pleasure as the *telos* of the human condition. As Christians we certainly may argue that worshiping God will bring us the most enduring form of human pleasure, but this pleasure itself is not the ultimate goal of humanity. Christians are called to community as the body of Christ, as an expression of Christ in community. The radical individualism espoused by hedonism—whether enduring or short term (or Christian)—falls unquestionably short in this regard.

Classical Hedonism: Epicurus

The Epicurean Garden

After Plato and Aristotle came a number of philosophers who were disillusioned with society. The political ideals of Plato and his followers had proved to be no more than utopian dreams. Stripped of the belief that the reasonable person could change the world, hedonists became increasingly inclined to withdraw from society. One such philosopher who favored the solitary lifestyle was Epicurus (341–271 BC), the most well-known proponent of hedonism. Epicureans did not seek harmony with society but rather the harmony of the individual with himself or herself and with nature. They wore simple clothing to avoid personal conceit, and they eschewed personal status in all forms to prevent troubling the soul. The Epicurean "Garden"[4] was an oasis of calm where people could spend time with friends and enjoy discussing art and philosophy. As stated in Acts 17, Paul met the Epicureans in the Athens marketplace (which was a bit surprising considering their tendency to withdraw from society).

---

3. John Piper, *Desiring God: Meditations of a Christian Hedonist* (Sisters, OR: Multnomah Books, 1986), 33.
4. The Epicurean school and philosophical community came to be called "The Garden." The school began in Epicurus' home and garden.

Epicurus supported an ethical theory of personal survival. In essence he was an *enduring* hedonist in that he drew attention away from the pursuit of pleasure and toward the avoidance of pain. He defined pleasure as "the absence of pain in the body and of trouble in the soul."[5] This gave rise to a very sober, almost ascetic lifestyle. Prevention was deemed better than cure. Epicurus encouraged people to follow a simple diet of bread and water: "Plain fare gives as much pleasure as a costly diet, when once the pain of want has been removed, while bread and water confer the highest possible pleasure when they are brought to hungry lips."[6] A sober diet would ensure that people remained healthy so that they would not need to worry about missing out on pleasure later in life. The resulting peace of mind was the tranquility that Epicureans sought to achieve.

For Epicurus, the philosopher understands the art of distinguishing between founded and unfounded desires. Humans cannot fulfill all of their desires without self-destruction. If we opt for short-lived, intense pleasures, it will most likely lead to intense misery. For example, if we drink too heavily, it leads to a hangover. Instead, we must take pleasure in a measured dose to avoid addictions and turbulent living. To help people in this regard, Epicurus drew a distinction between three types of desires and their related pleasures.[7] First, there are the natural necessary pleasures that fulfill unavoidable desires, such as the need for food, rest, and warmth. Failure to meet these desires inevitably leads to pain. Second, there are natural unnecessary pleasures, such as the desire for delicious food or a comfortable bed. Epicurus also included sexuality in this category. We can manage fine without these things, provided that intense suffering does not follow without them. Third, there are unnatural unnecessary pleasures that we are enticed by society to enjoy, such as fashionable clothing and the seeking of power and prestige. These are the most dangerous and must be avoided at all costs. (See illustration below.)

In the previous chapter we pointed out the link between worldview and ethics. The primary worldview underlying Epicureanism is materialism. This does not necessarily mean devotion to material objects, but rather a philosophical conviction that matter is the essence of all reality. Epicurus

---

5. Epicurus, *Letter to Menoeceus*, translation found in *Greek and Roman Philosophy after Aristotle*, ed. Jason L. Saunders (New York: The Free Press, 1966), 51.

6. Epicurus, *Letter to Menoeceus*, 51.

7. Ibid., 51–52, and also see André Laks, "Epicure," in *Dictionnaire d'éthique*, 1:650.

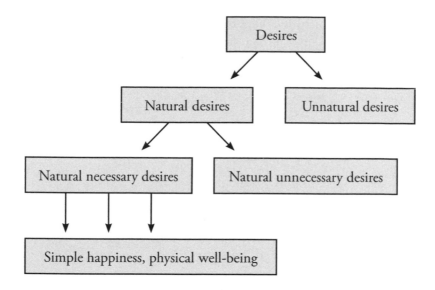

was influenced by the atomism of Democritus that had been developed a hundred years earlier. Democritus (460–370 BC) believed that reality is fundamentally material, a configuration of small particles that he refers to as atoms (derived from the Greek word for "indivisible"). For Democritus, everything—including people and their souls—is composed of a countless number of atoms. When we die, our unique combination of atoms simply disintegrates. To die is simply ceasing to exist. Death cannot therefore cause us ultimate pain. Epicureans drew on these "comforting" notions to help overcome humanity's fear of death. Epicurean ethics focuses on the temporary experience of pleasure for this life, since there is nothing beyond it that we can aspire to. There is no moral judgment to be applied to the life we live; all that matters, ultimately, is the here and now. This sentiment was aptly expressed by contemporary religious philosopher Don Cupitt when he claimed, "It is high time we learned to be less hard on ourselves and on each other; it is high time we learned how to love this life and live it well. It's all we'll ever have."[8]

---

8. Don Cupitt, *Life, Life* (Santa Rosa, CA: Polebridge, 2003), 66.

Evaluation

The essential feature of hedonism is self-seeking pleasure—*my* experience of pleasure. Much of what goes on inside our heads and the activities we observe in human behavior seem to be readily explained by hedonistic motives. When we fly in an airplane or drive a car for several hours in order to lie down on a towel and soak up the sun and swim in a warm pool, our actions seem to be the result of hedonistic calculations.

At first hedonism may seem animalistic and uncivilized—an ethic that focuses only on our basic urges. However, this does not do justice to the subtle distinctions offered by this philosophical school. The Epicureans present us with an opportunity to cultivate our hedonistic motives in order to develop a more refined lifestyle, to provide an ethics of aesthetics. An *enduring* hedonism moves us beyond short-lived pleasures to consider life in its entirety. Indeed, the hedonistic criticism of unnatural and unnecessary desires is highly relevant to a culture in which we are continuously bombarded by sensual advertising attempting to awaken our every immediate desire.

Of course, there are many shortcomings as well. The hedonist depends on circumstances to create pleasure and avoid pain. Each person must create his or her own safe garden. Disillusionment is never far away when various sensual stimuli daily offer new products and new ways of experiencing pleasure in our media-driven culture. If we are in constant pursuit of pleasure (whether short term or long term), without any regard for our Creator, sooner or later unfavorable circumstances will leave us high and dry with emotional failure and pain. If pleasure is seen as the goal instead of as a byproduct of grace, it will ultimately bring disappointment. If you use your family as simply a source for increasing personal pleasure, it will be disastrous. Rather, when the family is regarded as one context in which to give loving expression to others, you will most likely experience times of pleasure along the way. The most enduring pleasure often follows the hard labor of perseverance.

Hedonism evades the important moral task of building and encouraging a just society. The fact that the early Epicureans chose to withdraw from society is an obvious illustration of the irrelevance of their ethics. Political hedonism is also not the answer to socially accepted pleasures. No matter how you slice the pie, hedonism is still focused on the pleasure of the individual rather than the good of the community. It is difficult to imagine how such a perspective will not lead ultimately to alienation and, in the end, isolation.

For the Christian, hedonistic materialism is obviously not a viable alternative since it excludes the spiritual world and spurns the blessed hope of resurrection. By definition hedonism advocates a perspective that is contrary to Christian community and to ultimate dependence on a personal God. This is not to say that there is absolutely nothing that we may critically appropriate as Christians from hedonist notions. Often by denying, ignoring, or hiding immediate pleasures, we have failed to do justice to the expression of the beauty of God in our daily lives. We sometimes deny ourselves personal pleasures in community by ignoring pleasures altogether. Hedonism as a system falls completely short, but it does highlight this aspect of momentary pleasures we would do well to recontextualize. As Qoheleth teaches us in the book of Ecclesiastes, we should find satisfaction in our days, be happy in our work, being kept "occupied with gladness of heart" (Ecclesiastes 5:20). Rather than renouncing all desire and beauty, let us remember to stop and smell the flowers or gaze at a nice painting, embracing these simple pleasures as gifts from God for our enjoyment in communion with him.

Modern Hedonism: Thomas Hobbes

The Secularization of Society

Metaphysical materialism enjoyed a huge success in England in the seventeenth and eighteenth centuries, bringing a revival of hedonism. Along with his French contemporary René Descartes, the Englishman Thomas Hobbes (1588–1679) is regarded as the founder of modern thought. Hobbes differed in many respects from Descartes, however. According to Hobbes humans are composed only of matter (materialistic monism) and not, as Descartes reasoned, of soul and matter (dualism). Descartes showed almost no interest in moral philosophy, preferring to devote his attention to constructing a new, mathematically oriented theory of knowledge. Hobbes' interest was in sensory experience and in understanding human nature. In contrast to Epicurean hedonism, Hobbes' new form of hedonism included a strong social vision. He attempted to reconcile typical human selfishness with the role of the state. Many of today's political and economic theories are, in fact, founded in varying degrees on Thomas Hobbes' modernist ideals.

Leviathan (1651) was Hobbes' primary moral-philosophical work. What is most striking about this publication is its radical departure from the highly structured nature of medieval society. According to traditional medieval Christian ethics, humanity was created in the image of God, and God himself had established the sociohierarchical order. The place and time of your birth determined your lot in life, and social mobility was practically nonexistent. The state was God's state. The king was God's anointed. If you were born a servant, that was your call in life. In ancient philosophy Aristotle had confirmed this static worldview by affirming the good as that which fulfilled our natural potential. Thus, "once a peasant, always a peasant." In contrast Hobbes emphasized the unbridled freedom of the individual and humanity's power to overcome outdated sacred structures.

In *Leviathan* Hobbes rejected the traditional ethical view that nature and society operate in perfect harmony. Instead, he presented a picture of chaos. Nature does not teach us order but rather teaches the enmity of every individual toward the rest of humanity. Nature is a tough environment in which we are locked in a basic fight for survival. Consequently, Hobbes drew a clear distinction between the natural state and political society (the commonwealth). There is no supernatural reality that we can look toward for moral guidance. People are simply "matter in motion," and their relationships are determined by mechanical laws, not by some higher purpose. Inspired by Galileo's insights into astronomy (without Galileo's theological motivation), Hobbes viewed people as individuals who relate to each other in the same way as forces and counterforces or as actions and reactions in the physical universe. By nature we fight for goods that are in short supply in order to improve our condition. The government can do nothing to change this harsh state of affairs. We must resign ourselves to the fact that criminal behavior is essentially a part of the political system and that people will always fight among themselves. The threat of violence and anarchy will always be lurking around the corner.[9]

The Right of Nature and the Law of Nature

So are we destined to be victims of our own urges? No. Hobbes does recognize a need for morality, but the source of that morality is not to be

---

9. See chapter 13 of Hobbes' *Leviathan*. Thomas Hobbes, *Leviathan: With Selected Variants from the Latin Edition of 1668*, ed. Edwin Curley (Indianapolis: Hackett Publishing, 1994), 74–78.

found in the church or any externally imposed order, but within humankind itself. His ethic is radically anthropocentric. The first section of *Leviathan* is titled "Of Man," with Hobbes' materialist anthropology paving the way for a new theory of the state. The only constant in Hobbes' ethics lies in human "appetites and aversions," which is why his system may be considered simply as downright selfishness. By nature's law we are driven by an urge for self-preservation, accompanied by a deep-seated fear of dying a painful and untimely death. Typically, humans will desire more and more until death finally draws the line. Reason is not a means to discover the ultimate good; it only shows us the most direct route to our next desire.

This is the context in which Hobbes placed a new interpretation on the law of nature. He drew a distinction between the right of nature and the law of nature, deeming the former to be more fundamental than the latter. The right of nature states that we all have unlimited freedom to protect our own lives, avoid pain, and find pleasure. Everything that we *can* do in this regard is also lawful for us to do. From the perspective of nature alone, there are no rules forbidding us to subject others to slavery or even to slaughter them. Freedom is the absence of all external hindrances. However, the law of nature places restrictions on the freedom afforded to us by the right of nature. In this context Hobbes quoted Matthew 7:12: "So in everything, do to others what you would have them do to you." In reality Hobbes' interpretation has nothing to do with Christian love; it is simply an admonishment to respect others as a means of ensuring that they will treat us with similar respect. This presupposes that we are happy to have our right of nature curtailed, which only works if others are also willing to comply with self-restraint. It is simply due to the law of nature that we strive for peace. In doing so, we improve our chances of survival and avoid the results of war.

For Hobbes, morality is our decision to lay aside our right of nature—our greedy attempt to acquire endless material possessions—and to place limitations on ourselves, on the condition that others are prepared to do likewise. It is precisely in our voluntary restriction of our right of nature that we create for ourselves a form of morality, the basis of which lies not in our natural state (since we are already radically free) but in our undertaking to pursue peace. So justice is not founded on the nature of God but on the sum of free-will decisions taken by human individuals. In Hobbes' eyes injustice results from inconsistency. It is the discrepancy between promising to exercise self-restraint and yet choosing to claim our right of nature that places the other under threat. This is what constitutes immoral behavior according to Hobbes.

The Contract and the State

In the context of voluntary submission Hobbes proposed his famous "social contract." Our fear of death and our desire for a good life drive us beyond our savage natural state. Common sense compels us to negotiate conditions for peace. When we give up rights, we enter into a covenant of mutual trust. Our moral duties arise out of agreements we enter into with each other on a voluntary basis. When people create social ties, there must be a contract to which all parties involved voluntarily subscribe. Reason is merely an instrument used to come up with the most opportune contract. Morality is nourished by the frightening contemplation of what life would be like without any such agreements. So morality is a form of slavery we enter into voluntarily, albeit under pressure. Justice is then defined as acting according to that contract, and injustice is failure to comply with the terms of the contract.

Hobbes' hedonism results in a reciprocal contract. How did he ensure that people would abide by such a contract? Our very pursuit of happiness and fear of death drive us to submit to an absolute ruler, a sovereign, the *Leviathan*, who is above the contract and will protect it. This is the only way to avoid full-scale war. This sovereign is an artificial symbol that ultimately represents the state in general, not necessarily one particular leader. So the power is a fictional state, and it is the state's obligation to preserve peace and safety. Although the state is essentially a charade, it derives its authority from a contract entered into by everyone; therefore, it is treated as a reality. The state is not completely sovereign or despotic; it cares about protecting its citizens and serving their interests. After all, citizens have given up their natural rights in exchange for the state's protection and safety. If the state can no longer guarantee them these things, the treaty is dissolved and revolution inevitably ensues. People then revert to the right of nature until a new contract can be drawn up.

Evaluation of Hobbes' Hedonism

Hobbes' most significant contribution is probably the ethics and state theory he founded not on static metaphysics but on psychology and anthropology. Although his general philosophy did not attract many followers, his political philosophy exercised a huge influence. The task of government was to create an order that served the interests of the individual as well as it could. But it was precisely for the sake of self-interest that we created a certain moral order. Society was composed of a complex network of egoists. To a degree, Hobbes succeeded in reorganizing base selfishness into a form whereby people were able to live together peaceably. His theory helped convince extreme egoists that it was in their best interest to honor agreements. It is not without reason that Hobbes is sometimes (along with Machiavelli) referred to as the father of the "Realpolitik," but this is based more on practical than ideological factors.[10]

Hobbes attempted to bridge the gap between human selfishness and a just society, bringing to the fore issues such as the legitimacy of political authority. But did he succeed? He painted a picture of humans being completely at the mercy of the emptiness of their own desires, aimlessly drifting from desire to desire, never stopping to question the deeper meaning of life.[11] The result was a view of society in which everything came down to contracts and an eternal struggle between the interests of individuals—a meager definition of peace, to put it mildly.

What strikes us here is the high level of opportunism, the arbitrariness of the law, and the need for aggressive power. The welfare of the people may be the highest law, but how is that welfare ultimately defined? The price we pay is the choice between total submission and war. We seem to be left in the untenable position of human freedom with radical subordination. We are incapable of living in freedom together as long as we allow ourselves to be led by our feelings. The leader proposed by Hobbes is subordinate to existing anthropological patterns and will ultimately put his or her own interests first, meaning that war is the only outcome we can realistically expect—a bleak prospect indeed.

Perhaps some of the most plaguing problems with Hobbes' proposal are found in his presuppositions. Humanity is seen as no more than a material presence driven by desires and stimuli. Objects bring movement to the senses, and via these movements they influence the brain and heart. As David Hume (1711–1776) would later suggest, reason becomes the slave

---

10. *Realpolitik* was a term advocated by Otto von Bismarck, referring to the unification of Prussia and Germany in 1871.

11. Alasdair C. MacIntyre, *A Short History of Ethics: A History of Moral Philosophy from the Homeric Age to the Twentieth Century* (London: Routledge, 1998), 138.

of our passions.[12] Ultimately, ethics boils down to a subjective experience of pleasure and pain.[13]

Another presupposition underlying Hobbes' hedonism is that genuine altruism does not exist or, at best, is unnatural. A genuine human being is not capable of true loving actions; all relationships between people arise from selfish motives. Certainly, we would see human selfishness and sinfulness as central to Reformed theological expression as well. But can self-interest be elevated to the status of universal dogma? Sometimes humans do perform spontaneous altruistic acts. When we hear of a stranger's diving into a river to save a small child from drowning, this heroic act is done without reflection. Parents often act altruistically toward their children even when their children are making terrible and rebellious lifestyle choices. At the very least, it is difficult to substantiate the content of human motives, and we find it unconvincing to deny that genuine altruistic acts may occur.

It goes without saying that Hobbes' hedonism enjoys considerable success in the ethics of policymaking. Political life is often centered around an electoral contract, with the idea of truth trampled underfoot in an effort to maintain a hold on power. In the ethics of management, the relationship between employer and employee is often seen purely as a give-and-take operation. Management seeks to maximize profits using rewards and punishments. Much of our modern medical ethics is also based on a form of hedonistic dogma with its empirical style of applying medical treatment for pain control. According to Henk Jochemsen and Gerrit Glas, consequential ethics is clearly at work in the contract between the physician and patient, with the focus of attention being on the consequences of the medical treatment rather than on any particular norms or the virtue of the parties involved. But the "care ethics" proposed by Jochemsen and Glas as an alternative presupposes a capacity for altruism, empathy, and the genuine pursuit of mutual involvement. Care ethics constitutes a serious challenge to contract thinking. Jochemsen and Glas make the point

---

12. David Hume, *A Treatise of Human Nature*, ed. L. A. Selby-Bigge and P. H. Nidditch (Oxford: Oxford University Press, 1980), 415.
13. Benjamin Wiker describes how Epicurean philosophy later formed the basis of Darwinism. The Epicureans set the trend of systematically excluding the divine from nature. The current moral decline of the West has to do with the embracing of materialistic hedonism. See Benjamin Wiker, *Moral Darwinism* (Downers Grove, IL: InterVarsity Press, 2002).

that Christian ethics purposefully takes altruism, rather than egoism, as its starting point.[14]

Utilitarianism: Jeremy Bentham and John Stuart Mill

Jeremy Bentham: Hedonic Calculus

Lawyer and philosopher Jeremy Bentham (1748–1832) has the honor of being recognized as the founder of utilitarianism. His principle work, *An Introduction to the Principles of Morals and Legislation* (1789), is still a classic for understanding this approach to ethics.[15] Like Hobbes, Bentham was of the opinion that laws cannot be based on natural rights, divine revelation, or the law of the strongest. We can characterize Bentham as a cautious psychological hedonist, given that he argued that we usually act out of self-interest. But he was definitely not an ethical hedonist, given his conviction that we must strive for the greatest happiness for the greatest number.

Bentham based his theory on modern anthropology, like Hobbes. Nature has placed humankind under two sovereign masters: pain and pleasure. By nature we generally tend to pursue the greatest sensory pleasure. In this respect Bentham was a confirmed empiricist. He then drew a link between utility and happiness. All individual and social actions should be weighed against the principle of utility: the greatest possible happiness for the greatest number of people. Only deeds that augment human happiness can be deemed morally good. According to Bentham the principle of utility provides the only answer to stuffy traditions, speculations, and superstitions. This radical form of consequential ethics rejects every law that is unable to prove its usefulness in terms of individual and communal happiness.

In order to make his theory work, Bentham had to come up with a way to measure happiness or pleasure. He presented six anthropological parameters for calculating pain and pleasure: intensity, duration, certainty or uncertainty, propinquity or remoteness, fecundity, and purity. For example, a person may get drunk and experience intense pleasure in doing so. This

---

14. See Henk Jochemsen and Gerrit Glas, *Verantwoord medisch handelen* (Amsterdam: Buijten & Schipperheijn, 1997), 147–48. The authors refer in general terms to consequentialism and utilitarianism. However, their criticism is particularly relevant to hedonism in the tradition of Hobbes and less so to the more subtle forms of hedonism proposed by John Stuart Mill.

15. Jeremy Bentham, *An Introduction to the Principles of Morals and Legislation*, ed. J. H. Burns and H. L. A. Hart (Oxford: Clarendon Press, 1996).

pleasure is certain and fairly immediate, but of limited duration. It is barren in the sense that it will not generate new forms of pleasure in the future, and it is impure given its negative long-term consequences.

Additionally, he proposed the seventh parameter of extent—focusing on the greatest happiness for the greatest number of people. This parameter marks the most distinct dividing line between utilitarianism and hedonism. Bentham even depended here on sympathy—the capacity of the individual to gain pleasure from the fact that something is bringing pleasure to a large group of people. This complex seven-parameter calculation is referred to as the pleasure calculus or the hedonic calculus.

It is important to note that Bentham saw no fundamental discrepancy between the interests of the individual and those of the community. In this regard he represented the classical liberalism of his day. Society acts in a reasonable fashion and represents the sum of individual interests. According to Bentham all sorts of social institutions that justify their existence purely on the basis of ancient traditions (such as the royal family) should be abolished. Every social institution should prove its usefulness to the citizens in practical terms. The government's job is to keep its distance and concentrate on the pursuit of safety and equality for the people. But it is the development of the individual that will benefit society in the long run. In Bentham's opinion government aid is only permissible in the case of extreme poverty. His ideas on this subject are in line with the economic theory developed by another utilitarian, Adam Smith (1723–1790), the father of the free-market economy.[16]

John Stuart Mill: Quality of Pleasure

John Stuart Mill (1806–1873) introduced us to a refined version of Bentham's theory, which attempted to overcome the criticisms directed toward traditional utilitarianism.[17] Mill qualified Bentham's emphasis on

---

16. Adam Smith taught moral philosophy at the University of Glasgow and was particularly influenced by the empiricist David Hume (1711–1776). Before Smith wrote his famous *An Inquiry into the Nature and Causes of the Wealth of Nations* (1776), he had already published a moral-philosophical work, *Theory of Moral Sentiments* (1759). It is often forgotten that this earlier work is an important key to understanding his second economic work correctly. Cf. Jean-Pierre Dupuy, "Smith, Adam: La science morale d'Adam Smith," in *Dictionnaire d'éthique*, 2:1792–98.

17. MacIntyre argues that every possible problem relating to utilitarianism falls onto the shoulders of Mill. See MacIntyre, *Short History,* 235. According to Arrington, Mill goes so

the quantitative aspect of sensory pleasure by suggesting that pleasure is also subject to a qualitative hierarchy. For Mill the level of quality ascribed to different pleasures corresponds to the structure of human capacities. For example, intellectual and social delights rank higher than basic sensory pleasures. Mill replaced the hedonic calculus with an even more complex hierarchy of values: "It is better to be a human being dissatisfied than a pig satisfied; better to be Socrates dissatisfied than a fool satisfied. And if the fool, or the pig, is of a different opinion, it is because they only know their own side of the question. The other party to the comparison knows both sides."[18] The question that clearly arises here is how Mill could apply this qualitative distinction in practice. He called on judges to perform this task, believing that their experience and wisdom would help them weigh quantity against quality. For Mill, only those following the practical knowledge of Socrates were capable of sound judgment!

Mill saw the individual as less isolated than Bentham did. The individual is part of a specific sociohistorical context. The ultimate goal is for us all to progress together toward a better society. This requires us to embrace the principle of impartiality. For Mill, Jesus' admonition to love your neighbor as yourself tallies perfectly with utilitarianism. The one who acts on this admonition contributes to society. But this higher motive is the exception rather than the rule. What matters most is that we always measure our actions against the contributions they will make to society. In this regard what Mill offered is a socialistic variation of utilitarianism. For example, he considered large-scale land ownership to be in contradiction to the good of society and, therefore, unethical. In contrast to Bentham, Mill proposed a far greater degree of state intervention to protect workers and guarantee education.

Evaluation of Utilitarianism

We may note many parallels between utilitarianism and hedonism. Yet perhaps the aspect of hedonism that is corrected by utilitarianism—and this is certainly a significant correction—is that of egoism. The principle of utility compels us to consider the collective and societal implications of

---

far in responding to criticism and introduces so many shades of meaning that what he comes up with is actually a more or less new theory. See Robert L. Arrington, *Western Ethics: An Historical Introduction* (Oxford: Blackwell, 1998), 334.

18. John Stuart Mill, *Utilitarianism* (1863), quoted in Arrington, *Western Ethics*, 338.

our actions. Utilitarianism has made a significant contribution to ethical reflection in this respect. In their outspoken resistance to the dogmatism of principle ethics, Bentham and Mill presented ideas that made us more receptive to the importance of an impartial and honest society. Bentham was an important advocate of universal suffrage and justifiably questioned the usefulness of all sorts of traditional social institutions. Mill was in favor of the division of power and advocated a parliamentary democracy with proportional representation. Despite these significant contributions, however, we believe utilitarian ethics has some critical shortcomings that may be linked to those also found in hedonism. In the following paragraphs we will consider five of these weaknesses.

First of all, Mill introduced external criteria that he was unable to relate to the principle of utilitarianism.[19] For example, he spoke of the common interest but did not succeed in defining that interest within a purely utilitarian framework. We are left to provide subjective interpretations of pleasure and pain. What Mill called a higher form of pleasure, such as reading quality literature, may well be a painful experience for others. Why are Mill's value judgments correct? Who or what determines the value of quantitative experience?

Second, there is the apparent presumption of the utilitarian approach in claiming to measure the seven criteria of pleasure empirically. But what about the measure of pleasure intensity? If we struggle to measure our own pleasure intensity, can we effectively measure the pleasure of others? Bentham attempted to get around this problem by speaking in terms of sums of money. If someone is willing to pay a large sum of money for a given pleasure, then that pleasure has a mathematical value. The same applies to the avoidance of pain. But the calculation of actual amounts is not the issue here; rather, the point Bentham wished to make is that there is a link between money and pleasure. More money means more pleasure. If we spend our money, we get pleasure in return. What is missing from Bentham's reasoning, however, is that the value of money and spending power are relative; a given sum of money is worth more to a poor person than to a billionaire.[20]

Third, it requires a degree of mastery to skirt around the latent selfishness in a utilitarian system. Utilitarianism may not be as brashly self-serving

---

19. MacIntyre, *Short History*, 237.
20. Arrington, *Western Ethics*, 332–33.

as hedonism since it attempts to link self-interest with the common good, but its success is highly questionable. In both theory and practice it seems clear that a shift from selfishness to interest in the common good does not come naturally. As an idea, utilitarianism certainly bears witness to the naive optimism of Mill's era. Mill depended on a natural sense of sympathy and a healthy awareness of enlightened self-interest, which he felt should lead to the realization that we can benefit from the happiness of others. Against the background of hedonist dogma, however, this represents a clear departure from the thesis that we are simply driven by the pursuit of pleasure and the avoidance of pain.

Fourth, utilitarianism may lead to the oppression, or at least the suppression, of minority voices. By way of illustration, suppose that a group of ten businessmen plan an elaborate extortion scheme in their company. Nine out of the ten criminals decide in advance that if they are caught they will place the entire blame on the oldest and sickest in their group, Simon, who is dying of cancer. He would be the fall guy. In their context this would be the best choice, because it is better that one person should be punished rather than the entire group. Plus, this man will not live much longer anyway. So the focus is not on the particular action of injustice but on the minimization of suffering.[21] If we were to apply a similar model to world politics, we might propose combating the problem of overpopulation simply by letting people starve to death. After all, it is not realistic to expect ten billion people to share the world's limited resources. Of course, there would be few who would find this an acceptable conclusion to draw.[22] Therefore, some form of principle ethics (such as the *Universal Declaration of Human Rights*) often accompanies utilitarianism.

Fifth, related to the above scenario, utilitarianism may lead to the destruction of individual rights. People are judged according to the contribution they make to the larger group. Employees get promotions not on the basis of individual merit but on the benefit provided to the group

---

21. Of course, there are shortcomings to this example. It fails to point out the anguish suffered by stockholders in the company or the emotional and legal problems faced by the innocent employees managing the absconded funds.

22. This is also referred to as "Lifeboat Ethics." See Garrett Hardin, "Lifeboat Ethics: The Case against Helping the Poor," *Psychology Today* 8, no. 4 (1974): 38–43. The poor are poor because they have too many children, and each nation should take care of itself. The rich nations have become lifeboats in which the poor try to escape. But the reality is that such an escape is impossible.

at large.[23] If it is does not help the group, there is no promotion.[24] This distinction between individual and group merit becomes more acute when we consider euthanasia. If terminal patients become psychological and financial burdens to those around them, it may be seen as appropriate to discontinue their lives.

In conclusion, we refer once more to the one-sided anthropological assumptions that utilitarianism seems to inherit from hedonism. Humans are basically seen as animals abandoned to environmental stimuli. Is it not far more reasonable to propose that humanity is at times selfish and at other times altruistic? Sometimes self-interest coincides with group interests; other times it does not. Even policymakers appeal to both our selfishness and our altruism at the same time. Duplicity characterizes our motives. We sort our trash, in part, to help with recycling efforts for the environment and also because we want to pay less for garbage collection. Perhaps it is better simply to accept the duplicitous nature of human beings as an indisputable phenomenon and an ongoing result of the fall.

Ethics of Responsibility: Hans Jonas

The Illusion of Progress

In his utopian novel *Nova Atlantis* (1620), Francis Bacon described how scientists would ultimately succeed in gaining complete mastery over nature. According to Bacon the discovery of the art of printing, gunpowder, and the magnetic compass would benefit humanity more than all of politics and religion together. Thanks to science and technology humanity could look forward to a future full of promise. In the House of Solomon (a research establishment on Bacon's utopian island) scientists not only dissect animals and carry out other medical trials, but they also breed intermediate species of animals and plants. This is an almost prophetic description of the genetic manipulation occurring today. In the New Atlantis Bacon saw people using new experimental science as a means of forcing nature into service. Through technological mastery we may free ourselves of all ills and burdens and return to our original, paradisiacal state. Science and technology will be our saviors.

---

23. Of course, in a deeply embedded system, this distinction may be unnoticeable because individual merit is a presupposition based on group benefit.
24. Example given by Scott B. Rae, *Moral Choices* (Grand Rapids: Zondervan, 2000), 88.

The later utilitarianism of Bentham and Mill bore witness to the optimism and faith in progress typical of the nineteenth century. But the ecological crisis and many problems linked to gene technology have dealt traditional utilitarianism a heavy blow. The future is less predictable and more whimsical than we had expected. The population explosion and the far-reaching implications of issues surrounding fossil fuels serve as a painful demonstration of the fact that we are deluding ourselves if we think we can calculate the amount of pleasure we may expect in years to come. This realization of our limitations forms the background for the ethics of responsibility formulated by German philosopher Hans Jonas (1903–1993). Jonas' life spanned almost the entire twentieth century, a period during which he was able to experience for himself both the blessings and the curses brought to us by technology. His ethics attempts to provide a qualification to technological and industrial power in a time of global challenges.

The Imperative of Responsibility

Hans Jonas' principal ethical work is entitled *The Imperative of Responsibility*.[25] Jonas writes that we can no longer rely on modernism-based ethical premises. Neither human nature nor the nature of things is fixed, so we are unable to give a clear description of the good we aspire toward. Ethics is the reflection of human actions, but the essence of human actions has drastically changed. Modern technology has expanded what we do and how we operate in our daily lives. Humans use aggressive technology to re-create their environment. By extending life, administering psychiatric drugs, and engaging in gene therapy, we are able to change ourselves. We have also acquired the ability to destroy ourselves many times over. Yet in such potentially perilous times we are without clear moral guidelines. For Jonas the combination of advanced technological resources and the absence of moral direction is life threatening: "Now we shiver in the nakedness of a nihilism in which near-omnipotence is paired with near emptiness, greatest capacity with knowing least for what to use it."[26]

In the scheme of Jonas, it is virtually impossible to predict where technology will take us. Our power is, ironically, far greater than our capacity

---

25. Originally published as Hans Jonas, *Das Prinzip Verantwortung, Versuch einer Ethik für die technolgische Zivilisation* (Frankfurt: Insel, 1979). For an English version see Hans Jonas, *The Imperative of Responsibility* (Chicago: University of Chicago Press, 1984).
26. Jonas, *Imperative of Responsibility*, 23.

to predict outcomes. We are overtaken by the ever-pressing immediate, without time to think carefully about the implications and side effects of new technologies. Traditional utilitarianism suggests that we can extrapolate and calculate consequences. In reality the more advanced our knowledge, the more difficult such estimations have become. Traditional ethics has focused primarily on the noncumulative effects of our actions, taking the view that each situation can be assessed more or less in isolation. Jonas' new ethics requires that we take into account the broader, more unpredictable range of consequences that may arise from our actions. One clear case in point is gene technology. Nobody knows precisely what the longer-term consequences of tampering with genetic information will be. Our technological ability to bring about self-destruction gives rise to a compelling norm of self-preservation. Ensuring that survival itself is not endangered is becoming the most important ethical principle. This is quite different from a consequential ethics that is committed to predetermined goals.

Moreover, we are deluding ourselves if we believe technology will solve its own problems or that humans will automatically adapt to every change as rapidly as those changes are fired from our constantly changing culture. Jonas, therefore, proposed two important guiding principles for a new ethics: responsibility and a focus on the future of humanity. By *responsibility,* Jonas referred primarily to self-control. The supreme principle of ethics makes no reference whatsoever to a superior God but is about ensuring the lasting survival of human beings. The very fact of our technological power has allowed us to turn our "wants" into "musts." What matters is the preservation of freedom. But our abilities and powers must never result in the destruction of our freedom. Responsibility does not mean obedience to principles but preservation of freedom in the face of growing technological power. Jonas challenged us with the ethical demands of future generations. He called for a new imperative along the lines of acting in such a way that our choices guarantee the future integrity of humanity as the fellow "object of our will."[27]

---

27. This is negatively formulated, "Do not compromise the conditions for the indefinite continuation of humanity on earth." Positively stated it is rendered, "In your present choice, include the future wholeness of Man among the objects of your will." Jonas, *Imperative of Responsibility*, 11. Jonas alluded to the principle ethics of Immanuel Kant, but the differences between Kant and Jonas are significant. The purposiveness of Jonas' model places it closer to utilitarianism. Unlike the traditional ethics of Kant with its emphasis on the individual, Jonas placed far greater emphasis on humanity as a whole.

Jonas sought to give a new metaphysical basis to the concept of responsibility. It can no longer be based on outdated philosophical or religious concepts. The ethics of responsibility must be an ethics of transience. Jonas was making a fundamental point: responsibility can exist only where things or people change and especially where the threat of ruin is present. We are not able to feel responsible for that which is static and unchanging, for that which exists in and of itself. In this Jonas was rejecting both the Platonic basis and the Judeo-Christian basis for ethics. Given that God is unchanging and perfect, we cannot, according to Jonas, feel responsible toward him. A self-sufficient God has no need of us anyway. So responsibility is not a vertical but a horizontal concept. It arises from within humanity itself, not from some supratemporal truth.

Jonas provided a basis for his concept of responsibility in his new ontology of life, or the "being that wills." Proceeding from this will to live, responsibility is not something that comes into being subsequently, like Hobbes' contract; it belongs to nature itself. Jonas discussed two paradigms of responsibility: parental responsibility and political responsibility, both of which seek the well-being of others. These have three concepts in common: *totality, continuity,* and *future. Totality* implies that we aim to serve the whole person, from basic needs to advanced development. *Continuity* is almost a tautology: it points out that we cannot stop taking responsibility, even for a moment. The ethics of responsibility does not get time off. The concept of *future* refers to the need to move beyond the pursuit of transient interests and think long term. The responsibility of the parent ends when the child reaches adulthood, but political responsibility extends to future generations.

Jonas departed from both the anthropocentrism of Enlightenment thinking and the existential strain of his teacher Martin Heidegger.[28] Humanity no longer holds a central position in the universe, and nature has its own intrinsic value. Since humans originate from nature, they also participate in nature's purposefulness. In this context Jonas described the continuity between mind and organism. Ethics is ultimately grounded in the life and breath of all that exists. Responsibility means that humanity respects the individuality and the intrinsic value of nature.

---

28. Hans Jonas, *The Phenomenon of Life* (Evanston: Northwestern University Press, 2001), xi.

Jonas proposed a "heuristics of fear" as a more appropriate alternative to modernistic optimism. When weighing the pros and cons of a given course of action, we should attach more importance to the negative effects of technology than to its benefits. The motivation behind this is the realization that our biosphere is an ecological time bomb, along with our awareness of the presence of destructive nuclear power. The heuristics of fear also implies that clear restrictions must be placed on the global economy. Jonas was extremely critical of a liberal capitalist economy, arguing in favor of a Marxist-inspired collective and economic intervention. Even democracy came under scrutiny. A liberal democracy is tainted by compromise and lacks decisiveness. It is better to place the future of humanity in the hands of enlightened experts. Jonas revealed himself to be an out-and-out utilitarian when he declared his willingness, in an emergency, to tolerate deception and lying in order to save the collective.

Evaluation

Hans Jonas gave an extremely keen-minded description of the power of technology and the failure of ethics to catch up with the events of the world. He can unquestionably be credited with placing future generations high on his agenda. In this respect he is one of a small group of moral philosophers to have found a receptive ear in a broader political and cultural setting. The themes he addressed are vital to the future—themes that a Christian ethic seeking relevance in today's society must not avoid. In particular a deep regard for future generations is a useful extension of the Christian love ethic. When it comes to ecological morals, it is most noble to view fellow human beings as both those who live now and those who are to come.[29] Jonas also made a significant contribution to the field of biomedical ethics. He pointed out that it is not enough to simply weigh the opportunities presented by genetic therapies within the context of an individual life as an intimate decision between patient and medical staff. Our ethical considerations must extend beyond the well-being of individual patients to include long-term implications for society as a whole.

Nonetheless, Jonas' ethics of responsibility is weighed down with several inconsistencies and obscurities, although for Jonas such inconsistencies did

---

29. Patrick Nullens, "Leven volgens Gaia's normen?: de verhouding tussen God, mens en aarde en de implicaties voor ecologische ethiek" (Ph.D. diss., Evangelische Theologische Faculteit, Leuven, Belgium, 1995), 312–15.

not pose a serious threat. He preferred to think of himself as one pointing people in a new direction rather than as the founder of an entirely new ethical system. The question remains whether his inconsistencies are of such magnitude that they call into question his project. On the one hand, Jonas emphasized the unpredictability of the future and the open-endedness of life in general. On the other hand, he wished to take the future as his starting point for developing a universal ethic. This ambivalence permeates his entire ethical model and, in our view, presents a problem difficult to resolve.

Another inconsistency is the way in which Jonas minimized classical anthropocentric ethics. In line with many eco-philosophers or depth ecologists, he was interested in biological life in general.[30] Yet with his ethics of responsibility he became outspokenly anthropocentric, placing emphasis on our responsibility for future human generations. Jonas did nothing to address this contradiction, nor did he discuss the discrepancy between what should happen in the interests of future generations and the wider interests of nature as a whole.

His proposed ethic of responsibility may present drastic options for people desiring to safeguard the future of the planet. For example, some may choose not to fight AIDS in Third World countries since it restricts population growth in regions where this is most needed. Of course, Jonas would never have proposed such a measure because his ultimate goal was to preserve the integrity of the individual, but the dilemma points to a potential weakness in his system just the same.

As well as giving marked precedence to the collective, the ethics of responsibility also creates the potential, in ideological terms, for an authoritarian polity. For Jonas the direction of the collective is best placed in the hands of the experts. Since Jonas used the parent-child paradigm as his starting point, his interpretation of political responsibility is strongly paternalistic. Rather than offering human redemption, Jonas' model seems to be pointing more toward a green dictatorship with global power.

---

30. Nullens, "Leven volgens Gaia's normen?" 302–5. Deep ecology differs from "shallow ecology" in that it does not believe in a technical solution to our ecological problems. Technical and legal solutions can only be used to tackle symptoms, not the disease. In order to safeguard the future of the planet, we need a fundamental change in thinking and attitude. These terms come from the Norwegian philosopher Arne Naes. A standard feature of deep ecology is that it questions the unique and central position of humanity in nature and views humankind instead in terms of its place in the ecosystem.

Chapter 4

Principle Ethics

The Theonomous Principle Ethics of Thomas Aquinas

Unity between Reason and Faith

Thomas Aquinas (1225–1274) remains one of the most important figures in the history of Christian ethics, having had a tremendous influence on Roman Catholic moral theology. Aquinas is particularly noted for his unique insights into the relationship between faith and reason and the integration of philosophy and theology. He developed a detailed synergy between the rediscovered writings of Aristotle and the Christian faith tradition. His magnum opus, the *Summa Theologica*, was written for his students as an introduction to Christian doctrine and morality.

Like his teacher Albertus Magnus, Aquinas believed the primary focus of theology should be on supernatural or revealed truths. Natural reality, outside the sphere of faith, could be understood via reason. Although he recognized this distinction, Aquinas was strongly opposed to two orders of truth. Since God was the source of all reason, it followed that our articles of faith could not be unreasonable. The cornerstone of both reason and faith was God as Creator and Savior. Reason and faith were in tune with each other, but faith took precedence. Supernatural grace did not exclude reason but elevated it and brought it to completeness (*gratia naturum perficit*).

Aquinas placed philosophy in the role of a servant to theology. In this regard he did not deviate from the traditional Platonic-Augustinian perspective prevalent in his day. What was particularly radical about Aquinas' work was his critical integration of Aristotle's philosophy and traditional Scholastic theology. Consequently, Aquinas' ethical standpoint reflects a high degree of realism and social engagement. His positive approach to all that is earthly and human stands in stark contrast to Augustinian Neoplatonism.

But Aquinas was far more than simply a Christian principles ethicist.[1] Although he made law the central benchmark for human actions, he also advocated an ethics of virtues. Where the law provides the external basis for moral actions, virtues provide the internal basis for morality. Aquinas uniquely drew these two elements together in a general teleological theory of ethics. The task of ethics is to use reason to guide people toward happiness. The Christian commandments are allocated their place within this teleological framework. As mentioned before, Aquinas was strongly influenced by Aristotle, whose teleological ethics was focused on happiness (*eudaimonia*), a happiness including the full development of human potential. Aristotle proposed that happiness was achievable in this life and that its attainment was itself a goal. Aquinas disagreed; he saw the ultimate goal of human existence as being to manifest God's glory. Our ultimate goal lies beyond human life. Instead, our complete happiness and the entire purpose of humanity are found in beholding the Creator. Aquinas' theological intervention with its emphasis on the hereafter provided a Christian recontextualization of Aristotle's teleological ethics.[2]

Aquinas' position becomes clearer in contrast with the principle ethics of the medieval Franciscan theologian and philosopher William of Ockham (1285–1349).[3] For Ockham the essence of morality is neither

---

1. For a brief, yet perceptive discussion on this, see Norman Kretzmann and Eleonore Stump, eds., *The Cambridge Companion to Aquinas* (Cambridge: Cambridge University Press, 1993), 196–216. Also see Jean Pierre Torrell, "Thomas d'Aquin: La philosophie morale de Thomas d'Aquin," in *Dictionnaire d'éthique et de philosophie morale*, 4th ed., ed. Monique Canto-Sperber (Paris: Presses Universitaire de France, Quadrige, 2004), 2:1947–54.
2. Aquinas' unique contribution placed ethics in a wider metaphysical and teleological framework. Additionally, he combined principle ethics with the ethics of virtues, as we shall see in a later chapter.
3. Ultimately, this distinction boils down to the difference between Ockham's nominalism and Aquinas' realism. For Ockham, concepts have no absolute ontological status. Concepts (*universalia*) are purely products of the human mind. They are categories that we as humans designate. Ockham also took a stand against Aristotelian influences and taught a double (and almost disconnected) truth composed of reason and faith.

the attainment of happiness nor the achievement of a reasonable order. Morality is strictly heteronomous—based on the simple fact that God rules according to his sovereign pleasure. According to Ockham divine will is not subject to the laws of reason. The biblical commands appeal to our wills, not to our minds.[4] Ockham saw a direct link between the will and faith. To believe is essentially to obey. If faith disappears, the basis for all morality is lost. In contrast, Aquinas propounded a unique integration of autonomy and heteronomy. Ultimately, everything is dependent on God's will, yet ethics maintains an element of independence through the laws of morality and the reason within us. For Aquinas the will follows reason, rather than reason following the will as with the voluntarism of Ockham.

The Law as Manifestation of God's Government

According to Aquinas happiness is not to be found in the here and now but in the hereafter, although we can attain a certain degree of happiness in the present if we are guided by reason and God's laws. Aquinas regarded law and reason as a single entity, since both have their roots in God's order. God's law is the source of all laws.[5] Likewise, the law is a manifestation of reason that seeks the common good. The concept of *law* (*lex*), therefore, sums up both our goals and our reason. Aquinas defined law as "an ordinance of reason for the common good, made by him who has care of the community, and promulgated."[6]

It is natural to view human laws as instruments in the hands of the ruling powers whose task is to work toward the common good of humankind. If a mayor issues a prohibition against noise in the streets after 11:00 PM, this is done in the interests of the community. Aquinas magnified this idea and presented God as the Great Ruler of the community of the universe. In accordance with the ideas conceived by the divine intellect, God orders movements and acts in the world toward his end. So the eternal law is simply a manifestation of divine wisdom that directs all movements and acts. As a wise and compassionate ruler, God takes care of us by means of his law. There is no contradiction between God's law and his eternal love. It

---

4. The notion that the only possible basis of morality is God's will, whatever that may be, is referred to as *voluntarism*.

5. Thomas Aquinas, *Summa Theologica* 2.1, qq. 90–108.

6. Aquinas, *Summa* 2.1, q. 90, a. 4, New Advent (2008), http://www.newadvent.org/summa/2090.htm.

is precisely by obeying his law that we achieve our ultimate human purpose, freedom, and complete self-fulfillment.

Aquinas laid a metaphysical foundation for his law ethic: all laws participate in God's law. An individual act is not evil simply because it contravenes civil law, but because it fails to comply with the law on which all laws are based. All laws are derived from God's unchangeable law and must be applied correctly. In this context Aquinas described a hierarchy of God's laws. First is the eternal law (*lex aeterna*) within God himself, through which the whole universe was created and by which it continues to be governed. It follows then that the metaphysical logic of the universe is based on divine reason. Second, there is natural law (*lex naturalis*) that is knowable by humans. The order of nature is a manifestation of God's eternal law. Humanity is part of nature, created in God's image, and therefore capable of fathoming God's order. As rational creatures, humans participate in the eternal law. Therefore, the legal good is also the natural and reasonable good. Third, at the lowest level, is the human law (*lex humana*) revealed in the laws of the church and state. Human law comprises ethical norms that can be derived specifically from the natural laws. A law at this level is only valid to the extent to which it is founded on the natural law. Finally, there is divine law (*lex divina*), including the Ten Commandments, which can be known by revelation.

Aquinas drew a distinction between the imperfect law of the Old Testament and the perfect law of the New Testament.[7] The Old and New Testament laws function as ordering principles, leading us toward the positive goal of true happiness, which will finally be achieved in the next life. However, the law of the Old Testament focuses strongly on the earthly promise, while the law of the New Testament is more spiritually focused on the promise of eternal life. The motivation in Old Testament law is the fear of punishment, whereas the New Testament law is that of grace and love.[8]

---

7. This is another example of the dichotomous thinking typical of Aquinas.

8. Aquinas quotes Peter Lombard, *Sentences* iii.D.40: "For this reason, too, the Old Law is described as 'restraining the hand, not the will.'" But, "the New Law, which is the Law of love, is said to restrain the will." Aquinas, *Summa* 2.1, q. 107, a. 2, http://www.newadvent. org/summa/2107.htm. Aquinas concurs here with Lombard's *Magister Sententiarum* (*Four Books of Sentences*), the standard theological reference from the 12th to the 16th centuries.

The Rational Person and Free Will

Aquinas was convinced that by nature humanity is inclined to follow God's law (*inclinationes naturales*). By living according to rational law we fulfill our human potential and move ever closer to God.[9] Humans are purposive beings. Aquinas was not suggesting that we have a natural inclination to adhere to a detailed set of moral principles, but that we have a natural inclination to follow general natural principles. Reason brings us into contact with the law of nature—the law that reflects the eternal law. Everyone knows that good must be done and that evil must be avoided. Like all beings, humans strive for self-preservation, so the law of nature teaches us to protect life. Likewise, humans also have the desire to reproduce, so the law of nature teaches us to protect the relationships between husband and wife and between parents and children. The unique rational character of humankind creates a desire for social life and a longing to know the Creator. The dual commandment to love God and love our neighbor (Matthew 22:37–39) encapsulates the two most important precepts of the law of nature. Humanity's social predisposition implies that people do not wish to harm each other and do not wish to lie.

As well as highlighting the significance of humanity's cognitive faculties, Aquinas attached considerable importance to the power of the human will. The will and reason make humankind unique as the image of God. The human will must function in harmony with the divine will. Although humans have limitations, they remain independent beings with a free will. God can be glorified only when humans pursue the highest good, not because they are forced to do so but because they choose it out of their own free initiative. But the will must be guided by reason. The mind impresses truth on the will, and the will induces the mind to discover the truth. A harmonious existence is one in which the will and the mind are in agreement.

Evaluation

Aquinas was a brilliant thinker who succeeded in developing an impressive synthesis between Christian theology and Aristotelian philosophy. The Thomistic model still plays an influential role in Roman Catholic moral theology. For example, we recognize this Thomistic division of laws in the New Catechism:

---

9. Aquinas, *Summa* 2.1, q. 94. a. 3. Cf. *Summa* 1, q. 83, a. 3.

> All law finds its first and ultimate truth in the eternal law.
> Law is declared and established by reason as a participation in
> the providence of the living God, Creator and Redeemer of
> all. . . . There are different expressions of the moral law, all of
> them interrelated: eternal law—the source, in God, of all law;
> natural law; revealed law, comprising the Old Law and the
> New Law, or Law of the Gospel; finally civil and ecclesiastical
> laws.[10]

Christian ethics is not simply a matter of blind obedience to commands—
it revolves around obedience based on reason. For Aquinas scriptural
guidelines, the virtues, and the natural order all work together.

Broadly speaking, we are in sympathy with the Thomistic intention
of linking together these various aspects of ethics. Indeed, ethics is more
than a series of arbitrary precepts. God uses precepts to fulfill his loving
purpose in us. This Christian *eudemonism*, the pursuit of a fulfilling and
happy life in God's presence, is an invitation that is open to every person.
In this we find an association between the natural and the supernatural
realms. Nature itself provides us with certain guidelines for a happy human
existence. The challenge facing Christian ethics then is to consistently and
persistently integrate the natural with an encompassing theistic worldview.
This is an ongoing process requiring constant adaptation in response to
new findings in science and philosophy.[11]

Perhaps the most important criticism that can be leveled against
Aquinas is his willingness to embrace Hellenistic intellectualism, equating
intelligence almost completely with goodness: ignorance is evil and evil
is ignorance. Aquinas did not believe that the fall impaired humankind's
capacity to do good. What was lost was the original supernatural state of
grace. Considerable criticism has been generated by this perceived overes-
timation of human capabilities and underestimation of the power of sin,
particularly in Protestant Reformed traditions. The apostle Paul taught that

---

10. Quotation from articles 1951 and 1952 of the *Catechism of the Catholic Church* (Mah-
wah, NJ: Paulist Press, 1994), 473–74. See also the encyclical *Humanae Vitae* (1968) in
which frequent reference is made to the natural law. See *Catechism of the Catholic Church* at
http://www.vatican.va/archive/catechism/ccc_toc.htm.

11. Note that what is important here is the process of striving toward, not the ultimate
result. This position of unity between creation and redemption, the natural and supernatural, is also supported by Oliver O'Donovan, *Resurrection and Moral Order: An Outline for
Evangelical Ethics*, 2nd ed. (Grand Rapids: Eerdmans, 1994).

the foolish hearts of humans have been darkened (Romans 1:21): they do not choose good (Romans 3:11), and they are hostile to God (Romans 8:7). It follows that ethics cannot rely on nature alone, but its starting point must be God's gracious acts. Humankind is not capable of fully knowing and understanding God's norms, never mind acting in accordance with them.

The Theonomous Principle Ethics of John Calvin

The Seriousness of Sin

The reformer John Calvin (1509–1564) presents us with a completely different approach to Christian principle ethics, far removed from the realm of moral philosophy. The Reformation refocused attention on Scripture, and its initial attitude toward medieval Scholasticism was highly critical. Calvin took a far more dramatic view of the impact of sin than Aquinas. For Calvin the sin of Adam and its resulting original sin took possession of every part of the human's soul: "For our nature is not only destitute and empty of good, but so fertile and fruitful of every evil that it cannot be idle."[12] Not only fleshly desires were polluted at the Fall, as medieval tradition would claim, but also the mind and heart. If sin only had a hold over our desires, it was simply a matter of ensuring that our will and mind took the upper hand. Calvin, however, emphasized the spiritual source of Adam's fall: the sin of pride. In doing this he distanced himself from a long tradition of philosophy and also from the Renaissance humanism popular in his day. For Calvin reason was useful but could be severely misleading, since it was governed by sin. The will had been badly damaged and robbed of its power to resist sin. Only by faith were we able to lead virtuous lives, and that only by the grace of God. The solution to our ignorance was solely God's saving and elective work. But the focus of Calvin's work was not to berate humankind, but to highlight the magnificence of God's grace.[13]

As with the other Reformers, Calvin claimed that ethics did not determine the path to salvation. Good works cannot justify anyone before God. Instead, ethics belongs to the sanctification process as part of a life lived in

---

12. John Calvin, *Institutes of the Christian Religion*, ed. John T. McNeill, trans. Ford Lewis Battles (Philadelphia, PA: Westminster Press, 1960), II.i.8.
13. See Erich Fuchs, "Calvin, Jean: La philosophie morale de Calvin et le calvinisme," in *Dictionnaire d'éthique*, 1:230.

gratitude for the gift of salvation. The sanctification of the believer is firmly embedded in his or her communion with Jesus Christ—not in the law but in grace. God brings about change in the life of the believer, and nothing happens without Christ's knowledge and consent. Both the law and the process of sanctification by God's Spirit must be seen in the context of Christ's atoning work. The heartbeat of Calvin's ethics can be heard in the piety of everyday life: "Here indeed is pure and real religion: faith so joined with an earnest fear of God that this fear also embraces willing reverence, and carries with it such legitimate worship as is prescribed by the law."[14]

The Ten Commandments

Calvin distinguished himself from Luther in placing greater emphasis on the commandments as a source of Christian ethics.[15] His *Institutes* includes a lengthy and detailed exposition of the Ten Commandments.[16] For Calvin the Ten Commandments have unchanging and lasting worth, forming the heart of Christian ethics. They are an expression of grace that God extends to the world and to his church. Calvin identified three uses of the Ten Commandments. First is their role in the sphere of public life to help restrain evil. Second, they help us become aware of personal guilt and sin. Third, they help provide a standard by which we Christians can measure our own sanctification. Calvin extended his understanding of the law beyond a mere literal interpretation. The Ten Commandments are not simply about outward forms but about our deepest motives.

All persons have an internal law written on their hearts, but this writing has been severely distorted. God has therefore given humans a written law to clearly attest to that which has become obscured in the law of nature. The law as a source of revelation is much more than a dry text. Calvin was careful not to dwell exclusively on the external character of the law. Nothing is hidden from God's sight, and what he therefore requires of us above all else is inner obedience—obedience to the law, flowing from a

---

14. Calvin, *Institutes*, I.ii.2, 43.

15. For a comparison of Luther and Calvin, see John Hesselink, *Calvin's Concept of the Law* (Allison Park, PA: Pickwick Publications, 1992).

16. Calvin himself referred to this as a "short explanation." See *Institutes*, II.viii.1–50. See also Calvin's *Sermons on Deuteronomy* and *Commentary on the Four Last Books of Moses*. John P. Burgess, "Reformed Explication of the Ten Commandments," in *The Ten Commandments: The Reciprocity of Faithfulness*, ed. William P. Brown (Louisville: Westminster John Knox, 2004).

believing heart. The law should be understood in line with the character of the merciful king. In this regard the inner ethic of the Sermon on the Mount provides the hermeneutical key to a better understanding of the law.

Calvin's interpretation of the commandments recognizes the literary device of *synecdoche,* where the part is used to signify the whole. While the commandments prescribe or forbid particular acts, there are broader implications for their practice.[17] A positive command implies a corresponding prohibition and vice versa. If a certain act is pleasing to God, it follows that he will detest the opposite. Likewise, if God detests something, what he requires is the opposite. For example, "Honor your father and mother" is a positive command, so avoiding dishonor toward your father and mother would be the implied negative command. Ethical implications could expand from this. Honoring your father and mother would also seem to imply a proactive engagement with them, not a passive neglect.

A negative commandment is "Do not steal," but a radically positive implication of this injunction may be rendered, "Give generously." Not only are we not to steal from others, but also we are to give generously to those in need. We must continuously seek the underlying purpose and broader application of a given commandment. Above all, for Calvin religion precedes justice. Without true religion, justice is impossible. Righteousness apart from religion "has no more beauty than the trunk of a body deprived from its head."[18]

Evaluation

It would be difficult to overestimate the ethical influence of Calvinism. His aim was to demonstrate God's glory in all spheres of life. Calvin took Christian ethics and translated it into concrete terms for application in the daily life of the believer. With his emphasis on the Ten Commandments, Calvin is regarded as the father of Christian command ethics.[19]

While much of the criticism leveled at Calvin's command ethics is of a theological nature, moral-philosophical questions also arise, questions

---

17. Calvin, *Institutes*, II. viii.8–10.
18. Calvin, *Institutes*, II. viii.11.
19. This is the standard approach taken by Reformational ethicists. The international term *divine commandment theory* is often applied. See for instance, Richard J. Mouw, *The God Who Commands* (Notre Dame: University of Notre Dame Press, 1990); and Georg Huntemann, *Biblisches Ethos im Zeitalter der Moralrevolution* (Neuhausen, Switz.: Hanssler, 1999).

that pertain to the one-sidedness of a theonomous command ethic. Calvin made cautious reference to the continuity between the commandments and general moral awareness but neglected to expound the idea more fully. He agreed with Aquinas that all morality finds its source in God. He also agreed with William of Ockham that an act is either good or evil because God has commanded that it is so. But Alasdair MacIntyre complains that Calvin's presentation of God is devoid of insight. God is represented as a "cosmic despot"; something is good because God decrees it, and what he decrees is good. As a result, the law loses its essential purposefulness and seems to become completely arbitrary.[20] Ultimately, it appears that Calvin's ethics boils down simply to gratitude and an unquestioning obedience to God.

Calvin's ethics is also sometimes criticized as being too heavily focused on the Old Testament. Although Calvin's thinking was Christocentric, he did not regard Jesus as adding much new content to ethics. For example, he wrote, "The covenant made with all the patriarchs is so much like ours in substance and reality that the two are actually one and the same. Yet they differ in the mode of dispensation."[21] What was new, however, was that Jesus taught the internalization of the law, in the presence of Pharisees. The emphasis Calvin placed on the Old Testament lifted the Ten Commandments out of their specific historical context to the end-all of Christian morality. As a result, he may have failed to grasp the particularity of the commandments. By contrast Martin Luther was reluctant to use the law as the rule for gratitude and measure of sanctification. Anabaptist ethics placed the Sermon on the Mount and the ethics of love more centrally, introducing a greater degree of discontinuity with Old Testament command ethics. According to this tradition the Sermon on the Mount is more than an exposition of the Ten Commandments; it is a further moral revelation of the commandments or even a replacement for them.[22]

---

20. Alasdair C. MacIntyre, *A Short History of Ethics: A History of Moral Philosophy from the Homeric Age to the Twentieth Century* (London: Routledge, 1998), 123–24. MacIntyre seems unjustly to blame Calvinism (and Lutheranism) for dividing up morality between incomprehensible commands on the one hand and their own political and economic laws on the other. At best, this is a caricature. Calvin's entire aim was to make the commandments relevant to economic and political life. MacIntyre admits this somewhat grudgingly when he writes of Calvin's activities in Geneva. For a response, see Richard J. Mouw, "Alasdair MacIntyre on Reformation Ethics," *Journal of Religious Ethics* 13, no. 2 (1985): 243–58.
21. Calvin, *Institutes*, II.x.2.
22. Glen H. Stassen and David P. Gushee, *Kingdom Ethics: Following Jesus in Contemporary*

The way in which Calvin promoted the law as an expression of gratitude may unfortunately pave the way for Christian legalism. In practice it can lead to a heavy emphasis on external obedience, with love and grace relegated to the background. The stress on external precepts can lead to a suffocating church environment, leaving little room for human failure and personal growth. As we noted previously, Calvin directs us to a richer interpretation of the Ten Commandments by underlining unification with Christ and the ethics of the heart. When he writes of the regeneration process, he mentions his desire to write an extensive ethics of virtues—which he unfortunately neglected to do, referring the reader instead to what has already been written in the "Homilies of the Fathers."[23] Nonetheless, Calvin still seemed open to the idea of supplementing command ethics with the classical ethics of virtues.

Unfortunately, some make a logical link between ethics and the Calvinist dogma of election, using the *practical syllogism*. The argument goes like this: God's elect bear fruit. I bear fruit. Therefore, I am God's elect. Adherence to Old Testament law is taken to be evidence of regeneration. As a result, the believer is lured into seeking assurance of salvation by means of obedience to the law. Despite all the sweet words of grace, this way of thinking opens the door to a faith based on works and the pharisaical conceit that goes with it.[24] This is a real danger that arises when we lose sight of the primacy of God's promises and grace.[25]

The Autonomous Principle Ethics of Immanuel Kant

Knowledge

The purely philosophical ethical system propounded by Immanuel Kant (1724–1804) is significantly different from the theocentric command

---

Context (Downers Grove, IL: InterVarsity Press, 2003), 131–32.

23. Calvin, *Institutes*, III.vi.1.

24. John E. Colwell, *Living the Christian Story* (Edinburgh: T&T Clark, 2001), 57. Alister McGrath links the *syllogismus practicus* (practical syllogism) to the unique work ethic of Calvinism. See Alister E. McGrath, *A Life of John Calvin: A Study in the Shaping of Western Culture*, rpt. ed. (Malden, MA: Wiley-Blackwell, 1993), 241.

25. In this context, we refer the reader to "Lord's Day 32" of the Heidelberg Catechism. Our assurance of salvation is founded on the blood of Christ. The fruit of the Spirit is not so much an assurance for God, but rather an assurance for us, its purpose being to win others to Christ. In other words, the fruit is an additional *adminiculum*. We thank our colleague Dr. Jan Hoek for pointing this out.

ethics previously considered. Kant is one of the most important philosophers within the Western tradition and represents a milestone in ethical history. He is most noted for his attempt to reconcile the two main schools of the Enlightenment: Continental rationalism (René Descartes) and British empiricism (David Hume). Kant took on this challenge with the publication of his groundbreaking epistemology, *The Critique of Pure Reason* (1781). Kant refused to accept the skeptical rejection of all metaphysical concepts. He agreed with the empiricists that much of our knowledge is derived from experience but argued that it depends on the mind to organize this experience. Kant separated notions of pure intuitions (or concepts) and empirical intuitions.[26] As he put it, "Pure intuitions or pure concepts alone are possible *a priori*, empirical intuitions and empirical concepts only *a posteriori*."[27]

For Kant the mind is not passive (as argued by the empiricists) but active in imposing cognitive forms on the material of experience in the interpretive process. Categories give unity and clarity to our perceptions and allow us to obtain knowledge of phenomena. However, we can never know the *Ding an sich*, the thing-in-itself, that is, the supersensible noumena, because the categories are limited to the phenomenal world.[28] It is this line of reasoning that led Kant to utter his famous words: "I have therefore found it necessary to deny knowledge, in order to make room for faith."[29] Robert C. Solomon has described Kant's position as "transcendental pretense," the unsubstantiated presupposition that human experience is universal. Kant's position assumes that reason prescribes a set of morals or form of government that can be legislated and rationally defended for all humankind.[30]

---

26. Ronald T. Michener, *Engaging Deconstructive Theology* (Aldershot, UK: Ashgate, 2007), 22. See also David West, *An Introduction to Continental Philosophy* (Cambridge, MA: Blackwell, 1996), 18.

27. Immanuel Kant, *Critique of Pure Reason*, trans. Norman Kemp Smith (New York: St. Martin's Press, 1929), 92.

28. Michener, *Engaging*, 22. See Kant, *Critique of Pure Reason*, 55; and James C. Livingston, *Modern Christian Thought* (London: Collier, 1971), 65.

29. Kant, *Critique of Pure Reason*, 29.

30. Robert C. Solomon, *Continental Philosophy Since 1750: The Rise and Fall of the Self* (Oxford: Oxford University Press, 1988), 1, 2, 7. See Michener, *Engaging*, 22.

Moral Knowledge

Kant placed the self of humankind at the center of his moral philosophy. He received considerable criticism from those who believed he had made a mockery of faith in God and the possibility of a fixed morality. Kant argued that since religious and moral knowledge are of the noumenal world and not derived from the sensible world of experience, they have no justification. Nevertheless, Kant still wanted to assign ethics and religion a special and important place in our understanding. He took up this task in his work *The Critique of Practical Reason* (1788). Freedom was the achievement and central doctrine of the Enlightenment. But in order to create an ethical system, Kant had to reconcile duty and freedom. This was the goal of the ethics of duty, or *deontological* ethics.

The traditional ethics of Aristotle—and many who came after him—placed the main emphasis on happiness as the good we should strive toward. Kant objected to this because it was in conflict with the principle of freedom. The eudemonism of traditional ethics placed the demand for happiness outside of human control. Kant accused the empiricists and their utilitarianism of making ethics dependent on needs and pleasure. A need was obviously indicative of a lack of something, a personal deficit of some sort, the fulfillment of which could only be found externally to ourselves. Kant predicted with almost prophetic foresight that industrialization and consumerism would ultimately lead to emptiness and boredom. The greatest danger that threatened ethics was the utilitarian confusion of the useful with the good.

In Kant's search for a moral alternative, he focused on the enlightened consciousness of humankind. The fixed point of morality was not an object that we ought to desire or a God who must be obeyed, but the moral subject itself. For Kant pure ethics was driven by duty, not by results. Moral action was led by an inner sense of moral duty and not influenced by fickle desires. The essence of ethics lay not in consequences or in deeds but in the goodwill of the free, autonomous individual. What precisely was the nature of this inner sense of duty? As an Enlightenment thinker, Kant stood by the central role played by reason. Reason was the only means to freedom. Inspired afresh by the natural sciences, he went in search of the universal laws of the moral life. Laws of reason constituted the subject of humanity's duty.

And what are the laws that impose themselves on every reasonable being? Kant divided these imperatives into two types: the hypothetical and categorical.[31] The hypothetical imperative focuses on an end result or purpose: I must do *A* in order to achieve *X*. A student studies to pass an exam. A laborer works to earn a living. A child refrains from lying to avoid punishment. Although much of our morality centers on choices like these, in Kant's view they do not count as true moral acts. These rules are simply a matter of common sense, teaching us how we ought to live. The categorical imperative imposes itself on every moral and reasonable person, regardless of the person's self-interest or the possible consequences. This categorical imperative stems from reason and autonomous freedom. Reason influences the will: "Reason's true vocation must therefore be to produce a will which is good in itself, not just good as a means to some further end."[32]

Kant focused exclusively on the form (the formal aspect) of the rule and not on its content (the material), since the latter could change depending on the circumstances. He identified formal characteristics of this categorical imperative. A rule must comply with three formulations to qualify as being morally good. The first is "Act only on that maxim by which you can at the same time will that it should become a universal law."[33] In his formulations Kant used the term *maxim*, which stands for a "subjective [personal] regimen."[34] Kant allowed no exceptions. Lying, for example, is always wrong, regardless of the circumstances or consequences.

The second formulation of the categorical imperative is "Act in such a way that you treat humanity, whether in your own person or in any other person, always at the same time as an end, never merely as a means."[35] Every individual is a moral being; therefore, it is unacceptable to regard others as objects or merely as a means to an end. The third formulation is in a sense a synthesis of the first and the second: "the idea of the will of every rational being as will that legislates moral law."[36] This centers on the principle of autonomy. Reason formulates its own moral law and then submits to itself.

---

31. See Immanuel Kant, *Groundwork for the Metaphysics of Morals*, trans. Arnulf Zweig, ed. Thomas E. Hill Jr. and Arnulf Zweig (Oxford: Oxford University Press, 2002), 214–24. Thomas E. Hill, *The Blackwell Guide to Kant's Ethics* (Malden, MA: Wiley-Blackwell, 2009), 56.

32. Kant, *Groundwork,* 198.

33. Ibid., 222.

34. Kant, *Critique of Practical Reason*, ed. Mary Gregor (Cambridge: Cambridge University Press, 1997), 17.

35. Kant, *Groundwork*, 230.

36. Ibid., 232.

Here Kant emphasized the self and spoke out against a heteronomous ethic whereby God (or another external entity) sets the standards.

The categorical imperative is based on two presuppositions or postulates. First, humanity must be capable of choosing between good and evil. In stark contrast with the natural laws of causality, freedom means that humans can actually disobey the law. If this were not so, the issue of innocence and guilt would not arise. Freedom forms the basis for practical reason. Second, the categorical imperative presupposes immortality. Ultimately, humans cannot be judged within the boundaries of time and space. While the call to ethical behavior comes from within humankind, final judgment is the task of an entity outside of humankind. It follows that humanity's existence must extend beyond this life. Here lies the necessity for the existence of God for Kant. Morality presupposes the ultimate settlement of rights and wrongs and therefore also presupposes a God who acts as judge. Kant did not suggest that we can prove the existence of God; that would go beyond our mental capacity. All he claimed was that ethics required us to believe that God exists. More precisely, ethics did not presuppose the existence of God, but it did presuppose *belief* in a God. Whereas Aquinas saw God as the very foundation of all that is, Kant's view of God was restricted to the domain of obligation, not to existence or knowledge. God was the guarantor of morality. Conversely and significantly, autonomous morality was the norm for the divine.

Evaluation

Kant investigated the nature of morality with thoroughness unequaled by any of his predecessors. His critical analysis of the moral subject led him to a deeper understanding of duty. He explained that there was no discrepancy between freedom and dutiful action. He demonstrated an extremely perceptive grasp of the antithesis between the Enlightenment doctrine of freedom and a new ethic that rendered humans slaves to their sensory experiences. He recognized that as long as humans were dependent on the senses, they could never be free. A striving for happiness could not offer the universal and objective stability needed for an ethics founded on reason. Kant gave full consideration to the motivations behind moral acts, a consideration that proved to have a profound effect on the course of moral philosophy from that point forward.

Additionally, Kant's unshakable belief in the sacrosanct value of human life is laudable. With the Christian principle ethics propounded by Aquinas, the dignity of the individual relied to a large degree on a relationship with God (as beings created in his image). Enlightenment thinking brought into question the entire existence of God; by implication human dignity rooted in the image of God also came under threat. Kant's humanist rescue operation enabled humans to retain their sacrosanct value without that value's being dependent on a specific belief in the Creator. Human dignity then acquired a secular basis apart from religious and philosophical belief.

Kant laid the foundation for the common division between science and technology on one hand and ethics and faith on the other. Pure knowledge belonged to a different world from that of moral speculation and faith. In his attempt to elevate the position of ethics, however, he seemed to isolate both ethics and religion. Yet Kant still allowed room for belief in God. God, freedom, and immortality were the postulates of practical reason. God was not an object of metaphysical knowledge or speculation but arose as a postulate of rational, practical faith.[37]

It is remarkable to note the way in which Kant's ethics came to be taken as the standard for religion. The divine could be understood only from the perspective of the good. As a result, religion was based on morality, not vice versa. Kant did not acknowledge any clear form of knowledge by revelation, much less a Word of God. Kant dismissed as religious mania and pseudoreligion the claim that God might be thought to require anything of humanity over and above the good life led by a reasonable person.[38] Kant seems to close religious belief in the cage of our moral consciousness.

The picture Kant painted of the freethinking individual seems quite sterile. He referred to people who were never guided by feelings, who made impartial decisions, not influenced by the age in which they lived. Yet our subconscious inclinations, backgrounds, memories, and inclinations are psychologically complex. Whether for good or bad, partiality and emotions often guide our decisions in daily life. Philosophers such as Nietzsche, Max Scheler, and Herman Dooyeweerd would later level criticism at Kant's one-sided rationalism and paltry anthropology in particular. Dooyeweerd also pinpoints the danger of a pathological morality that completely separated

---

37. Peter Byrne, "Kantianism," in *The Blackwell Encyclopedia of Modern Christian Thought*, ed. Alister E. McGrath (Oxford: Blackwell), 296, 298.

38. Immanuel Kant, *Religion within the Boundaries of Mere Reason*, trans. Allen Wood, ed. Allen Wood and George Di Giovanni (Cambridge: Cambridge University Press, 1999). For instance, see his discussion about miracles, pp. 122–25.

feelings from ethics.[39] Kant appears to neglect one of our deepest human motives: our capacity to love. In fact, Kant took an extremely negative view of all human feelings and the desire for a happy life. At the same time he also rejected asceticism and morbid obedience. Instead, for Kant obedience stems from personal freedom, which by definition entails rejecting the illusion of happiness dependent on circumstances.[40] The question remains, however, as to whether that is how a deontological ethics works in practice.

Post-Kantian Theonomous Principle Ethics: Karl Barth

While Aquinas and Calvin are without question important representatives of theonomous principle ethics, they were both pre-Enlightenment theologians. In their time the concept of unity among thought, faith, and ethics was widely accepted. In the modern era faith in God no longer occupied the same prominent place in society. Religion became a private matter barred from the public forum, especially when it made ethical claims. Mature, responsible people were deemed capable of forming their own judgments regarding good and evil. Knowing and believing became two completely different worlds. This was the eighteenth-century context that shaped Immanuel Kant and subsequently influenced the ethics of Karl Barth. In his attempt to reconcile radical empiricism with Enlightenment rationalism, Kant elevated ethics to a standard against which all future theology should be measured.

Karl Barth (1886–1968) accepted Kant's basic thesis that humans of themselves can never know God. Barth identified Kant's work *The Critique of Practical Reason* as the first book he had read that had made a genuine impact on him.[41] However, Barth did not agree with Kant that God was a

---

39. Herman Dooyeweerd's attack is sharp: "Kant's rigid separation between morality and natural feeling-drives is in serious danger of legitimizing such pathological disintegrations of the inner act-life. It is inhuman and a-moral in its logistic formalizing of the meaning of ethical duty and ethical law." Herman Dooyeweerd, *A New Critique of Theoretical Thought*, vol. 2, trans. David H. Freeman, William S. Young, and H. De Jongste (Jordan Station, Ontario: Paideia Press, 1984), 150–51.

40. For a response to this criticism, see Monique Castello, "Kant, Emmanuel," in *Dictionnaire d'éthique et de philosophie morale*, 4th ed., ed. Monique Canto-Sperber (Paris: Presses Universitaire de France, Quadrige, 2004), 1:1029.

41. John Webster, *The Cambridge Companion to Karl Barth* (Cambridge: Cambridge University Press, 2000), 6.

postulate of ethics and merely the source of our moral behavior. Humanity could not possibly be the measure of the divine. Liberal Protestantism, to which Barth was reacting, had thoroughly embraced Kant's moral religion. Christian ethics had found expression primarily in the heeding of Jesus' moral principles and his social engagement. Barth sought a way out of this theological humanist liberalism. The source of theology could not be found in the thinking, acting, or feeling self, but only in God himself. Any theology that originated with humanity was a form of natural theology—humans attempting to understand God via rational thought. That kind of religion had nothing to do with true faith, only conceptual idolatry.

For Barth true theology had to begin from above, not from below. God was the "Wholly Other," who broke into our lives and revealed his Word to us. But Barth's "Word" could not be equated with the Bible. The Word existed in three forms: the Word of God revealed (Jesus Christ), the Word of God written (the Bible, through which we come to know Christ), and the Word of God proclaimed (the preaching of the church). But only Christ himself was infallible. Christ alone remained before us as the perfect one, he whom we were unable to control. As Barth said, "Revelation in fact does not differ from the presence of Jesus Christ nor from the reconciliation accomplished by Him. To say revelation is to say, 'the Word has become flesh.'"[42] Reason could not in any sense be taken as the measure of theology. Theological expression could never provide precise explanations; it had to resort to dialogue and the use of paradoxes. One such paradox was Christ as the eternal God who had revealed himself within temporal reality.

Barth was vehemently opposed to any attempt to emancipate ethics, as Kant had seemed to do. For Barth, Aquinas had also been guilty of giving ethics too much of an independent position within natural reality. Humans could not be understood outside the context of what God required of them. Ethics formed an integral part of the dogma relating to God, since it primarily had to do with God's ruling over humanity. Typical of Barth's dogmatics was the prominent position he gave the doctrine of the Trinity, which had its own particular impact on theological ethics.[43] The Trinitarian

---

42. Barth, *Church Dogmatics I.1*, 2nd ed. (New York: T&T Clark International, 2004), 119.

43. Friedrich Schleiermacher, by contrast, had given low priority to consideration of the Trinity. For Barth, the Trinity was a doctrinal prolegomenon, as the formal and moral criterion of the whole of Christian theology. For the significance of the Trinity in Barth's ethics,

doctrine was founded on the command of God as Creator, Reconciler, and Redeemer. Barth based his discussion of ethics on this broad dogmatic framework.

The Word of God was as central to Barth's ethics as it was to his dogmatics. Barth looked to revelation alone, keeping moral philosophy at a distance. He illustrated his view with Israel's mandate to occupy the land of Canaan, goods, culture, and all. However small, insignificant, and intellectually unimpressive Israel may have been, it had the Word of God. God's commands and his promise were sufficient.[44] The Word of God was an invasion into the world, in response to which reason could only bow.

For Barth Christian morality boiled down quite simply to obedience to God's commandments. But this was not a blind obedience to a "text"; that would only lead to legalism, casuistry, and an idolatrous use of the Bible. Nor was he advocating orthodox ethics, whereby general biblical principles were applied to specific contemporary situations; that would simply lead to using Scripture to confirm our own moral views. Rather, the command of God comes to us, breaks in to us, at specific moments in life as an event.[45] In such moments the absolute, personal, living will of God is revealed to us. Such commands remain completely unambiguous, because God's commands are by definition crystal clear, not some complex applications of a general rule.[46] No interpretation, as such, is required. It is not a "deliberation ethics," as if a person could contribute something, like a wise judge.[47] God reveals himself in his actions, whereby he has chosen humankind as his covenant partner. God's very being and his actions are one, which is why ethics must not be founded on universal abstractions. Barth opted for a highly narrative interpretation of the Bible as the history (*Geschichte*) of God's covenant of grace. For Barth God shows himself in the specific, the climax being his concrete revelation in Jesus Christ, the only Lord, in the face of a totalitarian state seeking to usurp the role of the church.

---

see Nigel Biggar, "Barth's Trinitarian Ethic," in Webster, *The Cambridge Companion to Karl Barth*, 212–27.

44. Barth, *Church Dogmatics II.2,* 518–20. Cf. Karl Barth, *Ethics*, ed. Dietrich Braun, trans. Geoffrey W. Bromiley (New York: Seabury Press, 1981), 56.

45. Barth, *Church Dogmatics II.2*, sect. 38, p. 661. Cf. Robert E. Willis, *The Ethics of Karl Barth* (Leiden, Neth.: Brill, 1971), 170–71.

46. Barth, *Church Dogmatics II.2*, sect. 38, p. 739.

47. Willis, *Ethics of Barth*, 183.

For Barth this Word always confronts—it is the voice of the Other. The Bible can become the living Voice of God. Our task is not to make clever calculations but simply to listen and obey. Even this confrontation with God's will is an act of grace on God's part, whereby he justifies us and accepts us. God demonstrates his love through his commands. Christian ethics, then, embraces command ethics and life by grace.

Evaluation

Barth made a huge contribution to the deeper theological considerations of Christian ethics. It is impossible to evaluate him in a few paragraphs, especially since his ethics and dogmatics form an integral whole.[48] Barth's integration of the doctrine of the Trinity into ethics has made an enormous contribution to biblical and theological ethics. Few have explained God's grace and revelation with such powerful depth and then gone on to place these doctrines in such a broad redemptive-historical context. With Barth, dogmatic theology formed the basis for Christian ethics. His positioning of revelation in Jesus Christ at the very heart of his theological ethics is an example worth emulating; it serves to balance the overly strong emphasis on the Old Testament typical of Calvin's ethics.

At the same time, the tension in Barth's understanding of God's hiddenness as "Wholly Other" and God's revelation of himself affected Barth's view of the application of Scripture in ethics. He did not provide biblical principles from which concrete daily applications could be derived but rather advocated using paradigmatic stories to confront people with the Word. For Barth, all biblical texts refer to concrete, historical events and must not be detached from their particular contexts. As Barth put it:

> For precisely in Holy Scripture the command of God does not confront us in the guise of rules, principles, axioms and general moral truths, but purely in the form of concrete, historical, unique and singular orders, prohibitions and directions. Their common import consists in the fact that it is always the same divine Overlord who in this way confronts various men . . . and, in the content of His command, of the ordering of these

---

48. For ambivalent attitudes toward Barth taken by evangelical (and Reformational) theologians, see Gregory G. Bolich, *Karl Barth and Evangelicalism* (Downers Grove, IL: InterVarsity Press, 1980).

men to conform in their actions at a definite time, in a definite place and in a definite way to the history of the covenant and salvation controlled by Him.[49]

Barth's vagueness here stands in sharp contrast to the more concrete use of Scripture practiced by both Jesus and the apostles.

In discarding the concrete, historical, and rational aspects of Christian faith, perhaps Barth was overly inclined to give way to the Kantian division between knowledge and faith. He extensively engaged with Scripture and entered into dialogue with tradition, but he banished reason and experience, ignoring two important sources for Christian ethics. In practice, reason and experience are impossible to ignore in the long term—they are sure to sneak in the back door eventually.[50] In fact, as most of us will find, they have both been living with us the entire time.

Dialogue with Emil Brunner

The Barth-Brunner debate on natural theology is familiar to many students of theology. Brunner was searching for a legitimate form of natural theology, whereby he made use of the concept "point of contact." Barth gave his emotionally laden response to Brunner in the form of a book succinctly titled *Nein!* (1934). Unfortunately, Barth's emphatic disapproval brought an end to their lengthy friendship. According to Barth there is no point of contact that is inherent to human nature. The only point of contact is what the Holy Spirit works in us. Brunner shared Barth's disdain for the separation of ethics from theology, seeing such movement as nothing less than an outworking of the consequences of the fall. He also joined Barth in his critique of Scholasticism and the role of reason. However, he was less radical than Barth in his isolation of Christian ethics. According to Brunner there is an anthropological point of contact between the believer and nonbeliever. All persons are created in God's image with a sense of responsibility and a basic awareness of good and evil. Many simply need to put God back at the center of their lives.

Brunner rejected the natural theology and natural ethics propounded by Aquinas and others. But he did teach a universal natural revelation.

---

49. Barth, *Church Dogmatics III.4*, p. 12.
50. Richard B. Hays, *The Moral Vision of the New Testament: A Contemporary Introduction to New Testament Ethics* (San Francisco: HarperSanFrancisco, 1996), 238.

Brunner's ethical theory addresses the created order, that is, the context or environment within which we should follow the commands.[51] God's command is obeyed within the context of a concrete reality. This reality determines in part how we act. Ethics is not limited to the individual but should manifest itself in society. Brunner refers not simply to areas of life practice in general but also to the divine order that governs each of these areas.[52] This created order includes marriage and the family, work, economic life, the state, culture, and the church. These are the structures of life. It follows that ethics must not only grasp the meaning of the commands but also fathom these very structures of life.[53]

Like Barth, Brunner focused primarily on specific commands in specific situations, yet he was more specific than Barth in his interpretation of what that meant. The command to love is the greatest command that contains all others. What God requires of us cannot be determined beforehand; his commands are not repeatable. We cannot use the law simply as a reference book. "God's Command does not vary in *intention*, but it varies in *content*, according to the conditions with which it deals."[54] The *why* is love; the *what* is always "occasional," to be received on each occasion afresh through the working of the Holy Spirit. The Spirit brings to life the letters of the biblical commands. In this sense Brunner was a forerunner of situation

---

51. See Emil Brunner, *The Divine Imperative: A Study in Christian Ethics*, trans. Olive Wyon (Cambridge: Lutterworth Press, 2002), 208–12. Helmut Thielicke also takes Brunner's side in the debate, pointing out, for example, Barth's inconsistencies in the area of political ethics. For Thielicke it was precisely his fundamental repudiation of secular moral knowledge that made Barth uncritical of the facts. Helmut Thielicke, *Theological Ethics* (Grand Rapids: Eerdmans, 1979), 321–23.

52. Barth saw this as a regrettable reversion to natural theology.

53. This is also Herman Dooyeweerd's main criticism of Barth's theological ethics. Morality has its own place within temporal reality and must not be swallowed up in the religious aspect of reality. Morality encompasses juridical and faith aspects and cannot be reduced to either one of the two. See Dooyeweerd, *New Critique*, 148–49.

54. Brunner, *Divine Imperative*, 134. We find a similar standpoint taken in the ethics of Helmut Thielicke, but Thielicke criticizes the concept "created order" in that it implies a perfect state of affairs. Thielicke emphasizes that these "orders" are necessary structures put in place because of the hardness of heart of humankind. They are not, therefore, free from sin and as such can better be referred to as "emergency orders." We live in this age according to these imperfect structures and look forward to future perfection. Thielicke, *Theological Ethics*, 434–51. Dietrich Bonhoeffer preferred the term "mandates" since it conveyed a more dynamic understanding. A mandate is a divine commission grounded in the revelation of Christ that calls us to be a representative of Christ in all aspects of life. Dietrich Bonhoeffer, *Ethics* (New York: Macmillan, 1965), 207–13, 300.

ethics, which we will consider in a later portion of the book. But in the following chapter, we transition our discussion from principles to character and virtues.

Chapter 5

Character Ethics
and the Virtues

The Classical Virtues: Aristotle

We cannot hope to gain any real understanding of Aristotle (384–322 BC) without at least some knowledge of his teacher Plato (427–347 BC). As befits a brilliant pupil, Aristotle was both Plato's follower and his antagonist. We recall that for Plato the good is an idea or form from the higher and changeless world of universals. Virtue is about acquiring insight into these absolute notions of beauty, goodness, and justice. Rigorous contemplation releases us from this temporal and changing world. According to Plato, then, ethics has a source beyond the visible world. In the world of universals the highest good exerts its erotic attraction on the human soul, causing humans to strive for perfection.[1]

This insight into the world brings harmony to the soul. The soul is made up of three components: in order of significance, reason, spirit, and

---

1. The Greek word *eros* is used here in its broadest sense to refer to the desire for personal development to make up for one's own shortcomings. It does not carry the sexually suggestive connotation we normally associate with the term. In this sense, virtue ethics is erotic self-realization.

desire. Plato compared the soul to a chariot pulled by two winged horses. The mind (reason) wants to advance upward to the realm of ideas, but desire (human appetites) is pulled toward the world. Virtue is that quality of allowing reason, the highest domain of the soul, to dominate. Plato referred to those who truly live by reason as "golden souls." These are the philosopher-kings equipped to lead society. The chief virtue of the leaders of society is reason or wisdom. Silver souls are bent on renown and power. They are the sentinels and soldiers responsible for maintaining order and security. Their chief virtue is courage—an essential quality for the warrior. The vast majority of people are bronze souls: those making sure that their own desires are satisfied. Everyone has these three facets of the soul within and must allow them to be guided by the virtues of insight, courage, and moderation. This will result in inner harmony in the form of the highest virtue of justice. According to Plato what applies to the individual applies also to the state. So a well-organized society will exhibit a harmony of genuine justice.[2]

Aristotle expanded virtue ethics, disconnecting it from the dualism of Plato. He freed it from ideological speculation and brought it down to earth. Aristotle criticized his teacher's thesis that the idea of the good is an unattainable ideal, given his own belief that ethics should focus on attainable wisdom for practical daily living. The Platonic model had distracted us from the business of practical philosophy.[3] There is a splendid illustration of this key difference between Plato and Aristotle in the fresco by Renaissance painter Raphael, *The School of Athens* (Vatican Museum, 1509–1510). The two masters Plato and Aristotle are positioned in the center. Plato is carrying his dialogue, the *Timaeus,* under his left arm—a work including his well-known address on the immortal soul. With his right index finger he is pointing upward to the world of ideas, as if to say that the *real* world is above and *this* world is a copy. Aristotle is holding his *Ethica* under his arm and gestures his hand horizontally to the world around him, as an indication that the real world is right here before us.[4]

---

2. Justice later became a central theme in radical postmodern ethics. Deconstructionist Jacques Derrida said that justice was the one thing that could not be deconstructed. See John D. Caputo, ed. *Deconstruction in a Nutshell: A Conversation with Jacques Derrida* (New York: Fordham University Press, 1997), 131–32.

3. Gabriel Richardson Lear, "Happiness and the Structure of Ends," in *A Companion to Aristotle,* ed. Georgios Anagnostopoulos (Oxford: Blackwell, 2009), 388.

4. John D. Caputo, *Philosophy and Theology* (Nashville: Abingdon, 2006), 13–14.

Teleological and Eudemonistic Ethics

Two of Aristotle's ethical works are available to us: *Nicomachean Ethics* and *Eudemian Ethics*, of which the former is generally deemed the more important.[5] Aristotle's ethical thought is an extension of his broader perspective on nature and metaphysics. Natural processes can be properly understood only in the context of their final destination. His ethical theory fits into a larger framework of purposiveness and is therefore referred to as teleological ethics. All things strive toward self-actualization or self-fulfillment. An acorn's purpose is to become an oak; a bee is made to be able to sip nectar. All things together form a hierarchical order at the top of which is God, the Unmoved Mover and Supreme Cause of all things. This God ensures that everything in nature moves toward a certain goal. Aristotle tended to refer to God as "It," not "Him," an impersonal primary mover that only thinks itself.

The purposiveness at work in nature is automatic. It happens without consultation, the various ends being moved by the Unmoved Mover's attraction. A human is by nature a deliberative being and must therefore select goals with conscious decision, using both the mind and the will. The opening sentence of Aristotle's *Nicomachean Ethics* is telling in this regard: "Every skill and every inquiry, and similarly every action and rational choice, is thought to aim at some good; and so the good has been aptly described as that at which everything aims."[6] All that we undertake is ultimately determined by our goals. Our short-term goals are more akin to means: we hunt in order to live. But the moral good is not a means, but rather an intrinsic goal that occupies a position outside the realm of usefulness. It is valuable in and of itself.

The higher goals are beauty and goodness. In more concrete terms, the goal of humankind is happiness or *eudaimonia*, which literally means "to have a good spirit." Aristotle was not referring here to hedonistic pleasure but to a state in which humans fully reach their purpose and achieve complete fulfillment. We exercise our abilities to the full by living a life of reason. Our focus should not be on immediate sensual pleasure but on

---

5. An important addition to these two primarily ethical works is Aristotle's *Politics*. Aristotle understood ethics as part of a political philosophy since the human was in essence a political animal, comparable to bees and ants. *Politics* 1252a24–1253a19.

6. Aristotle, *Nicomachean Ethics*, ed. Roger Crisp, *Cambridge Texts in History of Philosophy* (Cambridge: Cambridge University Press, 2000), I.1, p. 3.

overall goodness and beauty. Aristotle warned against becoming slaves to all sorts of immediate desires. True happiness is an activity of our highest faculty, the intellect, and is to be found in the contemplative life of searching for unchangeable truths.[7]

But Aristotle did not recommend a hermitlike existence in the contemplative life. Humans are social beings and can experience happiness only within the framework of the city-state (*polis*). People must unite in pursuit of the social ideal. The goal of the state is the good life for everyone. Aristotle went so far as to make the individual subject to the state and advocated reciprocity or even a fusion between the individual and the community. The purpose of each individual is to contribute to the common good. The state is an organic whole and can function only when each individual achieves his or her individual goal. So politics must do all it can to promote the happiness of the citizens. Practical philosophy (*phronēsis*) and ethics will lead us to function at our best, which is happiness.

Virtue Ethics

Aristotle's ethics of virtue should be understood against the background of consequential ethics and eudemonism. Virtues are about the nature of excellence of character.[8] Virtue is strongly linked to humanity's political responsibility. Aristotle followed the classical Greek tradition in which virtue is associated with civil duty, political leadership, and even war.[9] Although the virtues to which Aristotle referred are individual qualities, the emphasis is still placed on their impact on the community.

Aristotle defined virtue as "a state involving a rational choice, consisting in a mean relative to us and determined by reason."[10] Virtue is a disposition, an attitude to life that can be practiced and can become habitual. If we make the right choices, virtue becomes an integral part of who we are. So it is not an isolated good deed but a permanent state of being or character. Nor is virtue a spontaneous reaction, since it entails a deliberate choice. But it is more than learned behavior; it is a way of life in which a person is guided by the rational principle of prudence (*phronēsis*). Ethics is not

---

7. See Aristotle, *Nicomachean Ethics* X.7, pp. 194–99.
8. See Aristotle, *Nicomachean Ethics* II.6. For a full exposition see II.5–6, pp. 28–31.
9. The ancient meaning of *aretē*, "moral goodness" or "virtue," implied bravery and exudes the atmosphere of Homeric heroes.
10. Aristotle, *Nicomachean Ethics* II.6, p. 31.

simply a question of purely logical knowledge and theoretical contemplation but entails practical knowledge. Aristotle was most concerned with
gaining insight into our ends and seeking the right means to achieve those
ends. Only the prudent person who is experienced in the practicalities of
daily living can determine what is virtuous. What matters is not learning,
but insight, common sense, and even good taste. Unlike Plato, Aristotle did
not become absorbed in abstract contemplation but related morality to the
concrete, contingent circumstances of life.

Typical of Aristotle's ethical theory is the concept of the "mean" (the
middle)—the art of moderation.[11] As we see in all aspects of nature, it is
always important to seek a delicate balance. When anything is taken to
extremes, it goes wrong. The same is the case with virtue. Fanaticism and
impulsiveness are as bad as apathy and laxness. The virtue of bravery is the
mean between recklessness and cowardice. The virtue of generosity is the
mean between miserliness and extravagance. Discerning the mean has to
do with knowing how to react in a balanced, measured manner in every
situation. Virtue is not a mean in mathematical terms, but it is rather a
situational mean. For example, it is not an act of bravery if a woman simply
throws herself onto a land mine. But it is brave if she does this to save a
group of children. So the circumstances of the situation help determine
whether or not an act is virtuous.

Which virtues did Aristotle identify? Certainly, there are too many to
count, and there is no such thing as a fixed canon of virtues. However, we
can name the main virtue groups that he divided into the two categories
of rational virtues and ethical virtues. Under the rational virtues, he drew
all sorts of subtle distinctions between learning, skill, wisdom, intuitive
reason, and theoretical wisdom. Under ethical virtues, he spoke of courage,
moderation, friendship, and justice. The virtue of *justice* was considered by
Aristotle to be the most important.

Aristotle's *Nicomachean Ethics* is still considered one of the most important works in the field of moral philosophy. His methodical and analytical approach to morality turned ethics into a science. Aristotle employed
reason with exquisite precision to guide us from phenomena to abstract
distinctions. This high form of abstraction does not result in an irrelevant
and otherworldly ethical theory. We cannot but admire Aristotle for the

---

11. Gavin Lawrence, "Human Excellence in Character and Intellect," in *A Companion to
Aristotle*, ed. Anagnostopoulos, 425–33.

levelheadedness and clarity of mind with which he laid out highly practical ethical ideals. It is also remarkable that Aristotle's ethics was completely devoid of principles or commands. It was a full-fledged character ethic, placing the moral subject at the center while guarding the importance of community.

In practice, however, people often behave on the basis of their own cultural norms and then call what they do virtue. But is a virtue ethic always sufficient to persuade people to adhere to justice? Laws of some sort always seem to be an essential element of any functioning society. A society's ethics is also closely connected to its legal system. Ethical reflection today must unquestionably address issues such as duty, penalty, and repentance in greater depth than Aristotle's virtues. It is often assumed that Aristotle had rational and natural arguments for what were, in fact, generally accepted ideas of his own culture. Aristotle's perspectives were clearly derived from his anthropological interpretation that reason was the essence of humanity. Humans attained happiness by living according to reason. But is rationality the only route to happiness? Furthermore, is our greatest goal the attainment of happiness? And what exactly constitutes happiness anyway?

The Christian Virtues: Thomas Aquinas

We have already discussed Thomas Aquinas as a representative of theonomous principle ethics. Although Aquinas did not attribute a primary or exclusive role to virtue ethics, his exposition of Aristotle's *Nicomachean Ethics,* along with his *Summa Theologica* and *Summa Contra Gentiles,* devoted considerable attention to the theory of virtues. A pure Christian ethics of virtues completely unassociated with commands would have been unthinkable in the classical Christian era. It was generally acknowledged that God had revealed his moral will in his commandments. Virtue ethics tended to fulfill a more supplementary role, with a strong focus on spirituality and pastoral theology as essential qualities of a Christian leader.

Influence of the Stoics on Christianity

Before we look more closely at Aquinas' theory of virtues, we should point out the major influence that the ethics of the Stoics had on Christian thought and on Aquinas' virtue ethics. Stoicism's influence on the classical world cannot be overestimated. Stoic philosophy not only paved the way for Christianity but also joined Neoplatonism in shaping early Christian perspectives.[12] Virtue ethics found acceptance primarily via the practical ethics of Stoicism.

The Stoics' basic proposition was that a human life is supposed to follow the natural order. The virtuous life is a life lived in accordance with the principles of the cosmic order, and such a life brings us happiness. Again, a close link is made between reason and morality. Humans should not give in to their base feelings and desires but instead live according to rational obligations.

Virtue ethics as propounded by Cicero (106–43 BC) and Seneca (4 BC–AD 65) had a particularly far-reaching impact on early Christian ethics. From Cicero onward a sort of canonization of the four cardinal virtues took shape.[13] A virtuous life could be summed up by the qualities of wisdom, bravery, moderation, and justice. Virtue was closely linked with the rationality of the human soul. For instance, Clement of Alexandria (AD 150–215) defined virtue as "a state of the soul rendered harmonious by reason in respect of the whole life."[14] Following in the footsteps of his master Ambrose, Augustine also devoted considerable thought to a Christian theory of virtues. Augustine's ideas on this topic included a mixture of Stoic, Neoplatonic, and New Testament thought. This mixture was demonstrated when Augustine discussed the four rivers of paradise as referring to the four cardinal virtues: prudence, fortitude, temperance, and justice.[15] All virtues were summed up in the primary virtue of love.[16] The character of a Christian was evidenced by success in directing all feelings toward love for

---

12. Everett Ferguson, *Backgrounds of Early Christianity*, 3rd ed. (Grand Rapids: Eerdmans, 2003), 363–69.

13. See Cicero's influence in this regard in Marcia L. Colish, *The Stoic Tradition from Antiquity to the Early Middle Ages,* 2nd ed. (Leiden, Neth.: Brill, 1990), 2:79–89.

14. *The Paedagogus,* bk. 1, chap. 13, trans. William Wilson. In vol. 2 of *Ante-Nicene Fathers,* ed. Alexander Roberts, James Donaldson, and A. Cleveland Coxe. Rev. and ed. for New Advent by Kevin Knight (2009), http://www.newadvent.org/fathers/02091.htm.

15. Augustine, *On Genesis, A Refutation of the Manichees,* 2.10.14. Cf. Colish, *The Stoic Tradition,* 215–16.

16. This is how we have to understand his famous dictum *"Dilige et quod vis fac"* (Love and do what you will). Love has to be the very root of our moral actions. Augustine, *Homilies on the First Epistles of John,* Homily 7.8, trans. H. Browne. In vol. 7 of *Nicene and Post-Nicene Fathers,* ed. Philip Schaff, New Advent (2009), http://www.newadvent.org/fathers/170207.htm. This quote is often misunderstood as if love obliterates all other virtues and commandments. Marcia Colish comments on this phrase, "In the confidence that this kind of hearer will understand that he speaks not of obligation of man's moral duties but of their total transvaluation and irradiation by charity." Colish, *Stoic Tradition,* 220.

God. The virtues of the unbeliever were not true virtues because they did not lead to the proper end. According to Augustine the Romans had two sources for their ethics, "namely, liberty and the desire of human praise, which compelled the Romans to admirable deeds."[17] Christian ethics, on the other hand, took love as its central feature:

> As to virtue leading us to a happy life, I hold virtue to be nothing else than perfect love of God. For the fourfold division of virtue I regard as taken from four forms of love. For these four virtues, . . . I should have no hesitation in defining them: that temperance is love giving itself entirely to that which is loved; fortitude is love readily bearing all things for the sake of the loved object; justice is love serving only the loved object, and therefore ruling rightly; prudence is love distinguishing with sagacity between what hinders it and what helps it. The object of this love is not anything, but only God, the chief good, the highest wisdom, the perfect harmony.[18]

Virtue as the Perfection of Humanity

A notable feature of Aquinas' virtue ethics is that it combines Aristotle's teleological thought with Augustinian virtue ethics. Like Aristotle, Aquinas also considered the uniqueness of humans to lie in their intellectual faculties and will. Humans are masters of their own actions as "self-moving potentiality" and therefore responsible for the way they attain their goals. Despite their similarities, the differences between Aquinas and Aristotle are worthy of attention. Unlike Aristotle, Aquinas believed that individuals are not able to attain their goals without the gift of grace. The virtues are a result of God's infused grace that enables us to live a just life: "Infused virtue is caused in us by God without any action on our part, but not without our consent. This is the sense of the words, 'which God works in us without us.' As to those things which are done by us, God causes them in us, yet not without action on our part, for He works in every will and in

---

17. Augustine, *The City of God*, bk. 5, chap. 18, trans. Marcus Dods. In vol. 2 of *Nicene and Post-Nicene Fathers,* ed. Philip Schaff, New Advent (2009), http://www.newadvent.org/fathers/120105.htm.

18. Augustine, *Of the Morals of the Catholic Church*, chap. 15, trans. Richard Stothert. In vol. 4 of *Nicene and Post-Nicene Fathers,* ed. Philip Schaff, New Advent (2009), http://www. newadvent.org/fathers/1401.htm.

every nature."[19] No one can be saved without God's bestowing the virtues in his grace. But Aquinas did not neglect the importance of our own efforts. Virtue is a habit, a lasting inclination or disposition generated by much practice.[20] If we make the right choices in our lives repeatedly, this ability becomes a quality of character and requires less and less effort on our part. That is, we become more spontaneously good. Therefore, the dual spiritual exercises of ethics and spirituality become inextricably linked.

Natural and Supernatural Virtues

Aquinas made a distinction between natural and supernatural virtues. With respect to the natural virtues, Aquinas took his lead from Plato and Aristotle. The cardinal virtues are justice, prudence, courage, and temperance. These four virtues form the basis of a dignified human existence; they belong to the essence and power of the soul.[21] The difference between the natural and the supernatural virtues lies in the purpose they serve. The four natural virtues teach us how to live. Here Aquinas followed the Aristotelian approach, recommending a continuous search for the mean. To these he added faith, hope, and love, the three supernatural virtues given by God in order to help the Christian surpass human nature and participate in the divine nature.[22] The idea of moderation should not be applied to the theological virtues, for there is no such thing as an excess of faith, hope, or love.

Aquinas presents us with an impressive synergy between anthropology and a Christian ethics of virtues. The human soul is composed of the mind, will, and emotions. Our mind is guided naturally by wisdom and supernaturally by faith. Our will is guided both by bravery and by the love with which we serve God and our neighbor. Our emotions must be controlled by the natural virtue of moderation, while supernatural hope dictates what we ultimately desire. If we succeed in bringing all these together, the result is an inner harmony expressing itself in the virtue of justice.

---

19. Thomas Aquinas, *Summa Theologica* 1.2, q. 55, a. 4, New Advent (2008), http://www. newadvent.org/summa/2055.htm.
20. Ibid.
21. Ibid., I.2.56.1.
22. Thomas was referring to 2 Peter 1:4; *Summa Theologica* 1.2, q. 62, a. 1. Cf. Jean Porter, "Virtue Ethics," in *The Cambridge Companion to Christian Ethics*, ed. Robin Gill (New York: Cambridge University Press, 2001), 102–3.

Luther was extremely harsh in his criticism of Thomistic virtue ethics, which he regarded as a form of faith-works where grace becomes a human quality. For Luther justifying grace should be regarded as an acquittal rather than the means by which God enables us to do good works. In this sense Luther (and Calvin as well) proposed a more marked separation between salvation and sanctification. As part of his bid to return to scriptural roots, Luther preferred to speak of good works as evidence of the fruit of the Holy Spirit.[23] This is one of those hot topics where views vary considerably among evangelical scholars today. Wesleyan theology, for example, is critical of Luther's one-sided focus on forensic justification, favoring a stronger emphasis on the character-changing work of grace or, as Wesley called it, "therapeutic grace." This was a shift in emphasis, but not a departure from the premise of the Reformation: "justification by faith."[24]

Character Ethics: Stanley Hauerwas— Community, Narrative, and Character

American theologian Stanley Hauerwas serves as a model for a contemporary theological virtue ethics.[25] The strong psychosocial dimension of his ethical theory, however, and the considerable emphasis it places on personal development actually mean it has more in common with character ethics than with classical virtue ethics. As a moral theologian, Hauerwas is a multifaceted and fascinating individual. Although formerly a Methodist heavily influenced by the Wesleyan tradition, he eventually began considering himself an Anglican. Through his mentor John Howard Yoder, he grew to value the pacifist ethic of the Anabaptists. In his theology he is a kindred spirit with Barth, while also showing a strong affinity with Aristotelian-Thomistic virtue ethics. With this blend of traditions, Hauerwas' work represents an invigorating and contrasting alternative to the Calvinist command ethic.[26] His moral-theological model is centered on a small

---

23. Stanley Hauerwas, *A Community of Character: Toward a Constructive Christian Social Ethic* (Notre Dame: University of Notre Dame Press, 1981), 183–88.

24. Randy L. Maddox, *Responsible Grace: John Wesley's Practical Theology* (Nashville: Kingswood Books, 1994).

25. For an introduction to his work, see Stanley Hauerwas, John Berkman, and Michael G. Cartwright, *The Hauerwas Reader* (Durham, NC: Duke University Press, 2001).

26. In the Baptist tradition this approach is followed by James William McClendon, *Systematic Theology Vol. 1: Ethics* (Nashville: Abingdon, 1986); Joseph J. Kotva Jr., *The Chris-*

number of key concepts: narrative, community, character, and virtue. We previously noted Alasdair MacIntyre's critique on the loss of a coherent story in contemporary thought and the resulting relativism and emotivism. Hauerwas endorses this critique and takes it to the logical next step. A Christian ethic must return to narrative. But universal stories and grand narrative schemes will not suffice, since the notion of a universal ethic is a modernist fabrication. Rather, we need a specifically Christian morality within the community of faith.

According to Hauerwas ethics should not concern itself primarily with the specific decisions we make in a given situation. Its primary concern should be to answer the question, Who am I? What matters most is not the deed but the doer (moral agent). To limit ourselves to the consideration of concrete decisions is to reduce and impoverish ethics beyond recognition. Moral decisions are never made in a vacuum; they are consequences of our personality and an extension of our character, comprising the sum of our concrete inclinations and deeds. The personality—the moral subject—does not stand alone but is interwoven with its particular cultural and historical context.

Hauerwas offers a robust alternative to the rationalistic ethical decision making we often encounter in principle ethics influenced by Kant. His critique is leveled primarily at the pretensions of a liberalism that seeks to reduce ethics to rationally correct decisions. Such modernist reductionism ignores the diversity of life, assuming we can make moral decisions with perfect professional detachment. Hauerwas emphasizes instead the contingency of human existence. In his view there is no such thing as objective knowledge or universal reason. Character always precedes intellect. He advocates a subjective ethic, but by no means a private ethic. An ethics founded on rational decision making isolates the individual: "Morally and politically, we act as if we were not members of a community, did not share possessions and did not share a common history."[27] All that remains to bind us together is a sort of moral rationality, abstracted from a specific community and history. "Only from the perspective of an ethic that at-

---

tian Case for Virtue Ethics (Washington, D.C.: Georgetown University Press, 1996); and Glen H. Stassen and David P. Gushee, Kingdom Ethics: Following Jesus in Contemporary Context (Downers Grove, IL.: InterVarsity Press, 2003), 55–78.
27. Hauerwas, A Community of Character, 120.

tempts to separate morality from its historical context can virtue ethics be seen as a subjective threat to morality."[28]

For Hauerwas the essence of the Christian faith is not found in doctrines but in narrative. Doctrines are universal truth claims, whereas narratives focus on contingencies faced in the everyday. A story has a wide range of effects: it can unmask us, confront us, point out our limitations, or simply encourage us. Character derives its stability and unity from stories. Through stories we find and shape our identity. For the Christian this includes identification with the stories of Israel and, most importantly, the story of Jesus Christ. To live "in Christ" is to base our lives on the story of Jesus. Narrative is the means by which God chooses to make himself known. It is the medium by which he is pleased to change us and conform us to his image.

Experiencing narrative is not an individual matter. Those who live according to the story of Jesus create a new, story-formed community. The story binds people together and provides them with a communal orientation. Our character is shaped by being part of the community of Christ, called to live in love and peace. Only when the community determines to follow Jesus is it able to understand the story and derive moral direction from it. So obedience precedes comprehension, and the communal act precedes understanding. Scripture cannot be read properly outside the faith community.

Hauerwas challenges the prevailing individualist evangelical assumption that every believer has the right to read and understand the Bible for himself or herself. He goes so far as to contend that those who are not part of a faith community and who lack a virtuous character would do better to stay away from Scripture altogether.[29] Ultimately, it is the faith community that attributes authority to Scripture, and, conversely, it is Scripture that gives the community and the individuals within that community their identity. This dynamic can be seen as a continuous exchange, a dialogue through which we identify our own story with biblical stories. Outside the context of the community, Scripture is no more than an ancient text.

A character ethic finds expression in an ethics of virtues. Hauerwas points out that to date we have not succeeded in formulating a generally

---

28. Ibid.
29. Stanley Hauerwas, *Unleashing the Scripture: Freeing the Bible from Captivity to America* (Nashville: Abingdon, 1993).

accepted, unambiguous definition of virtue. Plato's understanding of virtue differs slightly from that of Aristotle, which differs again from that of Thomas Aquinas. The very fact that such different interpretations exist indicates how virtue ethics is context bound. An ethics of virtues is functional, meeting specific expectations, goals, and character qualities that happen to be valued in a given society. But it is more important to recognize a virtuous person than to be able to analyze specific virtues. The virtuous person is more than the sum of his or her virtues. Virtue is not merely a style or a way of acting out a role; it has to do with our ability or power to live according to our own traditional values and goals.

Hauerwas' insights into the relationship between narrative, community, and virtue can be usefully applied to moral education within the church. His ethics critically challenges the often-elevated position attributed to reason in the modernist paradigm. Principles and values can be judged by the fruits they produce in individual character and within the community. Hauerwas' virtue ethics portrays an intricate balance between the interests of the group and the development of the individual. He defies the arrogance of modernism that claims we can create our own stories. We do not construct our own stories or our own ethics; we are always shaped in and by the context of community.

According to Hauerwas the church takes on a unique role as the context for our moral education. Through the church we become part of God's story through moral preaching, sharing with one another, listening to each other's stories, and especially through the liturgy. As Hauerwas says, "Worship is the time when God trains his people to imitate him in habit, instinct and reflex. . . . In discussing whether, how, and when it is appropriate to speak in tongues or dance, or prophesy or use contemporary music, or pray extempore, the body [church] discovers when it is appropriate to campaign, denounce, protest or be silent."[30] This community-based virtue ethics offers us a Christian alternative to the radical individualism of Western culture. Hauerwas restores the church to its predominant position, without its becoming a dominant institution.

Nonetheless, we would like to offer some reservations about Hauerwas' proposals. Christian ethics has always emphasized a new and changed life. This entails far more than simply following a set of commands; our character

---

30. Stanley Hauerwas and Samuel Wells, eds., *The Blackwell Companion to Christian Ethics* (Malden, MA: Blackwell, 2004), 25.

and habits need to be transformed (Ephesians 4:25–5:2). The fruit of the Spirit produces virtues that stem from this transformed character (Galatians 5:22–23). But Hauerwas' virtue ethics has some traits that are foreign to classical Christian virtue ethics. According to Hauerwas character precedes commands. For example, he sees the prohibition against murder as an expression of the fact that we should respect the lives of others.[31] Certainly, our character influences our decisions. But conversely, our character is also shaped *by* specific decisions we make that become patterns of life.[32] Is it not also through obedience to commands that our character is shaped? Perhaps Hauerwas does not give this biblical dynamic sufficient consideration.

Hauerwas is critical of a strictly scientific, grammatical-historical approach to biblical exegesis. What matters the most is the morality of the church that enables us to understand the biblical narratives. Perhaps he is swinging the pendulum too far by placing an exclusive emphasis on narrative. The church is most certainly shaped by narrative and also by commands and theological paradigms. The intrinsic diversity of Scripture is important to Hauerwas because it demands the intervention of an inter-preting community. In order to acknowledge this diversity truly, however, we must acknowledge Scripture in the many and varied approaches by which it discloses itself in speech-acts of communication, whether doctrine, promises, commands, songs, laments, or narrative.[33]

---

31. Hauerwas, *Community of Character*, 119.
32. Dennis P. Hollinger, *Choosing the Good: Christian Ethics in a Complex World* (Grand Rapids: Baker Academic, 2002), 59; and Richard J. Mouw, *The God Who Commands: A Study in Divine Command Ethics* (Notre Dame: University of Notre Dame Press, 1990), 130.
33. Kevin J. Vanhoozer, *First Theology: God, Scripture and Hermeneutics* (Downers Grove, IL: InterVarsity Press, 2002), 34–35.

Chapter 6

Value Ethics and Personalism

The fourth model of moral reasoning we will discuss is value personalism. This approach finds its roots in Continental philosophy, especially in the school of phenomenology.[1] Value personalism has found its way into Catholic moral theology, but it is relatively unknown in evangelical Protestant circles.[2] It is interesting to note that the moral theologian Karol

---

1. The phenomenological method is essential for understanding value ethics. It is the philosophical school initiated in the first half of the 20th century by Edmund Husserl, Martin Heidegger, Maurice Merleau-Ponty, Jean-Paul Sartre, Emmanuel Levinas, et al. Literally, phenomenology means the study of phenomena: the appearances of things or things as they appear in our own experience. This method is a distinct tradition of the European continent. It differs from the analytical approach of the philosophy that is more successful in the Anglo-Saxon world. As William R. Schroeder remarks, "Far less emphasis is given to duty and obligation in Continental ethics and far more attention is paid to the cultural, psychological, interpersonal, and emotional conditions of a personal transformation that makes serious ethical achievements possible." William R. Schroeder, "Continental Ethics," in ed. Hugh LaFollette, *The Blackwell Guide to Ethical Theory* (Malden, MA: Blackwell, 2000), 375. See also John J. Drummond and Lester E. Embree, eds., *Phenomenological Approaches to Moral Philosophy: A Handbook* (Dordrecht, Neth.: Kluwer Academic Publishers, 2002).

2. Traditional textbooks of evangelical ethics limit discussion to relativism (emotionalism), consequential ethics (utilitarianism, hedonism), principle ethics, and virtue ethics. For example, see Kyle D. Fedler, *Exploring Christian Ethics: Biblical Foundations for Morality*, 1st

Wojtyla, better known as Pope John Paul II, wrote his second doctorate on Max Scheler, the main focus being a combination of Thomism and Scheler's phenomenological anthropology.[3] Value personalism complements the other three approaches in our matrix approach to Christian ethics. Moral reasoning of the heart goes along well with obedience to divine principles, a virtuous lifestyle, and the taking of responsibility for the consequences of our actions.[4] Previously, values have been defined as "the quality of being good, important or of human concern, or an entity which possesses this quality deserving of care."[5] We speak of value personalism, however, because of its close relationship with anthropology, as it investigates the person as a moral being. Personalism involves the discipline of understanding people in their natural and historical settings and understanding how people transcend their natural conditions by reflecting a higher world of values. As Emmanuel Mounier states, "Personalism is not a kind of spiritual doctrine, but rather the reverse. It includes every human problem in the concrete human life, from the lowliest material conditions to the highest spiritual possibilities."[6]

Max Scheler's Value Ethics

Criticism of Kant

Max Scheler (1874–1928) was a complex but fickle philosopher, sociologist, and psychologist who converted to Catholicism only to spurn it

---

ed. (Louisville: Westminster John Knox, 2006); Scott B. Rae, *Moral Choices: An Introduction to Ethics,* 2nd ed. (Grand Rapids: Zondervan, 2000); Glen H. Stassen and David P. Gushee, *Kingdom Ethics: Following Jesus in Contemporary Context* (Downers Grove, IL.: InterVarsity Press, 2003).

3. Jaroslaw Kupczak, *Destined for Liberty: The Human Person in the Philosophy of Karol Wojtyla/John Paul II* (Washington, D.C.: Catholic University of America Press, 2000); and Nancy Mardas, George McLean, and Agnes B. Curry, eds., *Karol Wojtyla's Philosophical Legacy* (Washington D.C.: Council for Research in Values and Philosophy, 2008).

4. It is unfortunate that Baptist theologian James McClendon mistakenly calls value ethics a "strong but obscure rival of virtue ethics." There is no need for rivalry between the two models, nor is value ethics more obscure than virtue ethics. James William McClendon, *Systematic Theology 1,* 2nd ed. (Nashville: Abingdon, 2002).

5. David A. Clairmont, "Glossary of Basic Terms" in *The Blackwell Companion to Religious Ethics,* ed. William Schweiker (Malden, MA: Blackwell, 2005), 582.

6. Emmanuel Mounier, *Personalism* (Notre Dame: University of Notre Dame Press, 1970), 9.

later.[7] His moral philosophical writings were a reaction to and a dialogue with Immanuel Kant and, to a lesser extent, with Friedrich Nietzsche. This dialogue is reflected in the title of Scheler's most important philosophical work, *Formalism in Ethics and Non-Formal Ethics of Values* (1913, trans. 1973).[8] An explanation of this title leads straight to the heart of Scheler's thought. He was dissatisfied with Kant's meager formalism, which he felt did not do justice to the intrinsic richness of our moral life. Humans required more than universal laws or formal principles; they also needed guidelines for the grind of daily life with its many-faceted challenges.

Scheler took the daily experience of morality as his starting point. Moral choices are made in the middle of a complicated world with conflicting values. According to Scheler, Kant's retreat into dry rational formulas cannot help us in this regard. Take for example one woman who decides to join the army to protect her country and is prepared to kill others in the process if necessary. Another person, however, may refuse to join the army precisely to avoid killing others. A furious internal battle rages within both persons, centered not on formal principles but on material (intrinsic) values.[9] Kant's maxims would not offer either of these people much solace. Although Scheler always held Kant in high regard, he maintained that retreating into formalism alienates us from the real internal battle that ethics should be addressing.

So how do we go about finding material content for ethics? Nietzsche identified our most deeply held values as the primary sphere of ethics. For him these values were highly arbitrary and could be changed as often as we saw fit throughout our lives.[10] Scheler learned much from Nietzsche about

---

7. For an introduction to Scheler's moral philosophical ideas, see Alfons Deeken, *Process and Permanence in Ethics* (New York: Paulist Press, 1974); and Peter H. Spader, *Scheler's Ethical Personalism: Its Logic, Development, and Promise* (New York: Fordham University Press, 2002).

8. Max Scheler, *Formalism in Ethics and Non-Formal Ethics of Values: A New Attempt toward the Foundation of an Ethical Personalism* (Evanston, IL: Northwestern University Press, 1973).

9. We can propose an even more complex scenario: What about the person who joins the army to fight against a malevolent dictator who is causing oppression in various countries (like a Hitler, for instance)? This person's primary motive would be to prevent oppression of others and to protect his or her family and the families of others.

10. Friedrich Wilhelm Nietzsche, *The Will to Power: An Attempted Transvaluation of All Values* (New York: Gordon Press, 1974); and *On the Genealogy of Morals* (Arlington, VA: Richer Resources Publications, 2008).

value experience, but he did not subscribe to the nihilistic project in which the *Übermensch* was free to destroy and create values at whim. Of course, an exaggerated reading of Nietzsche in this regard would be wrong headed. According to Nietzsche the will to live and have power is an absolute value to which all others are secondary. But this is not an abusive or tyrannical power by which to oppress, but a power to govern and lead—a responsible and disciplined use of power. It is power in the sense of self-mastery and self-discipline despite an understood death of God and lack of justification for morality or even existence itself.[11] Nevertheless, Scheler saw values as fixed, whereas with Nietzsche they were relative.

With such a focus on value experience and life, Ernst Troeltsch refers to Scheler as "the Catholic Nietzsche."[12] Scheler supported Kant's criticism of hedonism and eudemonism; values are fixed, and we should not allow ourselves to depend on variable circumstances. On the one hand, Scheler wanted the universal and fixed quality of Kant's ethics, and, on the other hand, he wanted an intrinsic theory of value along the lines proposed by Nietzsche. Herein lies the challenge of Scheler's value ethics.

For Scheler, Kant's greatest weakness was that he did not acknowledge the fixed and universal quality of values. This was because Kant made no distinction between *things* and the *value* of things. Kant was right to warn us against becoming dependent on things, but things are not the same as values. Things are just bearers of values, in the same way that things are bearers of color. Values are the qualities we perceive in things, but they do not become the things themselves. We can apprehend values in the same way that we can apprehend colors, without linking them to specific things. For example, we can talk about the beautiful, the sublime, harmony, sweetness, and so on without attaching these qualities to any particular object.[13] According to Scheler all values are material qualities, independent of the various forms in which they present themselves to us; they are the means by which we become acquainted with the thing. After observing something in totality, we then notice its other elements (the structures), and we begin to

---

11. Michener, *Engaging*, 33. See also James C. Livingston, *Modern Christian Thought* (London: Collier, 1971), 202–3; and Robert C. Solomon, *Continental Philosophy since 1750: The Rise and Fall of the Self* (Oxford: Oxford University Press, 1988), 125, 129.

12. Cited in Deeken, *Process and Permanence in Ethics*, 20.

13. Of course, we can argue that one most likely has certain things in mind when discussing such qualities.

gain a more intellectual insight into the matter at hand. If we come across a beautiful painting, we first perceive its beauty, and only later do we develop an understanding and further appreciation of what we are seeing in its rich complexities. If we paint a blue door red, blue does not stop being blue and become red. Individual friends can change and even desert us, but the value of friendship as a quality remains constant. In this regard, values are the fixed point of reference on which ethics should be based.

Axiology: The Order of Values

Scheler saw values as absolute, unchangeable quantities. It was the task of ethics to study these values phenomenologically, referred to as axiology (the theory of values).[14] Scheler attempted to prove that our value experience is in itself evidence of the reality of those values. We grasp values through direct experience or intuition, rather than by means of rational judgment or reasoning. Ethics is derived from the *ethos*, the inner perception of morality. The source of our morality, then, lies in our intense experience of the good, not in external principles or commands.

But this is only one side of the story. Ethics is not limited to inner morality; it is more than an existential, subjective experience. Following Augustine, Scheler went in search of the "order of love."[15] The internal points to the external, mirroring a higher reality. The order of love draws together the objective and subjective, the individual and the collective. It has a normative and a descriptive significance. It is normative in that it denotes the correct hierarchical order of values and descriptive in outlining the structure of human moral consciousness. It is the task of ethics to clarify this order. For it is our *ethos*, our sense of values, that forms the basis for theoretical ethics.

The order of love is reflected in the heart of each person as a microcosm of the kingdom of God.[16] Just as a snail is never without its shell, so individuals are always accompanied by their values.[17] The heart of humanity is not simply a pool of emotional chaos but a mirror or sounding board for

---

14. Scheler was influenced by the phenomenological method of Edmund Husserl.

15. Max Scheler, "Ordo Amoris" in *Selected Philosophical Essays*, ed. and trans. David R. Lachterman, Northwestern University Studies in Phenomenology and Existential Philosophy (Evanston, IL: Northwestern University Press, 1973).

16. Scheler, *Formalism in Ethics*, 396.

17. Scheler, "Ordo Amoris," 100.

the world of values. And the ultimate foundation of values lies in God.[18] All values are included in God's eternal love, and his eternal love keeps the order objective and unchanging. All values are fragments of the highest value of God's goodness and his kingdom. By choosing the right values, we participate in the actualization of the kingdom of God. In this sense philosophical ethics has a religious basis.

Ethics revolves around this axiology, focusing on gaining deeper insight into value structures and perceived values. History testifies to the ever-changing nature of value experiences and a dynamic switching back and forth of priorities. With respect to these unvarying values, Scheler identified four classes, ranking them hierarchically from lowest to highest:

1. Sensory values are our concrete experiences of pleasure or pain, the pleasant and unpleasant.

2. Vital values pertain to good health and the enjoyment of life. They go beyond mere sensory values; they include the noble and vulgar, the useful and futile. These values are linked to our general well-being and have as their goal the life comforts of the individual and the community.

3. Spiritual values lift humans beyond their biological environment. To attain these values we must be willing to sacrifice vital values. Spiritual values deal with deeply felt preferences of love and hate, the beautiful and ugly, and justice and injustice.

4. Religious values are at the top of hierarchy, referred to as holy or unholy. We experience these values as bliss or doubt, which go deeper than happiness and unhappiness. A person's state of bliss or doubt is an indication of how far removed he or she is from holiness. Through worship love takes on its most fulfilling personal form.

Interestingly, Scheler did not identify morality as an independent value because morality is about how we handle the above four classes of values. The more an individual is guided by the higher values, the more moral he or she becomes.

This list may come across as extremely abstract—a weakness that Scheler himself was aware of. After all, his ethics strives to address the concrete and

---

18. See Max Scheler, *On the Eternal in Man* (Hamden, CT: Archon Books, 1972).

the substantive. Scheler's personalistic approach helps compensate for the high degree of abstraction in his values. He described types of people and types of communities. Not everyone falls into one of the four categories, as if we can put people into boxes, but specific individuals demonstrate and personify certain values for us. Often it is not a single value category but a combination of values that takes shape in an individual who serves as a model. For example, Scheler argued that Augustine was a combination of genius and saint, while Frederick the Great was a mélange of hero and genius.

This approach is also referred to as "value personalism," since here values take shape in people and in personal relationships, the highest person being God. People have a greater impact on us than do laws or principles— rather than issuing orders, people demonstrate values in daily life. Moral transformation, then, happens by example, through identification with and participation in the life of another person.

It becomes somewhat confusing when, in his later writings, Scheler identifies five personality types, having previously referred to four value categories.[19] Unfortunately, Scheler never explained this apparent inconsistency. The five personality types are hedonist, leader, hero, genius, and saint. The vital values are found in the *hedonist* who knows best how to enjoy the fruit of his labors. This person is content with the simple things in life, neither striving to achieve higher goals nor asking deep questions. The second type, the *leader*, is interested in general progress. This person is probably not so much a political leader as a scientist, engineer, or economist focused on achievement and on making a contribution to the welfare and happiness of humanity. The third type, the *hero*, strives to live the noble life represented by the pure vital values. The hero demonstrates self-control and a desire for power. Heroes are generous and courageous, willing to sacrifice themselves for higher causes. Great statesmen, generals, and explorers would fall under this category. The fourth type is the *genius*, the one who values creativity and originality above all else. This is the only one who can be said to "create" all other types of work. The genius opens the world to us by helping us discover new values. Scheler gave examples that include Kant, Beethoven, and Dante. Finally, there is the *saint*. A saint transcends all temporal values. While the hero finds meaning in performing great deeds and the genius in producing masterpieces, saints focus on simply their own

---

19. For discussion see Deeken, *Process and Permanence in Ethics*, 204–5.

personality: who they *are*, channeling love to the holy. The greatest saints are the founders of religion. Their lives are examples to all of us of what it means to strive toward the holy.

Unfortunately, Scheler's Europe fell short when it came to prioritizing values. He saw misplaced value priorities as the most important cause of Europe's enormous social problems before and during the First World War. Values of usefulness and achievement were ranked above the higher values, while the highest value, the pursuit of human equality, wrongly neglected other cultural and life values.

Love and Resentment

Anthropology was the point of departure for Scheler. He viewed human life and ethics as an integrated whole. Humans were primarily *loving* beings rather than *thinking* beings, as Kant would have it, or *willing* beings, as Nietzsche had suggested. So the basis for ethics and the gateway to values are found in love. Our emotional relationships precede both the intellect and the will. Again Scheler used colors as a metaphor for values. The intellect is as blind to values as the ear is blind to colors. On this point he concurred with Pascal, who referred to the logic of the heart. Love is the highest human capacity and forms the basis for the sympathy required to develop a moral relationship with another person. Ultimately, love leads us to God and renders us willing to accept what he desires for us.

Love plays an important role in enabling us both to recognize values and to create them. Scheler described love as a movement that focuses on ever-higher values. Love is literally an "e-motion": a movement away from ourselves that transcends our ego. This ties in with Scheler's anthropology, where the capacity for self-transcendence is characteristic of humans as dynamic beings who are able to reach beyond themselves with the capacity to love.

Scheler's anthropological emphasis on love does not mean his portrayal of humankind is either naive or sugarcoated. On the contrary, being human all too often entails encountering broken love. It is precisely in his description of evil that Scheler is revealed as a master of phenomenological anthropology. The opposite of love is resentment, rancor, and spite, the autointoxication of the soul in which we are driven by jealousy, hate, deception, malicious pleasure, self-pity, and bitterness. This mindset develops when someone is not able to express negative emotions toward others (either individuals or organizations) and repeatedly experiences the same negative emotional response to others. Resentment leads to a confusion of values. Feelings of frustration and impotence therefore lead a person to create a negative value system. The worst form of resentment is vengefulness. Vengefulness is not active but reactive, with the intention of bringing pain to others. Scheler pointed out that a climate of resentment can develop in entire societies where people feel oppressed and powerless.

A second form of resentment Scheler described was jealousy. Again, the underlying cause is a sense of powerlessness. We are jealous of qualities we see in others that we are unable to develop in ourselves. Our jealousy of the virtue, character, or beauty of another disrupts our value experience. Things become important to us that have not been in the past. For Scheler noble people have a well-balanced self-image and are able to rejoice in the qualities of others. Unfortunately, common people allow their values to be determined to an unhealthy degree by the comparisons drawn between themselves and others. In our desire to bridge the painful gap between the high qualities of others and our self-limitations, we fabricate a scale of values to fit with our own desires and perceived shortcomings. Scheler's demonstration that morality has its own dynamic in this regard is quite insightful and avoids lapsing into relativism. Value experience is a unique means of relating to reality. His conviction that love is the key to understanding values and that ultimately God is the source of all values and love also aligns well with a Christian worldview.

Various other moral philosophers followed Scheler's lead in their quest for values and value experience. Nicolai Hartmann (1882–1950) presented an atheistic variation on Scheler's ideas.[20] Dietrich von Hildebrand (1889–1977) also wrote of the intuitive understanding of objective values, adding more subtle distinctions to his explanation of how we recognize and perceive values. But it is not enough simply to understand—a value demands an affective response. Hildebrand can also be counted as part of the school of German personalism. For Hildebrand as well, humans are self-transcendent beings who are continuously responding to values.[21] Within Catholic moral theology, Bernard Häring studied Scheler, looking closely

---

20. Nicolai Hartmann, *Ethics*, Library of Conservative Thought (New Brunswick, NJ: Transaction Publishers, 2003).
21. Dietrich von Hildebrand, *Christian Ethics* (New York: D. McKay, 1953).

into the area of religious phenomenology. Häring found the relationship between morality and religion especially fascinating.[22]

According to Scheler we come to understand values from a human perspective even though the foundation of all values is found in God the Personal Spirit.[23] With Scheler's emphasis on personal love relationships, he did not address the other side of the coin that Barth brought to the fore so radically. In evangelical Christian ethics, the point of departure for moral knowledge is revelation, not the intuitive experience of values. Anthropology is not seen as foundational but has a more supplementary and reinforcing role. God's Word speaks to us and demands total obedience. Revealed morality has to do primarily with the declaration of commands and prohibitions. Of course, we must keep in mind that these commands are always connected to our value experiences. It is in this regard that we view Scheler's value ethics as an insightful supplement to mainstream evangelical theonomous command ethics.

Scheler saw the relationship between God and humanity exclusively as a love relationship. He did not believe that God deals out punishments and rewards or commands love. God's love ethic is without commands. For Scheler a love command would be a contradiction. The ethical relationship is unmediated and without laws. In the depth of our being, we share in God's love. What matters is the "value manifestation of God addressing us in love" as seen in Jesus. Jesus is the highest type of value person. In his love he opens higher values to the entire world.[24]

Is Scheler's definition of love too confining? He focuses primarily on emotional and prerational aspects. But can love rightly be excluded from rational thought completely? Herman Dooyeweerd rightly points out that love is both rational and emotional. Our love often compels us to make complex choices within a network of social relationships. What is more, we

---

22. Bernard Häring, *Das Heilige und das Gute* (Krailling vor München: Erich Wewel Verlag, 1950).

23. A general criticism of Scheler's philosophy is its tendency to lean too heavily on religious presuppositions. Not everyone shares the view that humankind is by nature a "God-seeker." Scheler himself later wavered on his own religious perspectives. The incomplete and at times apparently contradictory nature of Scheler's work is confusing. In the moral-philosophical phase of his life, he placed a strong emphasis on God's personal being. Later, he regrettably turned toward pantheism. For a full discussion see Peter H. Spader, *Scheler's Ethical Personalism: Its Logic, Development, and Promise* (New York: Fordham University Press, 2002), 176–201.

24. Scheler, *Formalism in Ethics*, 305.

have an obligation to seek an ongoing balance between self-love and love for others.[25] According to Dooyeweerd it is characteristic of love (within temporal reality) that we seek the right proportional relationship between self-love and love of our fellow human beings. This proportionality and the complexity of relationships seem to propose a certain degree of rationality.[26]

It seems extremely difficult to pinpoint exactly how Scheler defined values. His quest for a fixed framework is utopian. In all fairness, however, Scheler was more concerned with pointing us in a general direction than with presenting a detailed system. He attempted to make the rather abstract notion of values more concrete by identifying individuals as models (or embodiments) of the values. McClendon points out that the biblical narrative precedes values, so the values themselves cannot be deemed primary. Values are "narrative dependent."[27] Perhaps McClendon's view is a bit too hasty. Simply because Scheler's model allows us to interpret biblical narratives as the personal embodiment of values does not necessarily imply that values are dependent on the narratives themselves or on the faith community. What it does imply is that narratives and the faith community *manifest* values, which is, in our view, closer to the truth. Biblical narrative has a hugely significant contribution to make to a Christian ethics of values.

Personalism

Scheler's influence is felt primarily in the moral-philosophical school of personalism.[28] Here the attention is drawn away from the objective world of values toward the person who translates these values into actions. Personalism is a multifaceted movement or a family of movements that "share a commitment to Christian theism" and understand the concept of personhood to be essential for properly understanding reality.[29] A distinctive feature of personalism is that humans, with values and responsibilities,

---

25. We will also address this later in this chapter in our discussion of Levinas.
26. Herman Dooyeweerd, *A New Critique of Theoretical Thought*, vol. 2 (Jordan Station, Ontario: Paideia Press., 1984), 160.
27. James William McClendon, *Systematic Theology 1*, 2nd ed. (Nashville: Abingdon, 2002), 347–56.
28. The relationship between Scheler and the school of personalism is quite complex. Cf. Deeken, *Process and Permanence*, 199–204.
29. Patricia A. Sayre, "Personalism," in *A Companion to Philosophy of Religion*, ed. Philip L. Quinn and Charles Taliaferro (Cambridge, MA: Blackwell, 1999), 129. See also pp. 129–35.

are always in relationship with others. Scheler closely linked anthropology and ethics, seeing humans as social beings who get to know others by means of relationships. Together with the irreducible nature of the human individual, this capacity to relate forms the central component of personalist ethics. The subtitle of Scheler's primary work, *Formalism in Ethics and the Non-Formal Ethics of Values*, is *A New Attempt toward the Foundation of an Ethical Personalism*. In Scheler's ethical personalism, values are put into practice by or even incarnated within specific individuals. At their deepest level, ethical values are passed on via inspiring individuals, not abstract ideas.

Scheler saw individuals as the sum of their deeds. But people can never be reduced to objects. It is not possible to take all a person's deeds and abstract them and so objectify them. In opposition to the traditional tendency to define humankind in universal terms, Scheler made a case for the uniqueness of the individual. Humans are able to transcend themselves and to be open to others. Religion plays a major part in his thinking here. The search for God and the longing for love lie at the heart of our humanity.

The term *personalism* came to the fore in Europe via the thinking of Catholic philosopher Emmanuel Mounier (1905–1950) in his primary work, *Le personnalisme* (1949).[30] A group of philosophers and intellectuals gathered around Mounier, one of whom was the Russian philosopher Nicolai Alexandrovich Berdiaev (1847–1948). Mounier and Berdiaev became noted for their opposition to collectivism and its habit of defining people according to their roles and positions.[31] Berdiaev's moral philosophy is highly relevant to the post-Soviet era, emphasizing the close relationship between individual freedom and responsibility. Personality is not material but is freedom of spirit; it is not egocentric but focused on others. Another important personalist was the Belgian priest and philosopher Albert Dondeyne (1901–1985), who became a source of inspiration for many Catholic intellectuals and political leaders.

Personalism is related to existentialism, but it is not identical. Personalism is strongly relationship oriented. The individual is not a

---

30. Ibid., 129–30. Sayre notes that American personalism was more systematic and suspicious of abstract philosophy divorced from concrete life experience. So through its founder, Borden Parker Bowne, American personalism was associated with reform movements such as women's suffrage and racial equality.
31. In 1934 the journal *Esprit* was founded by Emmanuel Mounier. See Sayre, "Personalism," 129.

thinking substance but an open being shaped by surroundings and context. Personalism is therefore critical of the calculable status given to reason in ethics. Personalism speaks to the fundamental moral attitude of humankind—the need to be open, loving, and respectful of the other. We need to make ourselves available to other persons and demonstrate solidarity as human beings. Scheler's thesis that we can attain moral knowledge only via acts of love lies at the very heart of personalism. The key to all existence lies in the structure of the human individual. We are not able to comprehend nature out of context, as a sum of facts. Rather we must seek to understand nature from the perspective of humankind.

The Personalism of Emmanuel Levinas

Biographical details are often brushed aside when considering the ideas of philosophers and theologians. However, to do this with Emmanuel Levinas (1906–1955) would be unfathomable. Levinas must be understood against the backdrop of the horrific despair of the Holocaust and the deep historical crisis of World War II Europe. The breadth of his cultural and historical experiences, combined with personal hardships, radically influenced this man's life and perspectives.

Levinas was born to Jewish parents in Lithuania, raised with both the Bible and the Talmud, and experienced the rich legacy of Russian culture. During his childhood his parents moved to the Ukraine, where as a young teenager he witnessed the Bolshevik Revolution of February and October 1917. He studied at the University of Strasbourg, where he was introduced to the phenomenological method of Husserl and Heidegger. He then studied with both Husserl and Heidegger in Freiberg before moving to Paris, which became his home for the remainder of his life. Levinas became an important spokesman in France for Husserl's philosophy. Along with his work in philosophy, he also made a contribution as a Talmud expert. His thinking was fundamentally Jewish, influenced by both Franz Rosenzweig and Martin Buber. Levinas derived continual inspiration from texts taken from both the Tanach and the Talmud, resulting in a spontaneous interweaving of the religious and the philosophical. But perhaps Levinas was most profoundly influenced philosophically, both positively and negatively, by Martin Heidegger's fundamental ontology in *Being and Time*.[32] Yet where

---

32. See Simon Critchley, "Introduction," in *The Cambridge Companion to Levinas*, ed. Si-

Levinas put ethics first, for Heidegger ethics was second.[33] This priority, as we will see, was critical for Levinas.

Levinas eventually broke relations with Heidegger, who had joined the Nazi Party. Sadly, most of Levinas' family was massacred in Lithuania during the Second World War. Levinas, who fought as a Frenchman, was deported to a German labor camp. It was during this devastating period of his life that his thinking began to change and develop.

Criticism of Western Philosophy

Levinas spoke out against the primacy of ontology in Western philosophy. Ontology draws all beings together into a single comprehensible reality. Independent beings therefore derive meaning from their position within the whole and their relationships with others in that whole.[34] He viewed this influence of Hellenistic ontology as laying the foundation for the destruction of the Jews. The National Socialist agenda attempted to destroy the Jews because they did not fit with the established definition of identity. Ontology assigns a place for everything, making everything equal, leaving no room for the other (person). That which is different must be broken down and controlled. This type of monolithic thinking is devastating to ethics. Western philosophy's preoccupation with the understanding and classification of being and reality, and then organizing that reality by means of technology and economy, is fundamentally *egological*—suppressing the uniqueness of the other.[35] For Levinas the point of departure for philosophy should not be found in ontology or epistemology, but in ethics. From the time of Descartes, the self had shifted toward the center stage of

---

mon Critchley and Robert Bernasconi (Cambridge: Cambridge University Press, 2002), 10–13.

33. Critchley, "Introduction," 13.

34. Levinas sharply distinguished ontology from metaphysics. Metaphysics was not a theoretical framework or some longing toward an external reality as was ontology. Rather it was the here-and-now, face-to-face relationship that was called by Levinas "metaphysical." In this sense metaphysics was the source of ethics. Emmanuel Levinas, *Totality and Infinity: An Essay on Exteriority*, trans. Alphonso Lingis (Pittsburgh: Duquesne University Press, 1969), 42–43, 77–78.

35. "Egology" for Levinas was a way of thinking that continuously sought to understand and dominate the other. The highest form of egology was ontology since all being was reduced to a totalizing system of reality, leaving no room for that which was different. See Levinas, *Totality and Infinity*, 44.

reality. Levinas expelled this full-fledged centered self of the Enlightenment and placed the other at the center.

The Appeal to Ethics

Meeting another person is a unique experience involving a certain level of knowing that extends beyond our knowledge of objects. We exchange greetings, a conversation begins, and then some level of personal relationship (however superficial it may be at the beginning) ensues. The other (person) is not simply absorbed into our periphery of knowledge. In this regard all personal encounters have a religious dimension: "The relation with the other (*autrui*) is not therefore ontology. This tie to the other (*autrui*), which does not reduce itself to the representation of the Other (*autrui*) but rather to his invocation, where invocation is not preceded by comprehension, we call *religion*."[36] The relationship encounter with the other cannot be reduced to my own analysis or assimilated into my understanding or reasoning. This religion to which Levinas was speaking "is the relation with a being as a being." It is not about "*conceiving* it as a *being* or as an act in which a being is already assimilated, even if this assimilation were to succeed in disengaging it as a being, in *letting it be*."[37] It is not the "I" that provides me with moral obligation but instead the other before me, who cries out to me with obligation to forsake my well-ordered world and accept responsibility—responsibility that is prior to individual freedom. It is in and through relation with the other that the whole abstract notion of *being* is broken. Ethics is done with corporeal sensitivity before real people with real bodies who are close, vulnerable, and experience pain.[38] Levinas' phenomenological sensitivities emerged with clarity when he simply stated: "Only a subject that eats can be-for-the-other."[39]

---

36. Emmanuel Levinas, "Is Ontology Fundamental?" in *Emmanuel Levinas: Basic Philosophical Writings*, ed. Adriaan T. Peperzak, Simon Critchley, and Robert Bernasconi (Bloomington and Indianapolis: Indiana University Press, 1996), 7.

37. Ibid., 8.

38. James H. Olthuis, "Face-to-Face: Ethical Asymmetry or the Symmetry of Mutuality?" in *The Hermeneutics of Charity*, eds. James K. A. Smith and Henry Isaac Venema (Grand Rapids: Brazos, 2004), 142.

39. Emmanuel Levinas, *Otherwise Than Being*, 74, as quoted in James H. Olthuis, "Face-to-Face: Ethical Asymmetry or the Symmetry of Mutuality?" in *The Hermeneutics of Charity*, eds. James K. A. Smith and Henry Isaac Venema, 141.

The face of the other displays the personal; it is where the realm of humanity is revealed, and it is through the face of humanity that we see the trace of the invisible God.[40] In the face of the other, I become aware of the idea of the infinite. This does not mean, as Roger Burggraeve points out, that God and the other are identical: "The face is not the Infinite One, but in its face I hear the Word of God who appeals to me towards responsibility. In this regard the ethical heteronomy of the face sets me on the track towards God."[41] The ethical call is rooted in the divine. It does not deny the self but drives the self from myself to neighbor-centered responsibility.[42]

Levinas' ethic is a radical call to the other. It is not a call to responsibility that assumes reciprocity in any form. As Levinas put it, "The responsibility for the other can not have begun in my commitment, in my decision. The unlimited responsibility in which I find myself comes from the other side of my freedom, from a 'prior to every meaning', an 'ulterior to every accomplishment', from the non-present par excellence, the non-original, the anarchical, prior to or beyond essence."[43]

This is not a command to horizontal relationships of symmetry or the I-Thou dialogical exchange of Martin Buber. There are, in fact, no assumptions of symmetry or reciprocity for Levinas. To be truly moral implies relationship that is disinterested in mutuality, balance, or remuneration; it is completely unconditional. The other must be faced as other in *asym*-metry.[44] This is a full-scale commitment to a personalistic, agapeic ethic.

Levinas' critical stance against the arrogant totalization of Western thought through ethics should be applauded and well considered by Christians today. It is an ethic that retreats "from the blind alleys into which radically pursued ambitions of modernity have led" and "readmits the Other as a neighbor, as the close-to-hand-*and*-mind, into the hard core of the moral self."[45] Levinas' vigorous defense of the unique and primary

---

40. Jens Zimmerman, *Recovering Theological Hermeneutics: An Incarnational-Trinitarian Theory of Interpretation* (Grand Rapids: Baker Academic, 2004), 232.

41. Roger Burggraeve, "'No One Can Save Oneself without Others': An Ethic of Liberation in the Footsteps of Emmanel Levinas" in *The Awakening of the Other: A Provocative Dialogue with Emmanuel Levinas*, ed. Roger Burggraeve (Leuven, Belgium: Peeters, 2008).

42. Ibid., 63–65.

43. Emmanuel Levinas, *Otherwise Than Being, or Beyond Essence*, trans. Alphonso Lingis (The Hague: Martinus Nijhoff, 1981), 10, as quoted in Zygmunt Bauman, *Postmodern Ethics* (Oxford: Blackwell, 1993), 74.

44. Bauman, *Postmodern Ethics*, 49, 48, 74.

45. Ibid., 84.

significance of ethical relationships involving concrete persons is critical for those living in a pluralist society. All men and women are created in the image of God and therefore deserve respect at a base level as living traces of our common Creator. Jesus called us to look into the faces of the poor, the widows, and the outcasts of our societies, to seek justice for them, and to care for them (James 1:27). In doing so, whatever we do for the least of these people, we also do for him (Matthew 25:40).

As Christians we are indeed called to an agapeic love for the other (Luke 6:35) without continually seeking reciprocity for moral action. However, did Levinas take this too far? James Olthuis is troubled that Levinas' insistence on the ethical priority of the other may result in a destructive forfeiting of the self and a guilt-laden moralism that may inadvertently end up doing more harm than good. If our own legitimate needs are always denied, they may resurface in disguised, angry, backhanded, and dangerous ways.[46] But for most of us, neglecting the self is not typically the problem. Taking care of ourselves is most often our first priority. In this sense we believe it is better to read Levinas as a postmodern prophet calling us out of the self-absorbed complacency that usually governs our everyday lives and challenging us to genuine neighbor love. Is this simply utopian? Indeed, but this preposterous goal must nevertheless remain the focus of our moral efforts as Christians. John D. Caputo understands well that Levinas went overboard by suggesting the impossible. But it is the hyperbolic poetics of it all that "strikes down my self-love and fills me with respect."[47]

Just the same, we should still take Olthuis' discomfort seriously. If we think exclusively in an agapeic fashion, it may create an excessive anthropological focus on guilt, rather than redemptive forgiveness. Of course, this has everything to do with motives. Do we serve others in appreciation of God's radical forgiveness through Jesus, or only out of a sense of the obligation before us? A theocentric Christian ethics takes as its point of departure a merciful God who grants forgiveness through Jesus Christ's atonement. It

---

46. Olthuis, "Face-to-Face," 143 and 143n.31.
47. John D. Caputo, *Against Ethics: Contributions to a Poetics of Obligation with Constant Reference to Deconstruction* (Bloomington and Indianapolis: Indiana University Press, 1993), 82. See also Olthuis' reference to Caputo in Olthuis, "Face-to-Face," 142–43. See also James K. A. Smith's insights on Olthuis' critique of Levinas in "The Call as Gift: The Subject's Donation in Marion and Levinas" in *The Hermeneutics of Charity*, ed. James K. A. Smith and Henry Isaac Venema (Grand Rapids: Brazos, 2004), 226–27.

is this same God, in grace, who calls us to serve others unconditionally in expression of our unconditional gratitude to him.

Chapter 7

The Triune God and the Good

Theocentrism and Ethics

The Basics of God's Moral Will

The prophet Micah gave us biblical morality in a nutshell: "He has showed you, O man, what is good. And what does the LORD require of you? To act justly and to love mercy and to walk humbly with your God" (Micah 6:8). Rather than undertaking deep philosophical speculation, he straightforwardly expressed what God revealed to him as "the good"—precisely what we are looking for in ethics! This passage deals with the relationship between the personal God, Yahweh, and the human being as his special creation. Christian ethics is developed in the context of relationship. The ultimate basis of Christian ethics is theocentric: God in the center. What is good is the will of God, who created all that is good. He is the Rock who is just and perfect (Deuteronomy 32:4). Wisdom requires that we do not simply lean on our own human understanding, but we are to trust in the Lord (Proverbs 3:5). Our ethics comes from God, who is beyond our human experience and understanding. Philosophical, immanent ethics is consciously limited to temporal reality and to our own perceptions. Our

Christian ethics is *fides quaerens intellectum*, meaning that it embraces a faith that seeks understanding from our Creator.

Returning to Micah's text, we find three interconnecting spokes to the wheel of theocentric morality: (1) to act justly, (2) to love mercy, and (3) to walk humbly with God. We will briefly consider each of these aspects and relate them to Christian ethics. The first spoke deals with concrete action, "doing what is just" (*mishpat*, in Hebrew). Among other things this word is used for the laws given by God through Moses (Exodus 21:1), with an emphasis on effective conduct and obedience. In prophetic literature the term is often used with reference to social tyranny and/or when God brings charges against his own people. This is the context in Micah: God is accusing the self-serving leaders of his people of injustices. God is more impressed with righteous living than he is with many offerings.

The book of Isaiah also confirms this: "Take your evil deeds out of my sight! Stop doing wrong, learn to do right! Seek justice, encourage the oppressed. Defend the cause of the fatherless, plead the case of the widow" (Isaiah 1:16–17). In the New Testament, James joins the prophets when he writes, "Religion that God our Father accepts as pure and faultless is this: to look after orphans and widows in their distress and to keep oneself from being polluted by the world" (James 1:27). Christian ethics always transcends theory and requires concrete, physical action.

The second spoke of ethics we find in the passage speaks to the heart: "loving mercy." The Hebrew word used here (*chesed*) is prominent in the Psalms. It bears a personal connotation centralizing a relationship in terms of faithful love or persevering goodness in the context of family and friendships. Love and faithfulness are closely connected. For example, we read, "Let love and faithfulness never leave you; bind them around your neck, write them on the tablet of your heart" (Proverbs 3:3). In this context we have an ethics of restored character. The term also holds the meaning of grace, mercy, or compassion.[1] This is also affirmed through the prophet Hosea: "For I desire mercy, not sacrifice, and acknowledgment of God rather than burnt offerings" (Hosea 6:6). As we shall see, it was typical of Jesus' ethics that he placed heartfelt mercy in the center. Jesus taught an ethics of grace and care for sinners, in contrast to the scribes, who empha-

---

1. The Septuagint usually translates the word as *eleos* (mercy) and the Vulgate translates it as *misericordia*.

sized outward appearances.[2] Christian ethics is called to move beyond rigid legalism to a morality of the heart that includes feelings of compassion. In this the Christian reflects the gracious character of God.

The third ethical spoke in Micah 6:8 relates to our positional attitude before our Maker: "Walk humbly with your God." *Walking* is simply an expression of daily life. Walking through life in humility before God—understanding that we are completely dependent on him for our every breath—should govern all we do. In this sense it is a misnomer even to call this a *spoke* of Christian ethics, for it is essentially the *hub* that turns *all* the spokes of our ethical character. This is completely in line with the opening words of Jesus' Beatitudes: "Blessed are the poor in spirit, for theirs is the kingdom of heaven" (Matthew 5:3). As humans we are not capable of building up and observing our own morality. Spirituality and ethics are deeply interwoven. Christian ethics is much more than a philosophical option; it is a heartfelt cry of surrender to God, asking him to guide us in giving grace to others in everything we do.

The Euthyphro Dilemma

A theocentric ethics is not without complications. Once we assume that the will of God is that which is good, we inevitably end up with what is known from ancient philosophy as the Euthyphro dilemma, derived from a dialogue recorded by Plato between Socrates and Euthyphro.[3] Euthyphro's father had allowed the death of one of his day laborers who had been languishing in a pit without any care. The worker, while in a drunken fit, had murdered a slave. The father did not believe neglecting the needs of his hired hand was a murderous crime, because the worker had murdered a slave. Nevertheless, Euthyphro believed that he needed to report the wrongdoing and help prosecute his father. Socrates was troubled that Euthyphro would show such disrespect by reporting the deeds of his father. After all, the worker who was killed was a murderer himself. Socrates sarcastically pointed out that Euthyphro must have had a great deal of wisdom in this matter to bring such charges against his own father.

---

2. Richard Hays speaks of a "hermeneutics of mercy." See Richard B. Hays, *The Moral Vision of the New Testament: A Contemporary Introduction to New Testament Ethics* (San Francisco: HarperSanFrancisco, 1996), 99–101.

3. See Plato, "Euthyphro: Piety and Impiety," in *The Works of Plato*, vol. 3, trans. B. Jowett (New York: Tudor Publishing, n.d.), 57–87.

But Euthyphro did not believe his family relationship was significant to the immoral act itself, the crime committed by his father. For reasons of piety, the rules of the gods, Euthyphro argued that he must bring charges of murder against his father. Socrates asked him how he could be so sure that something was good or evil. Euthyphro responded by saying that an act was evil if it was against the will of the gods. Socrates then probed him with deeper questions. If the gods held different opinions, how did we know which view was correct? Eventually, Socrates got to the pivotal question: "The point which I should first wish to understand is whether the pious or holy is beloved by the gods because it is holy, or holy because it is beloved of the gods."[4]

If we apply this dilemma to a Judeo-Christian ethic, the question is simply put: Is something good because God wills it to be so, or does God will it because it is good in itself? Which comes first, the will of God or the good? In the first case, whatever God wills becomes good *de facto*, by what seems to be the arbitrary decision of God, regardless of our understanding. The central concern is responding to and obeying the will of God.[5] Moral decisions in this model are justified by appealing to our interpretation of God's will. In the second case, God commits himself to what is good before willing it to be so. But if God wills something because it is inherently good, then God appears to be subject to the law of the good, just as we are. If this is the case, it appears that God is not free to decide what is good and what is evil. Without such freedom does God still remain God? Some would say that God is not necessary if ethics can simply appeal directly to the idea of the good.[6] Ethics simply becomes the normative framework in which religion is given permission to move, so religion does not provide any significant contribution to ethics.

Kant on Religion and Ethics

In many respects the Euthyphro dilemma still remains a challenge among ethicists today. From the time of Immanuel Kant, ethics has been seen as paramount to religion. In modern thinking ethics provides the

---

4. Plato, "Euthyphro: Piety and Impiety," 77.
5. In medieval philosophical debates, this was known as "voluntarism." For instance, this is seen in the divine command theory of William of Ockham.
6. Again, this notion was connected with Platonic "realism" in medieval philosophy. All that was "good" stemmed from an independently existing real *idea* or *form* of the good.

norms for the religious.[7] In Kant's work *Religion within the Limits of Reason Alone* (1793), he made it clear that religion is not necessary in order to know the good. The human being is a free, rational creature making autonomous moral decisions. In the opening sentences of his preface, Kant clearly stated his position:

> So far as morality is based upon the conception of man as a free agent who, just because he is free, binds himself through his reason to unconditioned laws, it stands in need neither of the idea of another Being over him, for him to apprehend his duty, nor of an incentive other than the law itself, for him to do his duty. At least it is man's own fault if he is subject to such a need; and if he is, this need can be relieved through nothing outside himself: for whatever does not originate in himself and his own freedom in no way compensates for the deficiency of his morality. Hence for its own sake morality does not need religion at all . . . by virtue of pure practical reason it is self-sufficient.[8]

Religion is subordinate to rational morality. Although Kant was skeptical about ultimate knowledge claims of actual things-in-themselves (*Ding an sich*), he remained optimistic about a phenomenological understanding of the sensible world.

Theologically there are significant problems with Kantian moral autonomy.[9] The danger of the Kantian approach does not seem to be

---

7. We find this in Protestant liberalism with Albrecht Ritschl (1822–1889) and later with Wilhelm Herrmann (1846–1922). This Kantian moral position is defended philosophically in Kai Nielsen, "God and the Basis of Morality," *Journal of Religious Ethics* 10, no. 2 (1982): 335–51.

8. Immanuel Kant, *Religion within the Limits of Reason Alone* (Chicago: Open Court, 1934), 3.

9. Max Scheler also warned of a distortion in the hierarchy of values. According to Scheler, it is impossible to deduce religion from morality. The good is a value that always points forward to the higher, the Holy. But by no means can the Holy be deduced from the lower value of the good. The good rather creates a desire for the higher, the Holy. The Holy must reveal itself to us, and if it does so, we acknowledge that it is the One we have desired from the value of the good. Only if the highest absolute value appears, will the essence of the good (moral value) reveal itself as a tendency to the highest value. Therefore, the Holy is both the crown and the foundation of all values. Bernard Häring, *Das Heilige und das Gute* (Krailling vor München: Erich Wewel Verlag, 1950), 192–94. Sharp criticism comes from Herman Dooyeweerd, who draws a distinction between the ethical and the religious. Almost all of

arbitrariness but an overconfident perspective on human capacity for moral discernment and civil decency. The sensible being is the virtuous being. The Christian gospel, however, speaks of a human being with moral ignorance, requiring God's wisdom and moral insight. The outcasts of civil society and structures are often the ones who find God's grace. Jesus' kingdom ethics is not a call for common rational sensibility. Instead, his ethical call seems resistant to common sensibilities and averse to the established order. But simply because a Christian theocentric ethic may be beyond human rational sensibilities and comprehension does not imply it is necessarily *unreasonable* or rationally absurd.

So if we return to the Euthyphro dilemma, which comes first, God's will or the good? Perhaps this question confuses the source *itself* with the results of, or the outworking knowledge of, that source. Consider, for example, the difference between a road map and an actual landscape. We read and understand road marks on the map, but the map is simply a description of what already exists.[10] Goodness is a descriptive quality of God's character, and his essence provides the basic structure for his creation. The good is not some independently existing thing that God serves. This is a confusion of categories. In this sense something is neither good because God loves it—as if something is arbitrarily good whenever God decides it to be—nor does God love something because there is some prior ontological goodness. Instead, goodness is inherently an aspect of God's character from all eternity, and he is the source of anything ascribed the attribute of goodness.

The Trinity and God's Absolute Love

The Triune God as Source of the Good

If God is the source of all that is good, why have so many terrible things, such as slavery and the exploitation of the poor, happened in the name of God? Obviously, simply giving a justification for an act in the name of God does not guarantee pure motives or a righteous morality. God's name is often invoked from behind a mask of duplicity and selfishness. The Bible

---

Dooyeweerd's philosophy resists Kantian autonomy and a still broader immanent philosophy in which there is no openness for the transcendent. Herman Dooyeweerd, *A New Critique of Theoretical Thought* (Jordan Station, Ontario: Paideia Press, 1984), 1:35–37; 2:141, 149–51.

10. Scott B. Rae, *Moral Choices* (Grand Rapids: Zondervan, 2000), 34.

speaks of many false gods, but only one true God, *Yahweh*. Humans have created many false conceptions of God throughout history, fashioning a God that aligns well with capitalism, monarchism, or socialism. We use the name of God through the lens of our personal, ecclesiological, or cultural comfort zones. We are guilty of conceptual idolatries, while still calling on the name of God.[11] This is not to say that we can never speak of God at all, for we are created in his image, and God has been made visible to us in the incarnate Jesus Christ.[12] The Trinitarian confession is uniquely Christian. A Christian speaks of the Father in the name of Jesus. A Christian is baptized in the name of the Father, the Son, and the Holy Spirit (Matthew 28:19) when joining God's community. By no means can we do justice to the doctrine of the Trinity within the scope of this book, but we will make a few observations relevant for our study of Christian ethics.

Through Jesus the disciples learned to understand God as Father. The risen and glorified Christ continued to be honored and worshiped as God. At Pentecost the apostles experienced the work of God's Spirit mediating Jesus' risen presence. The Christian's new life in Christ is a life in the Spirit, who is also confessed as a person of the triune God. The one name of God becomes unfolded into three names in Scripture. As Athanasius' confession of faith puts it, "That we worship one God in Trinity, and Trinity in Unity, neither confounding the Persons, nor dividing the Substance. For there is one Person of the Father, another of the Son, and another of the Holy Ghost."[13] Each of the three persons has particular characteristics. Luther's classic statement on the creed affirms that God the Father is Creator, the Son is Redeemer, and the Holy Spirit is the One who makes us holy.[14] Luther's distinction, however incomplete it may be, helps provide a dogmatic foundation for Christian ethics.[15] Within the framework of ethics,

---

11. See Bruce Ellis Benson, *Graven Ideologies: Nietzsche, Derrida and Marion on Modern Idolatry* (Downers Grove, IL: InterVarsity Press, 2002), 19.

12. Ibid., 21.

13. *Quicunque Vult or The Creed of St. Athanasius,* Medieval Sourcebook, http://www.fordham.edu/halsall/source/quicumque.html. We quote simply a small portion of the creed here. It is a Western formulation of the doctrine of the Trinity. See also Gerald Lewis Bray, *Creeds, Councils, and Christ* (Downers Grove, IL: InterVarsity Press, 1984), 175–94.

14. Martin Luther, Large Catechism: Part Second. Of the Creed, Christian Classics Ethereal Library, http://www.ccel.org/l/luther/large_cat/large_catechism13.htm. See also *Confessio Belgica,* art. 9; Karl Barth, *Church Dogmatics* 1.1; Roger E. Olson and Christopher A. Hall, *The Trinity* (Grand Rapids: Eerdmans, 2002), 65–72.

15. Of course there are other possibilities. In his work on the Trinity, Augustine ascribed

the Father is seen as Creator and Lawgiver; both the words of creation and the words of the commandments are interconnected and one in his perfect will.[16]

Unity in Love

We must be careful when ascribing any distinct actions to the three divine persons of the triune God. As Jesus said, "I tell you the truth, the Son can do nothing by himself; he can do only what he sees his Father doing, because whatever the Father does the Son also does" (John 5:19). The Father and the Son are perfectly one: "No one who denies the Son has the Father; whoever acknowledges the Son has the Father also" (1 John 2:23). Creation is not only the work of the Father; the Son was also present and instrumental in creation (Colossians 1:15–17). Likewise, redemption is not only the work of the Son, and sanctification is not solely the work of the Spirit.

The balance between unity and trinity is extremely complex theologically—an inscrutable mystery. In the Eastern Orthodox tradition, unity is principally viewed from the perspective of mutual indwelling (*perichoresis*). The Father is the source and origin of the Son and the Spirit. The Father generates the Son from eternity, and the Son is from the Father from eternity. This approach implies the eternal subordination of the Son to the Father. The Spirit also stems from the Father.[17] To a large degree the Western church agrees but differs by its focus on the unity of the three persons as one divine substance. The Western church sees primarily a substantial unity, and the Eastern church a relational unity of perfect divine love.[18]

---

power to the Father, wisdom to the Son, and goodness (or love) to the Spirit. Karl Barth related ethics to the main tasks of the three divine persons: Creator, Reconciler, and Savior.

16. Eleizer Schweid, "The Authority Principle in Biblical Morality," *Journal of Religious Ethics* 8, no. 2 (1980): 180–203.

17. In this respect, Eastern Orthodox theology is especially in line with the Cappadocian fathers. The Western church made the later addition of *filioque* ("and from the Son") to the Apostles' Creed. The Spirit is sent by the Father and the Son. The Eastern church preserves more of a hierarchy. The Spirit is only sent by the Father. For further clarification on the Eastern Orthodox Trinitarian perspective, see Vladamir Lossky, *In the Image and Likeness of God* (Crestwood, NY: St. Vladimir's Seminary Press, 1985), 71–96.

18. Jürgen Moltmann made an interesting attempt in this direction. The one-sidedness, however, is that the elevated place of the Father in the Eastern tradition seems to be too hastily reasoned away. Perhaps this is due to his forthright political hermeneutics that emphasizes emancipation and equality.

We believe there is much the Western church can learn from the Eastern church with respect to the Trinity, especially as it relates to Christian ethics.

The doctrine of the Trinity follows from the Christian message that God is love (1 John 4:8, 16) and that God demonstrated his love in his Son. Love seems to imply that God is plural, because love is a relational notion. The love the Bible speaks about is not self-love, but a giving love, a sacrificial love. The love of the three persons is eternal and immutable. Each person of the Trinity loves through the love received by the other. Because God is relational in essence, we find him in community. Perhaps the Trinity can best be described as the divine community of perfect love, love including both diversity and unity. A loving of the *same* is easier than a love for the *other* that demands sacrifice. God's inner love is so complete that it makes a perfect oneness. The intimate love between a man and a woman, love within a family, and love within a church body are all imperfect icons or shadows providing occasions for the pure love of the triune God.[19]

God's perfect love is the source of our love: "No one has ever seen God; but if we love one another, God lives in us and his love is made complete in us" (1 John 4:12). The love of God is shaped in us as we seek to imitate Jesus. We often forget that Paul's famous christological text of Philippians 2:5–11 is a moral appeal known as *parenesis* (exhortation).[20] It opens with the following: "Your attitude should be the same as that of Christ Jesus: Who, being in very nature God, did not consider equality with God something to be grasped" (Philippians 2:5–6). Through the incarnation the Son revealed the character of the Father, and the Father exalted the Son to the highest position. Christ is the second Adam, and he demonstrates what perfect human obedience means. Our imitation of Christ not only refers to Jesus' earthly life but also to the attitude of sacrificial love within the triune God. In this light it is utterly contemptible when Christianity clothes itself with unjust power and dominance in the name of God. The heart of Christian faith is rather about service, grace, and forgiveness.

Christian Trinitarian ethics, then, is social ethics. There is no *individual* Christian ethics per se; it is always social. Good conduct is conduct for the sake of the neighbor and ultimately for the glory of the triune God.

---

19. See Vigen Guroian, *Incarnate Love: Essays in Orthodox Ethics*, 2nd ed. (Notre Dame: University of Notre Dame Press, 2002), 28–31.

20. See Herman N. Ridderbos, *Paul: An Outline of His Theology* (Grand Rapids: Eerdmans, 1997) 253–7.

The popular expression "having a personal relationship with God" carries a great risk, because our relationship with God is always together with others. Now, it is *personal* in the sense that it involves the personal will of an individual before God within the community. But it is not as if we stand alone before God, detached from the community of believers in some sort of private relationship. Christian ethics is always already entangled with and embedded in a community ethics. The community, the church, is the people of God, the body of Christ, the temple of the Holy Spirit. It is in the context of God's community that we learn about the working out of unconditional love. In response the community is called to go outside its gatherings to do good works, to be salt and light. The community imitates God, who loves the world and gave his Son to redeem the world.

The Trinity and Theological Balance

The doctrine of the Trinity is essential for a well-balanced moral theology. If we speak of one biblical truth but suppress another, we lose the full richness of biblical revelation. This may happen by a certain emphasis, or lack thereof, as well as by direct omission. For example, if a certain passage is read out loud placing the wrong stress on certain words or neglecting to stress other words, our reading becomes skewed and perhaps unintelligible. In a similar fashion, if we stress only virtues while neglecting commands, values, and consequences, we are not providing a full and proper picture of the multifaceted aspects of Christian ethics. In this way the doctrine of the Trinity also reminds us to keep our moral theology in relational balance.

Richard Mouw submits that among Protestants various experiential emphases are attributed to each of the persons of the Trinity.[21] Mouw claims that Reformed Christians pay particular attention to God the Father as the One who revealed the law. This places a strong emphasis on the authoritative speaking of God and the need for unconditional human obedience. Here, the Ten Commandments are the timeless heart of Christian ethics. For people of the covenant, worship is experienced again and again as a gathering around Mount Sinai to hear the law of the Lord. God is the Creator, and the principles of the law refer to the structure of creation itself. The attention to God as Father gives Reformed theology a universal

---

21. Richard J. Mouw, *The God Who Commands* (Notre Dame: University of Notre Dame Press, 1990), 151– 52. Mouw appeals to an article written by H. Richard Niebuhr, "The Doctrine of the Trinity and the Unity of the Church," *Theology Today* 3 (October 1946).

tendency in the sense that God's moral commandments are good for the whole of society. God is not only the Father of all believers; he is the Creator of all people.[22]

Mouw observes in Anabaptist theology an emphasis placed on the Son.[23] This is also the general emphasis of mainstream evangelicalism. According to this emphasis, Christian ethics is, in the first place, about imitating Jesus. It is a Jesus-centered ethic placing a greater emphasis on the Sermon on the Mount than on the Ten Commandments.[24] In the Reformed model, Jesus is viewed more as the One who demonstrates the timeless morality of God's law. In the Anabaptist tradition there seems to be a discontinuity between the Old Testament and Jesus' call for ethical renewal. In evangelical circles we find the popular WWJD (What Would Jesus Do?) movement bids us to follow in the footsteps of Jesus when making everyday decisions.

Mouw notes the central position of the Holy Spirit in charismatic and Pentecostal circles. Here, it is the Holy Spirit who daily leads believers in making moral choices.[25] The will of God is found not only in Scripture but also in God's speaking to our conscience through his Holy Spirit, who both changes us and comforts us. An experience of God's presence is the primary concern.

Mouw remarks that, in practice, these systems tend to be more binitarian than unitarian. For example, the Reformed position tends to be Father-Son oriented and the charismatic position tends to be Spirit-Son oriented.[26] These are generalizations, but they nevertheless help us become aware of the significance of the relation between the Trinity and Christian ethics in various theological systems. We can learn a great deal about balance for our own perspectives if we remain in constant conversation with the rich variety of evangelical traditions. Keeping this in mind, we will now present our own attempt at a balanced Christian Trinitarian ethics.

---

22. Mouw, *God Who Commands*, 151.

23. Ibid.

24. We intentionally use *Jesus-centrism* instead of the more common *christocentrism* because of the emphasis on the earthly Jesus in personal discipleship. We find a recent example of this approach in Glen H. Stassen and David P. Gushee, *Kingdom Ethics* (Downers Grove, IL: InterVarsity Press, 2003).

25. Mouw, *God Who Commands*, 152.

26. Ibid., 154.

The Father: Creator and Lawgiver

Creation

The doctrine of creation is an essential aspect of Christian ethics at the level of worldview. As we noted before, specific values stem from worldviews. The Apostles' Creed begins with these familiar words: "I believe in God the Father Almighty, Maker of heaven and earth." The first *oeuvre* we note of God is that of creation. This is followed by his ongoing work of providential care for creation, through which God demonstrates his omnipotence.[27]

But there are at least three common pitfalls that often obscure a Christian ethics rooted in creation. First is the creed of materialism. Materialism is the basic belief that nothing exists other than matter. This is often reduced to a belief in natural and perceptible reality alone, with no place given to divine causation or the providential care of creation. Everything is explained by physics and chance.[28] Hendrikus Berkhof alludes to this as the "bunker" view of creation. God cannot get in. He is completely outside the realm of the natural laws. In a radically secular materialist mindset, God does not exist at all, either inside or outside of natural laws and creation.[29]

A second pitfall is placing undue emphasis on the divine as the manipulator of creation. In this case nature is seen as radically unpredictable, acting completely at the whim of some divine controller. This perspective is observed in animism and in the lives of superstitious Christians. Berkhof alludes to this as the "haunted house":

> Createdness by the God of holy love, who is changeable in his faithfulness and who works toward his goal along ever-new ways, means that our dependable world is at the same time open to surprises and changes. It is not a haunted house, but not a bunker either. Creation by this God means not only natural causality, but also room for a miracle. [30]

---

27. See John Calvin on common grace: *Institutes of the Christian Religion*, II.ii.17 and II.iii.3.
28. See Stephen M. Barr, *Modern Physics and Ancient Faith* (Notre Dame: University of Notre Dame Press, 2003), 1–3.
29. Hendrikus Berkhof, *Christian Faith: An Introduction to the Study of the Faith*, rev. ed. (Grand Rapids: Eerdmans, 1986), 169–70.
30. Ibid., 169. See also pp. 168, 170.

The third pitfall is dualism: thinking that God stands in conflict with the natural order of creation. God and nature are seen as two eternal principles facing each other in combat.[31] God is good, while the natural or physical is evil. To carry on in the footsteps of Berkhof's metaphor, we call this the "arena" model. This model has deep roots in Christianity under the influence of Gnosticism, where the material is seen as less good than the spiritual. Many early Christians were influenced by such Greek dualism without critical awareness of its destructive tendencies. This is noticed especially in the early fathers' views of human sexuality and the propensity of some toward asceticism.

Christians often give in to one of these basic pitfalls or misconceptions—the bunker, the haunted house, or the arena—when considering the relationship between God and creation. These basic mistakes cause serious havoc for value ethics. In the bunker model, nature is overrated; in the haunted house, it is unstable; and in the arena, it is rejected and fought. God is seen as absent, aloof, or opposed to the goodness of creation and nature. A well-balanced ethic must avoid these traps. God is not against creation but for the redemption of creation. God is pro-creation and pro-human. Humanity is the pinnacle of his creation, made in his image. God is the Creator and providential sustainer of all creation, but he provides natural or normal means by which this creation is governed and operated while under his care. This is not a deist reductionism. God is free and purposeful in our lives and chooses to interrupt and disrupt as he sees fit during his loving, care-filled, providential watch over creation. We do not have a God's-eye view of creation, so we do not understand *why* he interrupts or necessarily know *when* he interrupts via miraculous events.

In general, Protestant ethics has had an ambivalent relationship to the natural order, compared with Roman Catholic natural theology.[32] According to Bonhoeffer, this has "meant a serious and substantial loss to Protestant thought, for it was now more or less deprived of the means of orientation in dealing with the practical questions of natural life."[33] Because of Protestant theological stress on the fall and sin, it is as if the Word of God condemns the natural and unnatural alike. Bonhoeffer tried to recover the

---

31. Ibid., 170–71.
32. Stephen J. Grabill, *Rediscovering the Natural Law in Reformed Theological Ethics* (Grand Rapids: Eerdmans, 2006).
33. Dietrich Bonhoeffer, *Ethics*, trans. Neville Horton Smith (New York: Macmillan, 1965), 143.

importance of the natural order for ethics. He distinguished creation, as a broad concept, from the natural and unnatural. Through the fall, creation had became nature: "The natural is that which, after the Fall, is directed towards the coming of Christ. The unnatural is that which, after the Fall, closes its doors against the coming of Christ."[34] It is because of Christ's becoming human that we have the right to call people to natural life. Through reason we recognize the natural. But reason is not external to nature; it is embedded in the preserved life that perceives the universal in what is given in the particular.[35] So Bonhoeffer rooted human rights as God given in the natural order of biological life. We honor the Creator, not merely the creation, by respecting human life in its natural form.[36] God the Creator gives us precious life; creation is his work of grace, generating universal human rights. In this regard Bonhoeffer was one of the first Protestant theologians who considered human rights as of great import for Christian ethics.[37]

The Commandments

God the Father reveals himself as Creator and also as Lawgiver. Along with creation, the commandments are also a concrete expression of God's wisdom and goodness. In the grand scheme of things, the law does not simply begin with God's revelation to Moses, but with creation itself. Humans have been under the law from the beginning. They were allowed to eat from any tree in the garden, *except* one. In Paradise, the open relationship with God and abundant life experienced in obedience to God's law all worked in perfect harmony. God's law itself was not a curse but a blessing providing direction. After the fall, God helped restore life by revealing his law. The law has its ultimate source in the caring, loving, providential activity of God. If we bear this in mind, the oft-perceived contradiction between

---

34. Bonhoeffer, *Ethics*, 144.
35. Ibid., 146. The natural is recognized by reason, and it demands the consent of the "underlying will" that is also embedded in the fall. But as Bonhoeffer put it, "The natural is the safeguarding of life against the unnatural." *Ethics*, 146.
36. Bonhoeffer gave priority to rights of natural life as the source for duties. *Ethics*, 151.
37. See Larry Rasmussen, "The Ethics of Responsible Action," in *The Cambridge Companion to Dietrich Bonhoeffer*, ed. John W. de Gruchy (Cambridge: Cambridge University Press, 1999), 210; and G. M. Newlands, *Christ and Human Rights: The Transformative Engagement* (Aldershot, UK: Ashgate, 2006), 94; Heinz Eduard Todt, Ernst-Albert Scharffenorth, and Glen Harold Stassen, *Authentic Faith: Bonhoeffer's Theological Ethics in Context* (Grand Rapids: Eerdmans, 2007), 142–50.

the observance of the law and human happiness or between principle ethics and eudemonic ethics all seems to fade. The law is not simply about obscure commands but about the commands of a triune God expressing his love from the depths of his being for the care of his creatures. God's law is rooted in his creation and creative order, so following the law brings the most fulfilling happiness and joy (Psalm 119:164–165).

It is unfortunate that the word *law* has such suffocating, negative connotations for many. If we say something must happen "according to the law," it rings of authoritarianism. This is certainly not the case with the Hebrew word *Torah*. Torah connotes the giving of direction or instruction. This is quite important, for it connects the law with God's wisdom and love, deep values that God desires to share with us. Remember that these covenant "words" were given following, not before, the liberation of the people from slavery (Exodus 20:1). The law was given in the context of freedom already bestowed, not as the means to freedom.[38]

Since the commandments are an expression of God's love, and since God is love, it comes as no surprise that love fulfills God's law (Romans 13:8, 10). Love is not opposed to the law; love is the heart of the law. Only from God's love can we understand the ultimate meaning of the law. Love is the unifying factor that binds all laws together. Emil Brunner warned of taking an atomistic view of the law that would consider the commandments as separate entities. Instead they were "authentic 'expositions'" of the one law of love. In fact, it was a part of God's condescension toward our weakness that he was not telling us one thing to do—love—but "a variety of things."[39]

The Heart of the Law: Matthew 22:37–40

The Pharisees had been trying to trap Jesus by asking thorny questions. Then one expert in traditional moral theology asked, "Teacher, which is the greatest commandment in the Law?" (Matthew 22:36). Jesus' answer seems a bit ambiguous at first. He replied, "'Love the Lord your God with all your

---

38. We could also argue that following the law brings about a different aspect of freedom. If the law is the loving expression of God's wisdom and love, then following the law provides the deepest human satisfaction and purist moral freedom.

39. Emil Brunner, *The Divine Imperative: A Study in Christian Ethics*, trans. Olive Wyon (Cambridge: Lutterworth Press, 2002), 135.

heart and with all your soul and with all your mind.' This is the first and greatest commandment. And the second is like it: 'Love your neighbor as yourself.' All the Law and the Prophets hang on these two commandments" (22:37–40). Jesus did not say that the greatest commandment was loving God and that the second greatest commandment, in order of importance, was loving your neighbor. Rather, "All the Law and the Prophets hang on these *two* commandments" (italics ours). Relationship with God and relationship with our neighbor are inextricably linked, but one is not reduced to the other. The law is not simply a matter of outward obedience to static rules but of loving God with our entire being, complete and undivided.[40] And God desires that our love for him be expressed in love toward others in concrete actions of care. This summarizing double commandment becomes the hermeneutical filter and fulfillment of the Old Testament law (cf. Romans 13:9–10).

Law and Gospel

Both law and gospel have their origins in the same source: the God who creates and redeems. Jesus said, "Do not think that I have come to abolish the Law or the Prophets; I have not come to abolish them but to fulfill them" (Matthew 5:17). Jesus went even further to say, "Not the smallest letter, not the least stroke of a pen, will by any means disappear from the Law until everything is accomplished" (Matthew 5:18). Not the smallest aspect of the law would be neglected. As Christ, the Son of God, Jesus completely revealed and fulfilled the will of the Father, who is behind the law.[41]

Jesus was not preaching a radical antinomianism, as some believed. Jesus was fulfilling in his ethics that to which the literal meaning of the law pointed. By no means was he simply discarding the law as if it were now useless for a new era.[42] In fact, Jesus proposed an outworking of the law that surpassed that of the scribes and the Pharisees (Matthew 5:20)! Jesus'

---

40. Ibid., 133.
41. Continuity with the Old Testament is an important theme in the gospel of Matthew. Matthew's report is probably given in the context of a debate about the place of the law in the early church. In comparison with other gospel accounts, Matthew concentrates more on Jesus as teacher and on the moral aspect of imitation (Matthew 7:21–23). See Hays, *Moral Vision*, 94–96.
42. Keith Ward, *What the Bible Really Teaches: A Challenge for Fundamentalists* (London: SPCK, 2004), 23.

righteousness is radical and intense, getting to the deepest intent of the law. Where the law obliges us to love our neighbors, Jesus calls us to love our enemies. This passage follows Jesus' ethics of justice and love presented in the Sermon on the Mount. Jesus' law ethics is, first of all, an ethics of the heart, referring to the importance of our inward thoughts and deepest motives. Sin begins in the heart, so we must be cleansed from within, not remain concerned simply with external appearances. Through such deep-seated moral cleansing, Jesus' true disciples will reflect the perfection of the Father (Matthew 5:48).

The apostle Paul, a former Pharisee, often spoke about the relationship between law and gospel, especially when unbelievers became aware of God's righteous standards (1 Timothy 1:8–9).[43] Although the law itself is insufficient as a means to salvation, it leads us to Christ, who is the culmination of the law (Galatians 3:21–24; Romans 10:4). Jesus' love ethics brings the law to its fullest intended expression. Herman Ridderbos states that "in this respect, Paul's canticle love, no less than Jesus' radical commandments in the Sermon on the Mount, is a matchless unfolding of the deep and unmistakable content of the law, an unfolding that can be such a radical and previously unattained pinnacle because it forms the reverse side of the preaching of God's unimaginably great revelation of love in Jesus Christ."[44]

The Three Uses of the Law

Traditionally, Reformed ethics has used the Ten Commandments in three different manners.[45] The first function of the law is to direct social life. God subdues humanity's evil through his law (1 Timothy 1:9–10). This is God's provision for a common social order for daily life. Here we find again a close relationship between creation and law. People choose either to abide by social laws or to face punishment and/or ostracism from the community.

---

43. The literature on the subject of law and gospel is extensive. The last decade has stirred up many discussions on this topic with respect to the "New Perspective on Paul." See N. T. Wright, *Justification: God's Plan and Paul's Vision* (Downers Grove, IL: InterVarsity Press, 2009); James D. G. Dunn, *The New Perspective on Paul*, rev. ed. (Grand Rapids: Eerdmans, 2008).

44. Herman Ridderbos, *Paul: An Outline of His Theology* (Grand Rapids: Eerdmans, 1997), 282.

45. Calvin, *Institutes*, II.vii.6–15; Emil Brunner, *Divine Imperative*, 140–51.

The second function of the law is more pedagogically focused: to make people aware of their sins (Galatians 3:24). It is not the law itself that makes us conscious of sin, but God uses the law to convince us of our shortcomings. The law functions as a mirror in which we see our own failings. It is impossible for us to keep the full measure of the law, and so we are in need of God's grace.

The third function of the law is to provide a means for Christian living. The law is a standard for which we can be thankful because it shapes our Christian life. In the past we were unable to obey the law, but by God's Spirit we can live according to the intentions of the law. Martin Luther's Small Catechism began with a discussion of the Ten Commandments, and he emphasized the second use of the law (awareness of sin) to avoid any hint of legalism that might arise with the third use of the law. By faith we were free from the law. So if we were filled with the Holy Spirit, in Luther's view, we would do what was good spontaneously.

The danger of legalism is not inconceivable, especially if we regard the law as something to be feared because of the consequences of noncompliance. But this rests on a theological misunderstanding. Emil Brunner described the third function of the law as the law after faith, which is quite different from the law before faith. Brunner drew two important distinctions. In the first place, the law is now understood in the context of the great double commandment of love: love the Lord your God and love your neighbor (Matthew 22:37–40). The Sermon on the Mount is not merely a new law but a radical interpretation and consummation of the old law. Christian ethics seeks the will of God from love in faith. For this purpose we need the commandments in Scripture. Second, the law is now seen more as a loving provision of direction than the tight command of an oppressive master to a slave.[46]

Christ as Redeemer

Christian ethics is indeed Christocentric, but this does not minimize its Trinitarian emphasis. Jesus claimed that anyone who had seen him had seen the Father (John 14:9), and we understand that Christ is the mediator between God and humanity (1 Timothy 2:5). Christ represents the Father to the people and the people to the Father. Jesus was not only a great teacher

---

46. Brunner, *Divine Imperative*, 149–50.

and moral example, but, first and foremost, he reconciled us with the Father and gave us new life through his atonement on the cross (Romans 3:25; 5:19–21). Christ suffered as a human being and also as God, as a member of the Trinity. We recall Jesus' words in Mark 14:36 when he cried out to the Father, saying, "Everything is possible for you. Take this cup from me. Yet not what I will, but what you will." Jesus experienced a deep understanding of the agonizing temptation of the will, yet he held steadfast to the will of the Father. Scripture tells us that, as a son, Jesus "learned obedience from what he suffered" (Hebrews 5:8). Jesus came as the new Adam who accomplished justification, bringing life for all humankind through his act of righteous obedience (Romans 5:18). He is now our high priest in heaven who sympathizes with us, who understands what it is like to be tempted (Hebrews 4:15).

In connection with the cross, we see a relationship between the indicative and the imperative in the writings of the apostle Paul.[47] The new life (the indicative) is a work of God, originating in the death and resurrection of Jesus. Our ethics (the imperative) is then a response to God's grace of re-generation. The indicative and imperative are caught in a splendid ongoing dialectic. The new moral life is the result of the liberating work of Jesus and equally a command stemming from such redemption. But the imperative rests on the indicative, not vice versa. As Paul wrote to the believers in Colosse, "For you died, and your life is now hidden with Christ in God. When Christ, who is your life, appears, then you also will appear with him in glory" (Colossians 3:3–4). With regard to position (the indicative), they were new, redeemed creatures in Christ. As a result, they were to act accordingly (the imperative): "Put to death, therefore, whatever belongs to your earthly nature: sexual immorality, impurity, lust, evil desires and greed, which is idolatry" (Colossians 3:5). His cross becomes our cross, the beginning of new life and, consequently, new behavior. We prefer to speak of this as a "therefore-ethics."

The Resurrection: Affirmation of Redemption

Through the resurrection God broke the power of sin and death. This victory is also a reaffirmation of the goodness of God's creation. God did not give up on creation, but he sent his Son to redeem it. The bodily

---

47. See Herman Ridderbos, *Paul: An Outline of His Theology* (Grand Rapids: Eerdmans, 1997), 253–58.

resurrection of Jesus has a remarkable multidirectional significance. It looks back to creation with affirmation and looks forward to its renewal as a bright testimony of hope (Colossians 1:15–20). By proclaiming the resurrection, the apostles expressed their trust in the coming of a new creation. The resurrection teaches the value of God's creation and of the body, affirming our created life.[48]

The Kingdom of God: The Content of Redemption

In the Synoptic Gospels we meet Jesus Christ first and foremost as one who proclaimed the kingdom of God (e.g., Matthew 4:17; Mark 1:15). The kingdom of God was present in the presence of the Messiah (Luke 17:20–21). The Greek word *basileia* can denote kingdom or kingship.[49] The phrase *kingdom of God* is a broad theocentric concept that refers to salvation as well as to judgment and that ends with a condition of perfect peace and harmony. The kingdom is a symbol of victory over evil, sin, and suffering in the world. It is the reign of God in love and justice through his community. Some theologians try to force the kingdom motif into one primary category, either political, realistic, futurist, or spiritual. But the kingdom of God is both static and dynamic. It is present but not completely present, revealed but not completely revealed, current but also future oriented. It is a multidimensional and interrelated concept that involves each of these characteristics.[50] As some theologians have expressed it, it is *already,* but *not yet.*[51] Robert H. Stein puts it this way:

> The kingdom of God is both now and not yet. Thus the kingdom is "realized" and present in one sense, and yet

---

48. Oliver O'Donovan places the resurrection at the heart of his evangelical ethics. From this position, O'Donovan opens himself up to a natural ethics and fiercely resists an esoteric Christian ethics only relevant for believers. Oliver O'Donovan, *Resurrection and Moral Order: An Outline for Evangelical Ethics*, 2nd ed. (Grand Rapids: Eerdmans, 1994).

49. This is also the case with the Hebrew word *malkoeth*. See George Eldon Ladd, *A Theology of the New Testament*, rev. ed. (Grand Rapids: Eerdmans, 1993), 60.

50. Ronald T. Michener, "Kingdom of God and Postmodern Thought: Friends or Foes?" *Perichoresis* 6, no. 2 (2008): 224. For a concise overview of the kingdom theme, see Robert H. Stein, "Kingdom of God," in *Evangelical Dictionary of Biblical Theology*, ed. Walter A. Elwell (Grand Rapids: Baker, 1996), 451–52.

51. This approach is found in the work of Oscar Cullmann. See Oscar Cullman, *Salvation in History*, trans. S. G. Sowers (New York: Harper & Row, 1967). It is further developed by George Eldon Ladd; see Ladd, *Theology of the New Testament*, 54–132.

"consistent" and future in another. This is not a contradiction, but simply the nature of the kingdom. The kingdom has come in fulfillment of the Old Testament promises. A new covenant has been established. But its final manifestation and consummation lie in the future. Until then we are to be good and faithful servants (Luke 19:11–27).[52]

The kingdom of God is about the complete sphere of God's dynamic reign and reconciling work through his people, not about human empire building. Rather than focusing on the individual, it is concerned with God's redeemed community as it is enfolded into God's loving care. Certainly, there is an eschatological dimension that will continue to manifest itself in God's reconciling work in creation now and into the eschaton.[53]

The most important demand is that we seek his kingdom and his righteousness (Matthew 6:33). Righteousness is a summary of God's will as it is and will be manifested in his kingdom. The good works of believers do not create but rather manifest the kingdom of God. The community of God is the fruit of the kingdom of God, functioning as a herald of his kingdom.[54] The working out of the kingdom of God must not be reduced to mere religious humanism or social action.[55] Neither is the kingdom to be relegated solely to future consummation, completely detached from contemporary ethics.[56] The kingdom of God flows from the reconciling work of Jesus on the cross, which is just as relevant for the poor and oppressed of today as it will be for the future. When we pray, "Your kingdom come," this invocation must deeply touch our daily attitudes and perspectives. We are called to manifest God's kingdom as the salt of the earth and the light of the world. In this regard, the doctrine of the kingdom sheds great light on the purpose of Christian ethics for daily living. We must continually

---

52. Robert H. Stein, "Kingdom of God," in *Evangelical Dictionary of Biblical Theology*, 453. Also see Michener, "Kingdom of God and Postmodern Thought," 224.

53. Michener, "Kingdom of God and Postmodern Thought," 225. Also see Stein, "Kingdom of God," 453; and Ladd, *Theology of the New Testament*, 57–80.

54. The identification of the community and kingdom has become especially popular since Augustine. For a discussion of the relation between church and kingdom of God, see Ladd, *Theology of the New Testament*, 105–19.

55. For example, as we see in the work of Adolph von Harnack and Albrecht Ritschl.

56. Some traditional dispensational tendencies have only shown interest in social concerns insofar as they affirm a certain vision of the future. Some have even argued that the Sermon on the Mount as "law of the Kingdom of Heaven" was intended only for the Jews and cannot be applied to the community of Christ. Ladd, *Theology of the New Testament*, 60.

ask ourselves whether our decisions and actions contribute to or harm the manifestation of God's kingdom.

The Imitation of Christ: Response to Redemption

Christ demonstrated how we should live by both his words and his deeds. God's character was revealed in his Son. He demonstrated for us what it means to be completely subjected to the will of the Father. He is the Righteous One (1 John 2:1) whose life displayed God's original intention for human beings. Jesus gave us examples of the meaning of service and self-sacrificial love toward others.[57] Both Paul and Peter appealed to Jesus as our moral example (Ephesians 5:1–2; 1 Peter 2:21).

German theologian and martyr Dietrich Bonhoeffer gave the imitation of Christ a prominent place in his theology. Imitation means that we live in, with, and through Christ. This is not simply a higher or special call reserved for some; it is the essence of being a Christian. Through imitation we commit ourselves to the suffering Christ. The Christian life begins with suffering and the giving up of that which binds us to the world: "It is laid on every Christian. The first Christ-suffering that everyone has to experience is the call which summons us away from our attachments to this world. . . . The cross is not the terrible end of a pious happy life. Instead, it stands at the beginning of the community with Jesus Christ. Whenever Christ calls us, his call leads to death."[58] A disciple will also take up her own cross because she is no longer her own lord. According to Bonhoeffer imitation is not some ascetic or monastic activity, a way of leaving the world behind. On the contrary, it is about imitating Christ in the world and for the sake of the world, just as Christ himself suffered for the sake of the world.[59] We must also view the world from the perspective of God's kingdom and his righteousness. We become involved in God's work through the imitation of Christ. As Bonhoeffer wrote, "To flee into invisibility is to deny the call. Any community of Jesus which wants to be invisible is no longer a community that follows him."[60]

We also find this relation between imitation and social commitment to the world in the Wesleyan tradition. According to Wesley, the imitation

---

57. For example, Jesus displayed this in the washing of his disciples' feet (John 13).

58. Dietrich Bonhoeffer, *Discipleship*, vol. 4 of *Dietrich Bonhoeffer Works*, trans. Barbara Green and Reinhard Krauss (Minneapolis: Fortress, 2001), 87.

59. Georg Huntemann, *The Other Bonhoeffer: An Evangelical Reassessment of Dietrich Bonhoeffer*, trans. Todd Huizinga (Grand Rapids: Baker, 1993), 188–92.

60. Bonhoeffer, *Discipleship*, 113.

of Christ is not about an otherworldly mysticism, but about a practical religion in accordance with God's commandments. In his sermon on being salt and light, Wesley claimed that Christianity is a social religion: "Christianity is essentially a social religion and to turn it into a solitary one is to destroy it."[61] We cannot isolate the Sermon on the Mount from social action. Wesley viewed works of mercy as a means of grace enabling us to become more like Christ.[62] For John Wesley, there was "no religion but social religion, no holiness but social holiness."[63] Faith always included a social dimension.

The Holy Spirit: Sanctifier

The Dynamic Principle

Moral philosophy can at best describe a certain norm or standard. The law may instruct us to obey these norms, but only the Holy Spirit can change us "in Christ." Christian ethics is not merely about moral doctrine or theory but about moral capability; it is an ethics of transformation. Carl F. H. Henry expressed it this way: "The Holy Spirit is the dynamic principle of Christian ethics, the personal agent through whom God enters human life and redeems it from slavery, sin, death and law in a powerful way."[64]

The New Covenant comes into force following Pentecost. The law is now written in the hearts of believers. The Spirit creates a new way of thinking through which God's moral will may be discerned (Romans 12:1–2; Ephesians 1:17; Colossians 1:9). The Holy Spirit causes an incredible revolution of values and purposes. Under his guidance our daily efforts and life goals begin to take their lead from the direction of the kingdom of God.

The Holy Spirit gives new life, and he upholds and sustains our lives for his purposes. He is our source of hope (Romans 15:13), righteousness, peace, and joy (Romans 14:17). As Paul warned, we should not simply begin new life with the Spirit but continue to live in the Spirit (Galatians 3:2–3). Following regeneration, we are called to be "filled" with the Spirit

---

61. John Wesley, Sermon 24, "Upon Our Lord's Sermon on the Mount," discourse 4, in *The Works of John Wesley*, ed. Thomas Jackson (Grand Rapids: Zondervan, 1958), 5:296.
62. Wesley, *Works*, 5:296–310; and 6:51. Cf. R. Duane Thompson, "Social Involvement," in *Contemporary Wesleyan Theology*, vol. 2, ed. Charles W. Carter, R. Duane Thompson, and Charles W. Wilson (Grand Rapids: Francis Asbury Press, 1983), 693–732. Also see Kenneth J. Collins, *The Theology of John Wesley: Holy Love and the Shape of Grace* (Nashville: Abingdon, 2007), 267–70.
63. Wesley, *Works*, 14:321–22.
64. Carl F. H. Henry, *Christian Personal Ethics* (Grand Rapids: Eerdmans, 1957), 437.

(Ephesians 5:18). The works of the law do not justify us, but justification takes shape through the work of the Holy Spirit in our lives. Where the law was powerless, God's Spirit makes sure that "the righteous requirements of the law" are "fully met in us" (Romans 8:4). If we are led by the Spirit, we are not under the law (Galatians 5:18), and the promise of the New Covenant is thus fulfilled: "And I will put my Spirit in you and move you to follow my decrees and be careful to keep my laws" (Ezekiel 36:27).[65]

The Spirit of Community

The work of the Holy Spirit is not simply an individual matter. We already noted how the doctrine of the Trinity is the framework for a relational Christian ethics. In the Trinitarian formula at the end of Paul's second letter to the Corinthians, the community (*koinonia*) is specifically connected to God's Spirit (2 Corinthians 13:14). At Pentecost, a new moral community was born. When Paul spoke of the unity of the body of Christ, he wrote, "For we were all baptized by one Spirit into one body—whether Jews or Greeks, slave or free—and we were all given the one Spirit to drink" (1 Corinthians 12:13). This is profoundly significant for Christian ethics. God's Spirit breaks through social boundaries and creates a new community of mutual commitment. We cannot imagine how deep the divide was between Jews and Greeks and between slaves and free persons. The Spirit breaks through these radically disparate social boundaries. All members surround each other with loving care and mutual respect, experiencing joy and suffering together. Yet within this moral community of the Spirit, individual Christians still flourish. Jesus' ethics is thus visible in the work of the Spirit in this redeemed and reconciled alternative community. Stanley Hauerwas calls this the "community of character."[66] The words of Paul in his letter to the Romans are particularly apropos: "I myself am convinced, my brothers, that you yourselves are full of goodness, complete in knowledge and competent to instruct one another" (Romans 15:14).

---

65. In the following chapter, we will give attention to the fruit of the Spirit in the context of virtue ethics. On the role of the Holy Spirit in Paul's theology, and the relation between law and Spirit, see Gordon D. Fee, *God's Empowering Presence: The Holy Spirit in the Letters of Paul* (Peabody, MA: Hendrickson, 1994).
66. Stanley Hauerwas, *A Community of Character* (Notre Dame: University of Notre Dame Press, 1981).

Chapter 8

The Ethical
Human Being

Human Dignity and the Imago Dei

In the previous chapter, we considered the triune God as the heart and source of Christian ethics. Christian ethics is not exclusively anthropocentric. Christian theocentrism is, however, personalistic in its emphasis on relationship and community between God and humanity and among human beings. In this regard Christian ethics embraces a robust humanism. That is, it is human centered within a Christian framework of the *imago Dei*. Humans are morally fallen creatures, yet they are still created in the image of God and have significant value as created beings deemed "very good" by their Creator. The protection of human dignity in the gracious love of God—not human pride—is the affirmation of the *imago Dei*.

Augustine claimed that his life's purpose was to know God, the soul, and nothing whatsoever more.[1] As we have said, Christian ethics must duly consider both God and humankind, in relationship, love for God and love

---

1. Augustine, *Soliloquies* 1.7, trans. C. C. Starbuck. In vol. 7 of *Nicene and Post-Nicene Fathers,* ed. Philip Schaff. Rev. and ed. for New Advent by Kevin Knight (2009), http://www. newadvent.org/fathers/170301.htm.

for the other. It is both vertical and horizontal. We seek to understand the other, through the light of the Creator, as fellow human beings created in God's image. The horizontal (human to human) refers to the vertical (God) through the *imago Dei*, and the vertical (God) to the horizontal (human to human) through the incarnation, God the Son's becoming a human.

But the gap between Christian claims regarding the value of human dignity and the historical reality is horrifying. The carnage of the world's wars, from battles and bombs to the Holocaust, has scarred our memories. Human violence and terrorism continue to rage across the globe even today. We could cite countless examples, including the massacres among the Tutsis and Hutus in central Africa, the terrorist attacks on the Twin Towers in New York City, and the ongoing hostilities in the Middle East. Sadly, for most of us living in the relative comfort of the Western world, the children, women, and men who disappear in this savage bloodshed appear to be mere statistics rather than faces of once-living persons created in the image of God.

But the world's uncertainty regarding human dignity is not simply displayed in connection with war. Recent innovations in medical technology, stem-cell research, in vitro fertilization, euthanasia, and abortion-on-demand have also raised questions about human value and the beginning of human life itself. The issues are vast and complex. Where are the boundaries between human and not human or between life and death in biomedical ethics? The distinctions are becoming blurred. How do we make these difficult decisions?

In view of the *imago Dei* (Genesis 1:26–27), Christian ethics must hold to a robust perspective on the protection of human value and dignity. As the psalmist said, "You made him ruler over the works of your hands; you put everything under his feet: all flocks and herds, and the beasts of the field" (Psalm 8:6–7). For this reason, the Bible condemns murder: "Whoever sheds the blood of man, by man shall his blood be shed; for in the image of God has God made man" (Genesis 9:6). Murder is also listed later as the sixth of the Ten Commandments: "You shall not murder" (Exodus 20:13). It is God's will that we protect life and serve our fellow human beings. We are called to respect human dignity in view of God's gracious love to all people, people who are created in his image.

The dignity of humans because of the *imago Dei* must not be confused with salvific worthiness. Humans are not worthy of God's saving grace simply because they are created in God's image. But God loves all people, and he extends his offer of loving relationship to all people. In fact, his offer of salvation comes to completely *unworthy* humans who are guilty and fallen. But sin-scarred humans still have dignity as creatures bearing the image of their marvelous Creator. This is where God's redemptive work continues to restore his creatures and his creation to their original beauty.[2]

The *imago Dei* remains a mystery for Christians in many respects. How can humans be the image of God when God is spirit (John 4:24)? How can humans in any way be like God? In Ronald B. Allen's marvelous book *The Majesty of Man: The Dignity of Being Human*, he provides the following helpful insight:

> Theologians will continue to debate the concept of the image of God. Some attempt, erroneously in my estimation, to split bone and marrow in distinguishing "likeness" from "image" in Genesis 1:26. Some see the divine image solely in those moral and spiritual factors that distinguish man from beast. Others see the image of God reflected in the man-woman relationship as a mirror of the inner-relatedness of the Persons of the Trinity. Still others emphasize the rulership God delegated to man as the essential element of the divine image in man. In each of these suggestions there is one commonality: It is in the image of God that man has his dignity.[3]

The fact that each person was created by God in his image "is his differentia; it is his definition."[4]

We should not be too hasty to dismiss the significance of the body when considering the image. The image of God is about the entire human being, as whole persons, including male and female. We are created as soul beings with bodies. Jesus, the quintessential human, came in the flesh—and fully divine. The God-incarnate Jesus is the epitome of what it means to be fully human. We propose a view of the *imago Dei*, affirming a biblically based Christian humanism that "makes much of the Incarnation of the eternal Son of God," where "God takes on humanity which was patterned after

---

2. Ronald B. Allen, *The Majesty of Man: The Dignity of Being Human* (Portland, OR: Multnomah Press, 1984), 106–7.

3. Ibid., 91.

4. John Murray, *Collected Writings*, vol. 2, *Select Lectures in Systematic Theology* (Edinburgh: Banner of Truth, 1977), 13, as quoted in Allen, *Majesty*, 92.

his own glory."[5] This appreciation of corporeality distinguishes Christian humanism from classic rational humanism, where the essence of the human being is found in the rational soul.[6] God became fully, and physically, human.[7] Accordingly, our application of the love commandment must look to the needs of our fellow human beings, who are created in God's image, holistically, both physically and psychologically.

Another aspect of the *imago Dei* is commonly called the creation mandate. Humans were made dependent rulers and representatives of God on the earth, managing creation and other living creatures. As D. J. A. Clines writes, "The word calls the creation into existence; but the image of God is the permanent link between God and his world."[8] Clines compares the function of statues of the gods in the ancient Near East with the meaning of "in God's image and likeness." The statue was not merely a portrayal of a divine being, but the presence of divine power. Statues were dwelling places of the spirit or of a fluid that was derived from the being in whose image the statue was fashioned. In a similar manner, human beings could also become dwelling places of divine presence. Kings were viewed in such a fashion, as incarnate representatives of gods and therefore deserving of worship. In the book of Genesis, there is a wonderfully strange democratic move that describes all humans as representing God in "his image." This does not refer to the quality of the representation, however, but refers to the permanent link between humanity and God. Humans have received the breath of God and now in some way participate in God (Genesis 2:7) and are called to be God's representatives on earth.[9]

Stanley J. Grenz submits that scholars at one time directly linked the *imago Dei* with dominion, but that the consensus in recent years has been that it should rather be viewed as a result of being created in the image of God.[10] This commissioning to rule and manage creation is thus a

---

5. Allen, *Majesty*, 93.
6. We notice this all-embracing understanding of the word *image* (*tselem*) in Genesis 5:3: Adam had "a son in his own likeness, in his own image." Seth was not exactly his father but was a likeness of his father both psychologically and physically.
7. See Emil Brunner, *The Divine Imperative: A Study in Christian Ethics*, trans. Olive Wyon (London: Lutterworth Press, 1937), 193.
8. D. J. A. Clines, "The Image of God in Man," *Tyndale Bulletin* 19 (1968): 89.
9. Ibid., 53–103.
10. Stanley J. Grenz, *The Social God and the Relational Self: A Trinitarian Theology of the Imago Dei* (Louisville: Westminster John Knox, 2001), 197. Grenz cites the work of D. J. A. Clines, John Skinner, Gerhard von Rad, and Phyllis Bird.

consequential capability of humankind, not a part of humankind's inherent definition.[11] Scientific advancement and technological innovation have their roots in this creation mandate. But when technology and industry are used for personal gain and industrial power, they inevitably violate human dignity and the image of God.

The *Universal Declaration of Human Rights* (1948) is the most important manifesto of the United Nations.[12] Established on the ruins of the Second World War, it has served as a corrective and safeguard for general human dignity. The notion of human rights has been criticized at times as an overly individualistic Western utopianism. However, the intention of the *Universal Declaration* is primarily the protection of the weak. Although the declaration itself is not specifically Christian, we would do well to follow its call to remember the place of the weak and the poor in the kingdom of Jesus.

We previously referred to Dietrich Bonhoeffer's theological support for human rights as rooted in the life given to us by God. In contrast, postmodern philosopher Richard Rorty considers the grounding of human rights in human dignity to be outmoded and irrelevant. For Rorty, a theoretical defense or justification of human rights is neither possible nor desirable. Instead, we should evoke sympathy for the feelings of others.[13] Instead of seeking the right foundations, we should stress the pragmatic, telling sad and sentimental stories. Human rights, for Rorty, stem from social practices and cannot be grounded in ontology or a hegemonic interpretation of human nature. The Christian philosopher Nicholas Wolterstorff agrees that there is indeed no firm secular grounding for human rights. But instead of leaving them, with Rorty, as mere social constructs, Wolterstorff makes

11. Gerhard von Rad, *Genesis: A Commentary*, trans. John H. Marks, rev. ed. (Philadelphia: Westminster, 1973), 59, as cited in Grenz, *Social God and the Relational Self*, 197.

12. For the text, see http://www.ohchr.org/EN/UDHR/Pages/Introduction.aspx. For a discussion of the text and further literature, cf. Simeon O. Ilesanmi, "Human Rights," in *The Blackwell Companion to Religious Ethics*, ed. William Schweiker (Malden, MA: Blackwell, 2005), 501–50.

13. Richard Rorty, "Human Rights, Rationality and Sentimentality" in *On Human Rights: The Oxford Amnesty Lectures*, ed. Stephen Shute and S. L. Hurley (New York: Basic Books, 1993), 111–34. British philosopher Jonathan Glover describes the brutal history of the 20th century in a similar manner. He sees the only hope for the future not in a firm foundation of morality based in religion or philosophy but in a new human creation of morality based on sympathy. Jonathan Glover, *Humanity: A Moral History of the Twentieth Century* (London: J. Cape, 1999).

a strong plea for a theistic basis for human rights.[14] He claims that we should not base human rights on some interpretation of human capacities but on the relational property of being loved by God. Wolterstorff argues for an alternative, "bestowed worth." Just as relics have bestowed worth, because they point to the worthiness of a respected person in history, so all the more, humans have worth because of God's bestowed love. It is God's gracious giving of himself and his offer of relationship with humanity, not some set of special human capacities, that provide incomparable dignity.[15]

Relational Anthropology and Ethics

Theological anthropology offers tremendous insights for Christian ethics. John Wesley's anthropology is decidedly relevant in this regard, with his substantial focus on human relationships.[16] Enlightenment deism had triumphed in Wesley's day, with an inordinate emphasis on the human capacity for reason, which many theologians, unfortunately, uncritically endorsed. For Wesley, however, the essential attribute of the human being lay not in rationality but in love. Human beings received God's love and knew how to pass on this love to others through good deeds.[17] Like Calvin, Wesley used the metaphor of a mirror. The human being was the image of God, so humans should reflect God's being.[18] It was this reflection model that became the framework for Wesleyan personalist ethics.

The human being has four fundamental relationships according to Wesley: (1) God, (2) the neighbor, (3) the lower animal species, and (4) the self.[19] If a Christian lives a holy life, these four relationships will flourish. In

---

14. Nicholas Wolterstorff, *Justice: Rights and Wrongs* (Princeton: Princeton University Press, 2008), 311–62.

15. Ibid., 352–61.

16. Randy L. Maddox, *Responsible Grace: John Wesley's Practical Theology* (Nashville: Kingswood Books, 1994), 68.

17. John Wesley, Sermon 141, "The Image of God" in *The Works of John Wesley: The Bicentennial Edition*, vol. 4, CD-ROM, ed. Richard P. Heitzenrater (Nashville: Abingdon, 2005).

18. We find this in Augustine, Calvin, and Wesley. Grenz, *Social God*, 162–66. Theodore Runyon, *The New Creation: John Wesley's Theology Today* (Nashville: Abingdon, 1998), 13–18.

19. Maddox, *Responsible Grace*, 68. For the most part, we follow Wesley in his emphasis on relationships as key to human beings. However, we question his notion of relationship with the self. Is relationship with oneself really a *relationship*? Relationship by definition is not aimed at the self. It is rather from our self-consciousness that the other three relationships—

addition to the classical quality of the human being as a thinking creature, Wesley also emphasized freedom as a necessary quality for human functioning.[20] This should not be confused with free will. The human being has the freedom to choose to do good or evil only because of God's grace. Wesley does not so much base freedom on human nature, as some of his critics believe, as on the mercy of God. The will is a slave to sin through original sin. But God grants a degree of freedom through his universal prevenient grace, freeing our minds from sinful depravity enough to allow responsible choices for or against God.[21] So for Wesley freedom is not so much a human capacity as it is a gift from God.

More recent versions of theological anthropology that take a more relational approach are found in the writings of Emil Brunner, Helmut Thielicke, and Hendrikus Berkhof.[22] For Thielicke, three relationships—with the self, the neighbor, and the surrounding world—are the conditions for ethics. Christian ethics is about placing these three relationships under the will of God. Faith is not something abstract but is lived out in connection with myself, my neighbor, and my world. Saving faith comes to real human beings with personal histories, taking shape in these three interconnecting relationships.[23] Wolfhart Pannenberg, using the philosophical terminology of personalism, writes of "exocentric self-transcendence," the ability to experience that which is other than ourselves. This encounter constitutes the human personality.[24] Berkhof closely follows Brunner by describing the human as a "respondable" being who is created to meet God and able to respond to the Word of God.[25] A human is not a self-contained

---

with neighbor, animals, and God—depart.

20. John Wesley, Sermon 103, "What Is Man?" Ps. 8:4, in *The Works of John Wesley*, vol. 7, ed. Thomas Jackson (Grand Rapids: Zondervan, 1958): 167–73.

21. The typical Wesleyan dogma of prevenient grace uses the concept of *prevenio*, "to come before"; God's general grace precedes redemption, especially in the conscience. Cf. Runyon, *The New Creation*, 27–41.

22. See F. LeRon Shults, *Reforming Theological Anthropology: After the Philosophical Turn to Relationality* (Grand Rapids: Eerdmans, 2003).

23. Thielicke refers to Martin Heidegger's distinction between "Seienden" and "Dasein." The cosmos of being is the sphere in which our faith is manifested. Helmut Thielicke, *Theological Ethics* (Grand Rapids: Eerdmans, 1979), 465–81.

24. Wolfhart Pannenberg, *Anthropology in Theological Perspective*, trans. Matthew J. O'Connell (London: Continuum, 2004), 85, 105. Pannenberg bases his view on the philosophical anthropology of M. Scheler and H. Plessner. For a discussion see F. LeRon Shults, *Reforming Theological Anthropology*, 132–39.

25. Hendrikus Berkhof, *Christian Faith: An Introduction to the Study of the Faith*, rev. ed.

being who later happens to relate to other beings. For Berkhof, the image
of God consists of a triple encounter with God, neighbor, and nature. The
human is at once a child of God, a neighbor to other human beings, and a
lord over nature. We prefer to call these the three *constituent* relationships.
By *constituent* we mean that the human being is understood, established,
and developed through these three interactions. Through this development
we become fully human, finding growth, hope, and a longing for the good.
In the following sections we will more fully describe each of these constituent relationships.

Relationship to God: The Human Being as a Religious Creature

In the story of Genesis, God creates man by his word, using the physical matter of creation ("dust of the ground," Genesis 2:7). He touches man,
breathes in the breath of life, and then fashions woman from man. The
original humans lived in intimate fellowship with God. The Lord's walk
in the garden (Genesis 3:8) is symbolic of this initial intimacy. Following
their disobedience, God asks, "Where are you?" (Genesis 3:9). Adam and
Eve hide themselves, ashamed. To this day humans remain alienated, often
refusing to respond to God's personal call, "Where are you?"

Humanity cannot escape being dependent on God. All temporal reality stems from God: "For from him and through him and to him are all
things" (Romans 11:36). Humans are created for the glory of God (Isaiah
43:7) and are existentially connected to God. Paul, quoting Epimenides,
preached this universal truth in Athens: "For in him we live and move and
have our being" (Acts 17:28). The human being is created for God's glory
and cannot exist apart from God's sustenance. Religion—the seeking of
God—is inherently human; it belongs to our nature. Those who declare
the absence of God ultimately deny themselves. In a similar fashion the
commandments and values that we receive from God do not restrict our
humanness; they are structurally part of our humanity, freeing us to be
fully human. At the beginning of his *Confessions*, Augustine wrote, "You
move us to delight in praising You; for You have formed us for Yourself, and
our hearts are restless till they find rest in You."[26] Only by seeking God's

---

(Grand Rapids: Eerdmans, 1986), 186.

26. Augustine, *Confessions* I.1, trans. J. G. Pilkington. In vol. 1 of *Nicene and Post-Nicene Fathers*, ed. Philip Schaff, New Advent (2009), http://www.newadvent.org/fathers/110101.htm.

presence, *coram Deo*, do we truly learn to know ourselves. This is also the starting point of Calvin's dogmatics. If we seek the learning of ourselves apart from God, we will come to a false and prideful arrogance, lacking authentic judgment.[27] Only when God becomes the center of our entire being do we become authentically human.

Relationship with the Neighbor:
The Human Being as a Social Creature

Ethics nearly always refers to or involves others. The role we assign to this social element has a great impact on our ethical views. As we proposed earlier, human beings are created in the image of the relational triune God and so are, analogously, relational beings. From the beginning, humans were created male and female: "So God created man in his own image, in the image of God he created him; male and female he created them" (Genesis 1:27). The marital relationship functions as a paradigm for the social character of the human being to display the image of God, functioning as a symbol of the deepest love relationships: God and his people, Christ and the church. This is not to say that marriage is *the* essential characteristic of the image of God, however. After all, the perfect human, Jesus, was unmarried. So we should not make marriage the *sine qua non* of humanity. Yet celibacy is a gift from God, rather than an imposition, and for the purpose of sole dedication to the service of God's community (Matthew 19:12; 1 Corinthians 7:8).

Whether married or single, we are all called to the challenge of human relationships. In family and church relationships, Christian love is given the opportunity to flourish in the midst of radical differences. It is most often not through obvious similarities but through healthy polarities—learning appreciation of the other as other—that we are given the means to develop and mature as persons. This often involves pain, disillusionment, and emotional distress, things that contemporary hedonism finds difficult to cope with. But ultimately it is within the crucible and intensity of human relationships that we can fully blossom as persons.

---

27. Calvin, *Institutes* I.i.2.

Relationship with Nature:
The Human Being as a Creative Creature

We often mistakenly think of work as a consequence of sin. The curse is rather the "painful toil" of work (Genesis 3:17) that stems from the poison of sin. Work itself is a blessing from God and part of what it means to be created in his image: "The LORD God took the man and put him in the Garden of Eden to work it and take care of it" (Genesis 2:15). This refers to what we previously described as the creation mandate: to have responsible dominion and care for the resources of the earth. As human beings we are in constant interaction with the natural world around us, interwoven with it and called to be its caretakers. Our relationship with God is one of obedience and subservience, our relationship with our neighbor is one of equality, and our relationship with nature is one of dominion and care.[28] At the same time, humans remain dependent on nature for many daily needs, including food, water, and oxygen. Our physical destiny is connected with the destiny of the natural resources that we have been entrusted with.

Our relationship to nature and, by implication, to technology must be determined by certain values and principles. If this is neglected, we will be either lost in nature or destroyed by nature. This relationship has a strong instrumental character. We are allowed to use nature in order to serve our neighbor. We are even allowed to kill and eat animals and plants for food. But nature's resources must be a source of life for all people, not only for the rich and powerful. In this sense ecological ethics is a part of social ethics.[29]

---

28. This is not to say that there are no overlapping themes among these three. In the book of Hebrews, Jesus, the incarnate God, considers us "brothers" (Heb. 2:11). Among fellow human beings, we are equal as humans, yet we have various hierarchical structures to provide order in our communities and families (e.g., government leaders over citizens, parents over children).

29. We are cautious of the popular term *stewardship*. Human beings are the guardians and appointed rulers of nature who must maintain respect for God's norms and the interests of other people. This type of Christian anthropocentric position is defended in Patrick Nullens, "Leven volgens Gaia's normen?: de verhouding tussen God, mens en aarde en de implicaties voor ecologische ethiek" (Ph.D. diss., Evangelische Theologische Faculteit, Leuven, Belgium, 1995).

Relationships, Redemption, and the Kingdom of Jesus

Sin ruptured these basic relationships, causing alienation from God, neighbor, and nature. This resulted in idolatry, hatred of others, and the exploitation of nature. Redemption is about the restoration of these creational alliances. The kingdom of God manifests itself in these three relationships. When God rules, the world is in harmony with both neighbor and nature. Jesus came as the image of God (Colossians 1:15), as the new Adam, humanity in its most ideal expression. Jesus lived among us, teaching and demonstrating the kingdom of God. He taught his disciples how to pray and to live in dependence on the Father. He called himself the way to the Father (John 14:6), and he reconciled us to the Father through the cross. Our relationship with others is also restored through the work of the atonement. Jesus taught his disciples mercy, humility, and the importance of forgiveness—of loving one another as he had loved us (John 15:12). Jesus founded a new community of mutual equality and care. The gospel brings peace where there are divisions and liberation of the weak.

Jesus also canceled the curse on creation: "For God was pleased to have all his fullness dwell in him, and through him to reconcile to himself all things, whether things on earth or things in heaven, by making peace through his blood, shed on the cross" (Colossians 1:19–20). Redemption involves the restoration of the entire order of creation.[30] Currently, we live with an eschatological tension. We are still subject to illness and physical death, but Jesus' bodily resurrection has initiated the redemptive healing of the human being into complete wholeness, including the body. As a result, we live in hope, with full expectation of bodily resurrection, predestined for a fully restored creation. Oliver O'Donovan provides two points of reference for Christian ethics, pointing both backward and forward, to the original order of creation and its end. He then adds, "It respects the natural structures of life in the world, while looking forward to their transformation."[31]

---

30. Oliver O'Donovan, *Resurrection and Moral Order: An Outline for Evangelical Ethics*, 2nd ed. (Grand Rapids: Eerdmans, 1994), 56–58.
31. O'Donovan, *Resurrection and Moral Order*, 58.

The Moral Conscience

The notion of conscience has been a controversial subject through the centuries. Thomas Aquinas gave the conscience high esteem as the location of moral judgment and reasoning in humans. Kant viewed the conscience as the faculty whereby persons were able to make the "is" of universal law into the "ought" of the universal imperative. Freud viewed the conscience as an instrument of repression through the internalization of imposed prohibitions.[32]

The conscience is attributed an important role in Roman Catholic moral theology. It is the "inner core and the sanctuary of the human being."[33] The Second Vatican Council emphasized that God's law to do good and to avoid evil is written in the human heart. The *Catechism of the Catholic Church* quotes Vatican II, stating that the "conscience is man's most secret core, and his sanctuary. There he is alone with God whose voice echoes in his depths."[34] By no means can this be reduced to a mere feeling. The conscience is rather viewed as a "judgment of reason" in line with the Scholastic tradition. We hear God's voice better through prayer, study of the Word, and instruction by the church.

The Reformation emphasized the authority of Scripture as the only source of knowledge about the good (*sola scriptura*). The Reformers had become skeptical about the prevailing optimism regarding the human conscience. The human being was a sinner and therefore unable to fundamentally recognize ultimate goodness apart from the light of Scripture.[35] Oliver O'Donovan points out that the Greco-Roman understanding of conscience had the idea of a "self-consciousness" of wrongdoing. It was this notion that was introduced in the New Testament within the Pauline writings. However, the medieval and modern notions of conscience were expanded to describe moral understanding in general. Modern thinking emphasized the emotional "self-repudiation" of conscience, whereas the ancients stressed the self-critical, rational nature of the conscience. As O'Donovan

---

32. J. W. Gladwin, "Conscience," in *New Dictionary of Christian Ethics and Pastoral Theology*, ed. David J. Atkinson et al. (Downers Grove, IL: InterVarsity Press, 1995).

33. *Gaudium et Spes* 16, in *The Christian Faith in the Doctrinal Documents of the Catholic Church*, 7th ed., ed. Jacques Dupuis and Josef Neuner (New York: Alba House, 2001), 877–78.

34. *Catechism of the Catholic Church*, par. 1795, quoting *Gaudium et Spes* 16, http://www.vatican.va/archive/catechism.

35. G. C. Berkouwer, *Man: The Image of God* (Grand Rapids: Eerdmans, 1962), 148–50.

notes, both emphases are significant for the complex phenomenon of the conscience.[36]

With these things in mind, we suggest that for Christian ethics the moral conscience is the inner experience by which human beings make moral deliberations. Because humans are created in the image of God, they are moral creatures. We experience feelings of guilt and joy depending on whether we have done something right or wrong. This, in part, is what distinguishes us from animals, which seem to have no such awareness. Theologically, this notion refers to the moral function of the human heart. A person's being is completely caught up in the experience of responsibility and conscience as it relates to values, principles, character, and consequences. Wesley believed the conscience was the tribunal in the inner human being, a gift from God according to prevenient grace.[37] The conscience may be a gift from God, but it has been corrupted by sin and is in need of constant correction. Scripture and the church serve as filters for the conscience, confirming what is right and wrong. The conscience also needs correctives against the extremes of moral apathy and obsessive scrupulosity. In view of these ongoing needed correctives, the conscience must not be simply equated with the voice of God.[38]

The Heart and the Conscience

A basic anthropological term for conscience or the inner being in the Old Testament is the word *heart*. People think, feel, and provide moral judgments with their hearts. In some passages the Hebrew word for *heart* (*leb, lebab*) may be appropriately translated as "conscience."[39] For example, King David became "conscience-stricken after he had counted the fighting men" (2 Samuel 24:10). We see a similarity (but in a positive context) with Job, when he said, "My conscience will not reproach me as long as I live" (Job 27:6). Of course, we know from Jeremiah that indeed a person can be deceived by the conscience: "The heart is deceitful above all things and

---

36. O'Donovan, *Resurrection and Moral Order*, 114.
37. John Wesley, Sermon 105, "On Conscience," in *The Works of John Wesley*, ed. Thomas Jackson (Grand Rapids: Zondervan, 1958), 3:187, 189.
38. J. W. Gladwin, "Conscience," in *New Dictionary of Christian Ethics and Pastoral Theology*, ed. David J. Atkinson et al. (Downers Grove, IL: InterVarsity Press, 1995).
39. Alex Luc, "Leb, lebab," in *New International Dictionary of Old Testament Theology and Exegesis*, vol. 2, ed. Willem A. VanGemeren (Carlisle, UK: Paternoster, 1997).

beyond cure. Who can understand it? 'I the LORD search the heart and examine the mind, to reward a man according to his conduct, according to what his deeds deserve'" (Jeremiah 17:9–10). Certainty cannot come from the human heart or from the moral ways of a person. Only God can provide a final appraisal of our self-perceived righteousness.

The significance of Old Testament wisdom literature for ethics also becomes clear with this idea of the heart. Ethics and prudence belong together: "The wise heart will know the proper time and procedure" (Ecclesiastes 8:5). We must incline our hearts to understanding, so that our hearts receive wisdom (Proverbs 2:2–3). When young Solomon asked for wisdom, he literally asked for a "hearing heart" (1 Kings 3:9). The heart or conscience is not simply a matter of pure reasoning; neither is it a uniquely emotional perception or uncomfortable feeling. It is an activity that encompasses all of these things: thinking and feeling and rational, moral judgment that must be put in line with the mind of God.

The Conscience and the Holy Spirit

We have suggested that redemption is best understood as the restoration of three constituent relationships: with God, with neighbor, and with nature. Redemption also includes the restoration of the human heart and, therefore, the conscience. Here we find a close connection between the working of God's Spirit and our inner life. In this respect the conscience deserves a more exalted status in the New Covenant. The prophet Jeremiah announced that the law was no longer written on stone but in the human heart (Jeremiah 31:32–33). The Old Covenant was of the letter; the New Covenant is of the Spirit (2 Corinthians 3:6). A new ethics flows from the New Covenant, coming from within through the work of the Holy Spirit's indwelling presence.[40] It is an "inside-out" ethics!

The letter to the Hebrews indicates that the blood of Christ cleanses our conscience (Hebrews 9:14; 10:22). It becomes the point of contact between the self and the Holy Spirit in the life of the Christian.[41] Paul told his listeners that he spoke the truth when he said, "My conscience confirms it in the Holy Spirit" (Romans 9:1). Those who are "led by the Spirit of God are sons of God" (Romans 8:14), and "the Spirit himself

---

40. Ladd, *Theology of the New Testament*, 501–3; Gordon D. Fee, *God's Empowering Presence: The Holy Spirit in the Letters of Paul* (Peabody, MA: Hendrickson, 1994), 304–7.
41. In this regard the regenerated life becomes a "knowing-together" (*con-scientia*).

testifies with our spirit that we are God's children" (Romans 8:16). The Holy Spirit testifies to the believer's conscience, so that he or she receives another moral conscience.[42]

Nevertheless, the conscience remains fallible. As Paul affirmed, "My conscience is clear, but that does not make me innocent. It is the Lord who judges me" (1 Corinthians 4:4). The Word of God and the teaching of the community must continually shape the conscience. We must guard against an exclusively conscience-driven, individualistic ethic. The wise heart is always prepared to learn from others (Proverbs 15:22) in the context of community. A humble heart is the condition for a good conscience. Even in its fallibility, it is in the conscience where the matrix of ethics is manifested. With the divine commandments written on our hearts, we strive to be virtuous, and we become deeply aware when certain acts or thoughts oppose our redeemed character. We ponder the consequences of our acts. Finally, we become more and more attracted to those things that reflect the higher values, and we become more disgusted with things of lower value. In this sense ethics is deeply rooted in theological anthropology.

The conscience is a clear echo of God's voice in the Christian. It is more than simply an internal judge; it is the work of God's Spirit through the experience of our deepest values. As Wendy Reuschling points out, "The conscience is both necessary and shapeable, both antecedent and judicial."[43] For this reason Christians must allow their consciences to be shaped by the instruction of God's people in the community of faith. The conscience is developed as it submits to the influence of Christ, Scripture, and the faith community through the work of the Holy Spirit. This is not simply about blind obedience to the hard facts of the law, but it is about discovering joy in obedience to the purposes we were created for.[44]

---

42. Fee, *God's Empowering Presence*, 591–94.

43. Wendy Corbin Reuschling, *Reviving Evangelical Ethics: The Promises and Pitfalls of Classic Models of Morality* (Grand Rapids: Brazos, 2008), 150. See also pp. 145, 158.

44. Cf. John Wesley, Sermon 12, "The Witness of Our Own Spirit," in *The Works of John Wesley*, ed. Thomas Jackson (Grand Rapids: Zondervan, 1958), 5:134–44. This is a sermon on 2 Cor. 1:12, in which Wesley discusses the testimony of the conscience.

Chapter 9

The Use of the Bible in Christian Ethics

The Authority of the Bible and Ethics

Thus far we have proposed that Christian ethics proceeds from the love that exists within the triune God and from the human person as a responsible moral being created in the image of God. As we have noted, we must take into account relevant values and principles, along with the various influences on our character and the consequences of our actions. But what part does the Bible play in our ethical reflection?

Protestant ethics emphasizes the authority of the Bible in all areas of faith and life. It may appear strange to the nonbeliever that Christians consult a collection of old books when faced with contemporary dilemmas such as stem-cell research or same-sex marriage. For many people in our world of competing voices, studying the Bible to receive moral direction is not self-evident. Moreover, the Bible has been used—or rather misused—throughout history to support a variety of unjust and horrific activities.

A classical example of an immoral use of the Bible can be drawn from the apartheid regime in South Africa. The white pioneers identified themselves with the children of Israel in the exodus from Egypt. They felt they were, like the Israelites, predestined by God to possess the "promised land," in this case, South Africa. For these Reformed Christians, blacks were like the Canaanites, inferior and doomed to slavery.[1] This example, among many others like it, highlights an obvious need for deeper theological reflection on the use of Scripture in ethics.

Some disagree in principle, simply saying, "The Bible tells me so." And we can agree that some commands and prohibitions seem quite straightforward and uncomplicated.[2] But we still must ask the question of contemporary relevance, Are the injunctions in the Bible also injunctions for me? This leads us to the next question, What specifically *does* the Bible say to do in my particular situation and culture? Determining this and, at the same time, maintaining the integrity of the cultural context of Scripture is not so simple. As Wendy Corbin Reuschling aptly puts it, "Singing 'trust and obey' is one thing. Exercising trust and discerning the means and purposes of obedience when reading Scripture in all of its intricacy and richness is quite another."[3]

We wholeheartedly embrace the Protestant principles of "Scripture alone" (*sola scriptura*) and "Scripture in its entirety" (*tota scriptura*). God reveals himself in his written Word through the Holy Spirit. The Bible is the *norming norm* as we engage with Christian thought, tradition, and ethics. It is indeed the norming norm for our morality. This is not about building a foundational edifice on which to construct a morality, but rather about providing the interpretive framework for a mosaic of belief with interlocking doctrines.[4] Affirming the authority of Scripture is not worshiping a text. Our worship must only be directed to the personal triune God, and our chief ambition must be to follow Jesus. Without the testimony of Scripture, however, we could hardly say anything about Jesus.

---

1. This historical identification is by no means unique. Donald H. Akenson draws a comparison between Irish people, Jews, and South Africans, all of whom have identified themselves as people of the covenant. Donald H. Akenson, *God's Peoples: Covenant and Land in South Africa, Israel, and Ulster* (Ithaca, NY: Cornell University Press, 1992). See also Richard A. Burridge, *Imitating Jesus: An Inclusive Approach to New Testament Ethics* (Grand Rapids: Eerdmans, 2007), 347–409.

2. See this discussion in Wendy Corbin Reuschling, *Reviving Evangelical Ethics: The Promises and Pitfalls of Classic Models of Morality* (Grand Rapids: Brazos, 2008), 65–66.

3. Ibid., 66.

4. Roger E. Olson, *Reformed and Always Reforming: The Postconservative Approach to Evangelical Theology* (Grand Rapids: Baker Academic, 2007), 146–47. Olson draws on Stanley J. Grenz and John R. Franke, *Beyond Foundationalism: Shaping Theology in a Postmodern Context* (Louisville: Westminster John Knox, 2001), 24, 51. Again, this is why we prefer to refer to a "matrix" approach rather than a "foundational" approach to Christian ethics.

Furthermore, it is the Jesus of the Bible who reveals the triune God. As have we indicated before, Jesus spoke of the Old Testament Scriptures with the deepest respect, acknowledging that nothing will "disappear from the Law until everything is accomplished" (Matthew 5:18). Jesus frequently criticized his own Jewish tradition from Scripture but did not do this by appealing to new revelation. Instead, he preached the kingdom of God in line with the message of the Hebrew Bible.

The evangelical commitment to the authority of Scripture is a faith conviction within the framework of Christian discipleship and spirituality.[5] It should come as a result of imitation of Christ, not of scientific analysis. Walking in the Spirit, listening to Scripture, and prayer all work together. The Spirit works in a faith community where Christ is the center. It is risky to articulate this faith experience in precise dogmatic formulations where we may be more inclined to put our trust in clever definitions than in Scripture itself. We must avoid getting bogged down in the splitting of hairs, locking up the life-infused character of the Bible in our human categories of rationality. Scot McKnight provides the following instructive reminder: "The relational approach distinguishes God from the Bible. God existed before the Bible existed; God exists independently of the Bible now. God is a person; the Bible is paper. God gave us this papered Bible to lead us to love his person. But the person and the paper are not the same."[6]

The most commonly cited passage in the Bible about inspiration is 2 Timothy 3:16–17: "All Scripture is God-breathed and is useful for teaching, rebuking, correcting and training in righteousness." Because God breathed out the words of Scripture through human beings, we believe it is of divine and human origin, not simply of human origin. As 2 Peter 1:20–21 puts it, "Above all, you must understand that no prophecy of Scripture came about by the prophet's own interpretation. For prophecy never had its origin in

---

5. We see this Christocentric approach to scriptural authority in Glen H. Stassen and David P. Gushee, *Kingdom Ethics: Following Jesus in Contemporary Context* (Downers Grove, IL: InterVarsity Press, 2003), 84–86. In the Reformation period, the Anabaptist tradition (the "Radical Reformation") directly linked faithfulness to Scripture with the first disciples of Jesus. By refusing to acknowledge the authority of a developed credo or a catechetical handbook, the Anabaptists claimed they were dependent on the very words of the Bible. The Bible is the book of the church in the sense that we are the people this book speaks about. James William McClendon, *Systematic Theology Vol. 1: Ethics* (Nashville: Abingdon, 1986), 32.
6. Scot McKnight, *The Blue Parakeet: Rethinking How You Read the Bible* (Grand Rapids: Zondervan, 2008), 87.

the will of man, but men spoke from God as they were carried along by the Holy Spirit."

What is often missed in the 2 Timothy 3 passage is its clear moral focus. Paul was not providing his readers with a full discourse on the authority of Scripture or an explicit doctrine of inspiration. Paul already presupposed scriptural authority and inspiration. Rather, he was emphasizing that God's Word is useful for a virtuous life. The entire passage is concerned with our being "thoroughly equipped for every good work" (v. 17). It is about ethical actions—good works, not simply theological dogmatism. Good works, however, begin by listening to the voice of God.

Problems with the Use of the Bible in Ethics

Thirteenth- and fourteenth-century Catholicism and Scholasticism used reason to deduce religious truth from tradition. Protestants rejected the absolute authority of tradition in Roman Catholicism, but did they simply replace the hierarchy of the church with the Bible as their paper pope? Carl Raschke astutely points out:

> It did not alter the method of drawing implications from that authority. Thus, by the early-nineteenth century evangelical Protestantism found itself in an unusual place. It often reasoned from the precise texts of Scripture as if they were premises of Aristotelian syllogisms. Classical Protestantism was far more Catholic and hence medieval than it admitted. The focus on proof-texting betrayed those leanings.[7]

During the Enlightenment the authority of the Bible was radically questioned. The Bible became regarded more as a collection of religious literary texts than as the divinely inspired Scripture. In the spirit of modernism, it was unscientific to take into account the supernatural character of the biblical narratives. All notions of authority were required to submit to the tests of reason and empiricism. Theological liberalism responded to this challenge by filtering and demystifying the mythological elements of the Bible in order to discover the ethical essence of Christianity, making Christianity relevant to the needs and concerns of contemporary culture. Conservative fundamentalism (primarily in England and North America)

---

7. Carl Raschke, *The Next Reformation: Why Evangelicals Must Embrace Postmodernity* (Grand Rapids: Baker, 2004), 93.

responded by appropriating the realist philosophy of Thomas Reid, so that the plain sense of the Bible could be determined by commonsense rationality.[8] As a result, Raschke observes, "Evangelicalism unwittingly succumbed to the kind of facile and expedient rationalism that the Reformers had valiantly exposed in Catholic doctrine and sought to expunge from the practice of the Christian faith."[9]

As we can see, simply giving lip service to the Reformation tenet of *sola scriptura* does not erase all complication in the use of Scripture for ethical reflection. As we have attempted to point out, our background beliefs and presuppositions about how we should read Scripture greatly influence our applications. Simple bumper-sticker hermeneutics is not the answer by any means, nor is rigorous exegesis alone.[10] Those who think that they may discover "the proper ethical application of the Bible solely through more sophisticated exegesis are like people who believe that they can fly if only they flap their arms hard enough."[11] Our ethical character does not lie simply in our rationality, but in our relationship with God as his creatures created in his image.[12]

Again, the Bible has been used countless times throughout history to justify immoral behavior. This most often occurs when theological reflection in view of the three constituent relationships (God, others, nature) is neglected or when Scripture is simply cited as a proof text for complex decision making. Moreover, Christians with the Bible in hand often strongly disagree on ethical positions. Among others, these differences include perspectives on the role of women in the church, divorce and remarriage, the practice of euthanasia, pacifism and just war, and capital punishment. More is at stake than simply claiming "the Bible alone." Texts of the Bible are interpreted and applied differently. That which is clear and obvious to some people is unclear and ambiguous to others. This is readily noticed, for instance, in the debate on war and pacifism. The ethics of the Sermon on the Mount and its message of love for our enemies are the hermeneutical keys

---

8. Ibid., 28–30.

9. Ibid., 30.

10. Richard B. Hays, *The Moral Vision of the New Testament: A Contemporary Introduction to New Testament Ethics* (San Francisco: HarperSanFrancisco, 1996), 3.

11. This is credited to an unpublished lecture of Oliver O'Donovan by Hays, *Moral Vision*, 3.

12. See Stanley J. Grenz, *The Moral Quest: Foundations of Christian Ethics* (Downers Grove, IL: InterVarsity Press, 1997), 217.

for pacifists. But the mandate of the government and its right to carry the sword for the protection of the weak are the focus for just-war prescribers (Romans 13:1–7). We all make decisions as to what is most important and what is not, based on any number of factors, when we read and apply the Bible. Scot McKnight refers to this as the "pattern of discernment,"which is "rarely openly admitted and even more rarely clarified."[13] However, the church is still called to discern the Scriptures and to live with a faith appropriate to its time and culture.[14]

With the rampant technological development of our time, we are confronted with many ethical challenges as to which the Bible is silent. For example, if we did a concordance search on *genetic manipulation, virtual reality, in vitro fertilization, contraceptives,* or *nuclear warfare,* our search would produce no results. It would be naive to attempt to proof text the Bible on these issues in support of particular ethical guidelines. But this does not minimize in any way our stand on the authority of Scripture—in fact, it enhances it! If we view the Bible as a collection of strung-together vitamins we pull off the line when we need a boost, or a quick answer to a problem, we are not viewing the Bible as it was intended. To appreciate truly the authority of the Bible, we must understand it as the organically inspired story of God's redemption and reconciliation of his people, stimulating us to live out God's ongoing story today.[15]

God's story is, of course, composed of different stories and books, and each book has its own author, color, and character. With this diversity-in-unity within the canon of Scripture, we encounter dialectical tensions. The wisdom of Proverbs teaches maxims for living that often claim to result in abundant life and good health. However, the book of Job points to the limitations of proverbial wisdom and gives a poignant personal example of how sometimes very bad things happen to very good and godly people. Clearly, the four gospel writers present their own perspectives on their time with Jesus, providing their own particular accents on various events and on Jesus' teachings. In the letters to the Romans and Ephesians, Paul emphasizes that we receive our faith by God's grace. The book of James, however, emphasizes the importance of concrete actions to back up our faith. If we recognize that God used a diversity of authors and expressions to give us

---

13. McKnight, *The Blue Parakeet,* 144.
14. Ibid., 129.
15. Ibid., 57. See also pp. 55–65.

his incarnated story of redemption and reconciliation, we must understand that our own expression and discernment of that story will also be diverse. Whenever we say, "the Bible says," we must remember that it always "says" through a particular lens of understanding.[16]

The Diversity of the Bible

Each genre of Scripture provides its own contribution to Christian ethics. In Scripture we find rules, principles, paradigms, and symbols. We are morally addressed in different manners. Sometimes God issues direct commands as the divine judge. The command "You shall not commit adultery" (Exodus 20:14) is a specific injunction in the area of sexual purity. Elsewhere we may read a psalm that impresses us with God's promise to bless the righteous (Psalm 1, for instance). When reading the book of Daniel, we find ourselves identifying his world with our own in the midst of a culture seeking to impose its own perverse norms and values on us. The book of Proverbs throws out little nuggets of daily wisdom for direct application to our lives and relationships. The parables of Jesus paint vivid images with unforgettable lessons. The book of Revelation inspires us with tremendous hope for godly perseverance and makes us deeply aware of the destiny of the wicked. We do not give preferential treatment to one genre over another but respect each aspect of Scripture within its context.[17] In a similar fashion we find ourselves drawing on the resources of various genres and approaches in our matrix approach to Christian ethics.

Ethicists Glen Harold Stassen and David P. Gushee propose a framework of norms that functions on four levels: particulars, rules, principles, and basic convictions.[18] They argue that Christian ethics should strive for coherence and cohesiveness on these four levels: "Rules give reasons for particular judgments; principles give reasons for rules. Rules can also criticize particular judgments; principles can criticize rules, not the other

---

16. We are not saying that this leads to hermeneutical relativism. We rather affirm that the Holy Spirit uses our diversity and works through the interpretive process to display his Word. For further insights along this line of thought, see Peter Enns, *Inspiration and Incarnation: Evangelicals and the Problem of the Old Testament* (Grand Rapids: Baker Academic, 2005).

17. Hays, *Moral Vision*, 294–98.

18. Based on Henry David Aiken, *Reasons and Conduct* (New York: Knopf, 1962); and James Gustafson, "Context vs. Principle: A Misplaced Debate in Christian Ethics," *Harvard Theological Review* 58 (1965): 171–202. Stassen and Gushee, *Kingdom Ethics*, 100–118.

way around."[19] They claim that Scripture provides many examples of these different levels and how they interconnect. We will briefly consider these four levels and then refer to them again in our adapted proposal in the following chapter.

The first level is direct and concrete utterances in the Bible where there are judgments made without specific reasons provided. Stassen and Gushee give several examples. We recall how Nathan the prophet uses the parable of the rich man who steals a lamb from a poor man to make David aware of his own sin against Uriah and Bathsheba (2 Samuel 12). When Jesus calls Herod "that fox" (Luke 13:32), it tells us something about what Jesus thinks about the misuse of power by government leaders. This provides insight into his moral convictions. We can make similar judgments by means of analogy and identification. As Herod was for Jesus, so is politician X or state governor Y a dangerous "fox" for us. Many parables of Jesus belong at this level. Jesus often told specific stories, such as the parable of the good Samaritan. We may identify ourselves with a particular character in the story. As a result, we may consider either how we neglect to serve others or how we can improve our service to our neighbors in need.

The second level is simply about rules. Rules are direct commands about what should or should not be done. Rules do not render judgments about situations; they simply lay down the law and expect compliance. This is clearly represented in the eighth commandment, "You shall not steal" (Exodus 20:15).

The third level is made up of principles. These are more general than rules, yet they are also more profound. In contrast to rules, principles do not directly tell us what to do or not to do in specific situations. The double commandment of loving God and loving your neighbor (Matthew 22:37–39) is a principle, just as is the Golden Rule, "So in everything, do to others what you would have them do to you" (Matthew 7:12). Stassen and Gushee remark that rules are not absolute, but principles are. We should understand rules against the backdrop of principles and so remain open to exceptions. Rules exist based on well-determined reasons. The problem of legalism is often the application of rules without knowledge or reflection on the underlying principles.

The fourth level involves our basic convictions regarding morality. These include our perception of God's character, acts, and will. Christian

---

19. Stassen and Gushee, *Kingdom Ethics*, 103.

morality is governed by theological convictions. For example, Christian ethics will always make peace a distinct priority since we are required to reflect the gracious character of God: "Blessed are the peacemakers, for they will be called sons of God" (Matthew 5:9).

Stassen and Gushee's model looks for theological cohesiveness while allowing room for the diversity of biblical data. This avoids the pitfalls of rigid legalism on the one hand and the chaos of situation ethics on the other. Also, the relationship between ethics and worldview is maintained. In line with Anabaptist tradition, Stassen and Gushee have an eye for the renewing element of Jesus' ethics. They attempt to derive general hermeneutical principles from Jesus' approach to the law. Jesus reasoned from general godly principles rather than from a mass of particular laws, providing an ethics of the heart. He approached everything from God's gracious love and paid particular attention to sinners, the poor, and the oppressed.

This is not to say that Stassen and Gushee's model is free from weaknesses. Perhaps the greatest problem is that the lines between their four proposed levels seem vague and clearly contestable. For instance, they refer to Jesus' words in Matthew 5:41, "If someone forces you to go one mile, go with him two miles." We might expect these words to fit nicely into the level of direct judgment, where a particular situation is applied in an analogous fashion. However, Stassen and Gushee place these words in the second level, that of rules. Here they suggest that Jesus provided a rule with a broad field of application.[20]

Stassen and Gushee also seem to create an artificial distinction between principles and rules. Consequently, the Ten Commandments are viewed as mere rules, rather than as robust ethical principles. In our view, this fails to do justice to the significant central role or position of the Ten Commandments for biblical Christian ethics. Not all rules are created equal. Some function as basic norms, and others are applications of norms, expressed in specific injunctions. According to Stassen and Gushee, principles "do not tell us directly or concretely what to do."[21] Perhaps they do not provide the specific informative content for our actions, but we certainly desire to say (as Stassen and Gushee would most likely agree) that principles do indeed call us to some sort of action. Sometimes what Stassen and Gushee refer to as principles, we prefer to characterize as values. There seems to

---

20. Ibid., 102.
21. Ibid., 103.

be a close connection between principles and our deeper convictions. For instance, concepts of truth or well-being are not so much principles as they are values. Values do not tell us directly what to do, but what to cherish, and they describe how we organize our lives. Values do not appeal to the will, as principles do, nor are they to be equated with convictions. Values have, rather, a strong emotional component; they give general direction to our moral decisions, and they are the source of our principles and rules.[22] Listening, reflecting, and praying about Scripture within a community of fellow believers alters our entire value framework.

The Use of Scripture in a Theological Framework

Dogmatic Considerations

Is it anachronistic to use the Bible as a source for moral direction in the midst of an ever-changing world? As Richard Hays aptly asks, "How can we take our moral bearings from a world so different from ours?"[23] Indeed, the ancient world of the Bible is radically dissimilar to the world we face in the twenty-first century. This is why we emphasize that biblical morality cannot be contained in a list of immutable commands or propositions. There is a deeper theological and relational framework found in the character of the triune God as he reveals himself in Scripture. God sympathizes with us and accompanies us throughout history. But God is unchanging in his moral character, so his revealed moral will has permanent value. As humans created in his image, we also have a certain immutable singularity. Whatever our culture or background, our basic moral needs remain the same. Humans are remarkably capable of loving actions yet continue their struggle with selfish ambition and lawlessness. For these reasons alone we submit that biblical morality maintains a timeless and universal character.[24]

In view of the challenge of using Scripture in ethics, we must always strive to acknowledge the distinction between our interpretation of the

---

22. For example, the rule/principle "Do not store up for yourselves treasures on earth" (Matt. 6:19) is a concrete expression of "hallowed be your name"—our highest value.

23. Hays, *Moral Vision*, 6.

24. Terrance Tiessen, "Toward a Hermeneutic for Discerning Universal Moral Absolutes," *Journal of the Evangelical Theological Society* 36, no. 2 (1993): 189–207. We are not presuming to lay out a complete apologetic for the use of the Bible in modern ethics, but simply contending that our proposal is well suited to the presuppositions we have been working with in the course of this book.

Bible and Scripture itself. This insight is essential for avoiding a relativistic biblicism. Interpretation is ubiquitous, but it is still the means that God has given us to understand his Word. To use Scripture in ethics requires that we embrace a charitable and humble posture in our interpretation, maintaining a "Christian morality of literary knowledge" stressing virtues such as self-criticism and cooperation in community.[25]

How then do we make the move from the text of the Bible to moral application? Few people receive direct commands from God that tell them exactly what to do in the here and now. Nor should it be our intention simply to pick a passage and make a decision. Rather, the Bible provides a general wisdom map that guides us in our efforts of moral reflection. The transition from the descriptive in the Bible to the prescriptive of today comes from thorough theological reflection in the context of the church community. Richard Hays submits that we must be actively engaged in "metaphor making," putting the life of our community "imaginatively within the world articulated by the texts."[26] He proposes three concepts to bring out the unity in the diversity of the New Testament message: community, cross, and new creation. From these three metaphors we are able to discuss the whole of Christian ethics.[27]

Scripture and church are correlated concepts. As ethicist Allen Verhey aptly states, "Scripture is the book of the church, and the church is the community that somehow uses that book to preserve its identity and reform its common life."[28] He refers to Paul's words to the Romans, "I myself am convinced, my brothers, that you yourselves are full of goodness, complete in knowledge and competent to instruct one another" (Romans 15:14). The early churches functioned as communities of moral discourse, of moral deliberation, sharing a common memory of the death and resurrection of Jesus Christ.[29] It is impossible to separate ethical discernment from the general framework of a Christian view of reality as it is lived out in the Christian community.

---

25. Cf. Kevin J. Vanhoozer, *Is There a Meaning in This Text?* (Grand Rapids: Zondervan, 1998), 302.
26. Hays, *Moral Vision*, 6. Hays develops this idea more fully on pp. 298–310.
27. Ibid., 193–214. Hays speaks more of key images than of concepts or doctrines.
28. Allen Verhey, *Remembering Jesus: Christian Community, Scripture, and the Moral Life* (Grand Rapids: Eerdmans, 2005), 10.
29. Ibid., 15–18, 21–23.

The Wesleyan Quadrilateral

Scripture reading and theological reflection are embedded in the life of the church. This fundamental insight can help us avoid attempting to understand God's will as an individual matter, reading the Bible alone. As strange as it sounds, a well-considered theological use of Scripture involves more than Scripture itself. Certainly, we hold to *sola scriptura*, but this does not exclude other sources that must be used to enhance our understanding, interpretation, and application of Scripture. Scripture is the ultimate and primary authority, but not the sole source for all theological understanding. God has revealed himself to us generally in creation, history, and the *imago Dei*, as well as specifically in the Word. Doing interpretation honestly and carefully necessitates that we draw on other skills and resources. We find the Wesleyan quadrilateral—Scripture, tradition, reason, and experience—extremely helpful in this respect.[30] This is not to say that our understanding is derived equally from each aspect of these four theological sources. We follow Randy Maddox in his suggestion that Wesley's quadrilateral "could more adequately be described as a unilateral *rule* of Scripture within a tri-lateral hermeneutic of reason, tradition, and experience."[31] These three are interpreters of the one norming norm, Scripture. The Bible itself remains the primary source for the life and identity of the community.

The Reformation unmistakably intended a return to the primacy of Scripture in the formulation of church doctrine and practice. But as can be expected, the principle of *sola scriptura* was interpreted in a variety of ways. Luther desired reform from within the church, accepting everything that was not explicitly condemned by Scripture. Zwingli was more radical; he desired to reject everything not explicitly commanded by Scripture. Wesley appears to have followed Luther in this regard. Those matters about which Scripture does not speak were allowed as long as they agreed with the

---

30. The term *quadrilateral* originates from Wesley scholar Albert Outler. Wesley himself never expounded his method, but it can be defended from his writings.

31. Randy L. Maddox, *Responsible Grace: John Wesley's Practical Theology* (Nashville: Kingswood Books, 1994), 46. Maddox claims this was a phrase suggested in John Giffin, "Scriptural Standards in Religion: John Wesley's Letters to William Law and James Hervey," *Studia Biblica et Theologica* 16 (1986): 143–68. Richard Hays also refers to the significance of these three additional sources; see Hays, *Moral Vision*, 295–96. For the importance of this model as an alternative to fundamentalist use of Scripture among evangelicals, see Donald A. D. Thorsen, *The Wesleyan Quadrilateral: Scripture, Tradition, Reason and Experience as a Model of Evangelical Theology* (Grand Rapids: Zondervan, 1990).

conscience. Wesley believed in *adiaphora;* things about which Scripture was silent or indifferent required a search for general principles.[32]

Wesley was keenly aware that it was important to understand Scripture by considering other sources, including our own Christian tradition. For Wesley this tradition primarily consisted of two elements: the Anglican sources (the Anglican Articles and the Book of Common Prayer) and the writings of the early church.[33] He boldly claimed, "Every new doctrine must be wrong, because ancient religion is the only true one and no doctrine except for the one which was from the beginning can be true."[34] Wesley had a great liking for the early church because it stood closer to the time of the Bible. The Holy Spirit had worked powerfully among the leaders of ancient, persecuted Christian believers. Patristics was thus assigned an important hermeneutical role for the understanding of Scripture.[35] Tradition is critically important, but it must not hinder us from careful interpretation of Scripture in our current context. There must be a continual interaction between understanding Scripture from tradition and the critical questioning of our own tradition.[36]

Besides tradition, reason also played a crucial role for Wesley. But he restricted it to the work of "organizing and drawing inferences from revelation," rather than using it to provide a "rational foundation for the claims of revelation" in a metaphysical sense.[37] Unlike the Reformers, Wesley lived in the midst of the Enlightenment and the beginnings of industrialization. In England, deism was the prevalent mindset. People were hesitant to acknowledge God's action in history or to recognize the miraculous events of the Bible. Wesley combined the logic of Aristotle, in which he was trained at Oxford, with the conclusions of English empiricism. According to Wesley, reason is not the source of knowledge itself but a means by

---

32. Maddox, *Responsible Grace*, 39. Maddox makes reference to (among others) John Wesley, Sermon 12, "The Witness of Our Own Spirit," par. 6, in *The Works of John Wesley*, ed. Thomas Jackson (Grand Rapids: Zondervan, 1979), 1:303; and Wesley, "A Plain Account of the People Called Methodists," par. 2.10, *Works*, 9:263. Cf. Maddox, *Responsible Grace*, 270.

33. See Maddox, *Responsible Grace*, 42.

34. Wesley, Sermon 13, "On Sin in Believers," par. 3, p. 9.

35. Here we find a link with the Radical Reformation and the idea of restoration. The contemporary church must follow the early church. Maddox, *Responsible Grace*, 42–44.

36. As an example, Richard Hays mentions the tradition of just war. In his opinion, this is a departure from original New Testament ethics. Hays, *Moral Vision*, 297.

37. Maddox, *Responsible Grace*, 41–42.

which to arrange experience. The Bible is always the first source of our knowing (the norming norm), before other sources. Reason must not be construed as some separated source of revelation in addition to that of the Bible or creation; rather its job is to provide boundaries for responsible interpretation and application.[38] Wesley believed that it is important to testify to Christian faith and morals in a reasonable and clear fashion. Reason stands in the service of practice, rather than being simply an instrument for theological speculation. As with tradition, we must always keep in mind the ongoing limitations of human reason. We must always remember that on occasion, the gospel will seem "foolishness" to the wisdom of the world (1 Corinthians 1:25).

For some, Wesley's proposal of experience as a resource for theology is the most surprising. It was common practice in the Anglican tradition to do theology while drawing from Scripture, tradition, and reason. Wesley's added dimension of experience highlights the importance he gave to both the heart and the hands and accentuates the unity he saw between dogmatics, ethics, and spirituality. Some speak of the triadic nature of Wesleyan theology: orthodoxy, orthopraxy, and orthopathy.[39] The Bible is authoritative in doctrine, conduct, and the inner life. We not only think from the Bible, but we also act according to the Bible and feel what the Bible says.

Experience has a broad range of meaning in Wesley's thinking. The believer experiences and feels the love of God through the Holy Spirit. As new believers we first experience becoming a child of God. Then the conscience, through which the Holy Spirit speaks, becomes a part of our experience. Experience is phenomenological; it is shared and communal and serves to confirm the testimony of Scripture. For example, in Wesley's treatise on original sin, he draws on the obvious universal aspect of sin in human experience to confirm the objective account of sin in Scripture.[40] All in all, for Wesley pastoral practice in the experience of community cannot be separated from moral reflection. We believe Wesley's approach continues to be an exemplary model as we consider the authority and application of the Bible to a matrix approach in Christian ethics.

---

38. Ibid., 41.
39. Theodore Runyon, *The New Creation: John Wesley's Theology Today* (Nashville: Abingdon 1998), 147–48.
40. Maddox, *Responsible Grace*, 45.

Chapter 10

A Variegated Biblical Ethics

This chapter will further elaborate on the ethical riches found in the Bible, especially through the filter of the Ten Commandments. We desire to participate in the story of the Bible, moving beyond a mere deontological or "rules only" ethics, while at the same time guarding the commandment-centered character of many passages. Appreciating the richness of biblical ethics is, first of all, a pastoral assignment. Ethics often makes people think of commandments and prohibitions, a list of shalls and shall nots. Such a moralistic, "extinguisher" approach causes many to experience faith as an impediment to life's pleasures. Unfortunately, Christians often fail to recognize and demonstrate the unity between the commandments and the life-infusing good news of the gospel. We would like to highlight that unity in this chapter.

The Commandments and the Iceberg Model

A Traditional Tripartition

Christ's fulfillment of the law brought an end to the exclusive position of Israel as the people of God.[1] The incarnation initiated a transition from

---

1. This is not to say that Israel currently plays no role or is excluded from God's salvation plan.

the "holy nation" to a "holy church" drawn from many nations. Temple service was replaced by the worship and celebration of the church throughout the world. This transformation in salvation history had huge ramifications for the applicability of many Old Testament laws. At the Council of Jerusalem, the apostles determined not to place any burdens on the Gentile believers other than what was strictly necessary (Acts 15:28). Eventually, a distinction was drawn between ceremonial, civil, and moral laws. We find all three categories in the Torah, but only the last type, the moral, is usually considered to have enduring value for God's people today. This distinction can be roughly traced back to Justin Martyr (about AD 165). It was then refined in the Middle Ages, most notably by Thomas Aquinas, and it later reappeared with John Calvin (among others).[2]

Calvin called ceremonial law "a tutelage by which the Lord was pleased to exercise, as it were, the childhood of that people, until the fullness of the time should come when he was fully to manifest his wisdom to the world, and exhibit the reality of those things which were then adumbrated by figures (Galatians 3:24; 4:4)."[3] As for civil regulations, Calvin (a jurist himself) believed that all nations now have the freedom to make their own laws. However, the new laws must be made in accordance with the universal principle of love. The shape of particular laws will vary depending on time, place, and people, but universal principles of righteousness and respect for one's neighbor remain standing. Calvin called for equity and knowledge of the essential heart matter of the laws.[4]

In recent years this division between ceremonial, civil, and moral laws has been especially criticized in the biblical sciences.[5] Critics of this artificial division argue that the Old Testament law presents itself as a whole (for instance, in Leviticus 19). The ceremonial, civil, and moral domains often

---

2. Thomas Aquinas, *Summa Theologica* II-I.99, 2–4; cf. Calvin, *Institutes of the Christian Religion* IV.xx.14; and the Westminster Confession of Faith 19.3.4.

3. Calvin, *Institutes* IV.xx.15, Christian Classics Ethereal Library, http://www.ccel.org/ccel/calvin/institutes.vi.xxi.html.

4. Calvin, *Institutes* IV.xx.15. This is different from the oft-portrayed picture of Calvin as one who wanted to impose rigidly Old Testament laws in politics, as is the practice among theonomists and Christian reconstructionists (e.g., in the writings of R. J. Rushdoony, Greg L. Bahnsen, and Gary North). For a critical discussion of this movement see H. Wayne House and Thomas Ice, *Dominion Theology: Blessing or Curse? An Analysis of Christian Reconstructionism* (Portland, OR: Multnomah Press, 1988).

5. Christopher J. H. Wright, *Old Testament Ethics for the People of God* (Downers Grove, IL: InterVarsity Press, 2004), 288.

run together and overlap. This criticism certainly has some merit. After all, this kind of distinction never occurred in ancient Israel. But the fulfillment of the law in Christ had not then transpired either. Making a tripartite distinction of the law understandably presupposes reading the Old Testament from a New Testament perspective. The Ten Commandments formed the center and summary of an Old Testament moral law given and prescribed in a specific historical context. Regardless, we are convinced that the Ten Commandments remain central to the ethics of both Testaments, forming the cornerstone of biblical morality in general.[6] For instance, the fourth commandment to keep the Sabbath holy had ceremonial, civil, and moral implications in ancient Israel. But the Sabbath *principle* has an obvious and enduring moral dimension for the church today. Since the commandments are rooted in the character of God, they remain just as significant for our ethics and character development today.

The Iceberg

Biblical commandment ethics is a bit like an iceberg: we easily see the small portion of the whole, the commandments, floating on the surface—the tip of the iceberg—but we desire to uncover more and more of the mass beneath the water level to experience the depth and richness from which the commandments stem. Old Testament scholar Brevard Childs points out that the Ten Commandments were not revealed as general divine principles, but rather as particular imperatives for ancient Israel as the people of God. From that time forward, however, the commandments were used as a basis for reflection in narratives, wisdom literature, and prophetic texts. Similarly, we are suggesting that we should read the commandments in the larger framework of the entire canon.[7] The commandments describe God's

---

6. For example, Mark 10:17–22; Rom. 13:9; Eph. 6:2; 1 Tim. 1:8–11; James 2:11–12. After a study on the use of the Decalogue in the New Testament, Reginald Fuller concludes that the law maintains its prominence. He even recognizes the three Reformed functions of the law: "For the Old Testament and Judaism the law embraces the whole of the Torah, but for the New Testament writers the central part of it is the second table plus the love commandment. Although the New Testament writers never formulated a systematic doctrine of the law, they recognized the three functions which were systematized by the Reformers." Reginald H. Fuller, "The Decalogue in the New Testament," *Interpretation* 43, no. 3 (1989): 255. For examples from the Old Testament see Jer. 7:9–10 and Hos. 4:2. Cf. Patrick D. Miller, "The Place of the Decalogue in the Old Testament," *Interpretation* 43, no. 3 (1989): 229–42.

7. Brevard S. Childs, *Old Testament Theology in a Canonical Context* (Philadelphia: SCM

order, and so they are the antipode of chaos and sin. We do not find a strict juridical and direct use of the Ten Commandments, quoted as a literal codex. Designations such as the "fifth commandment" or "sixth commandment" are not used in the Bible. Yet we find many indirect references to the Ten Commandments in other literature of the Old Testament besides the direct context of the Decalogue. In fact, they resonate throughout the entire Pentateuch.[8] The prophets make reference to several of the commandments (e.g., Hosea 4:2; Jeremiah 7:9), but this is infrequent and presupposes a background of familiarity with the commandments. The prophets demonstrate concrete interpretations and applications of the commandments throughout their writings. Wisdom literature also gives us a deeper insight into the essence and utility of the commandments as practical daily maxims and principles.

The relationship between biblical stories and the commandments is vital. The biblical narratives provide a framework for the interpretation of the commandments. They function to uncover the depth of the iceberg. When Joseph withstands the seduction of Potiphar's wife, we see a positive example of the seventh commandment, "You shall not commit adultery" (Exodus 20:14). The tragic story of David, Bathsheba, and Uriah the Hittite provides a daunting picture of the negative results of failing to follow the tenth (no coveting), seventh (no adultery), and sixth (no murder) commandments.[9] We readily see the terrible consequences of one sin's leading to another through lust, illicit desire, adultery, deception, and murder. The relation between abuse of power and lust and murder comes distinctly to the fore in the story. The prophet Nathan's chastising parable vividly portrays how David abused his position and disobeyed God.

The Bible often speaks in terms of particular commandments rather than general moral-philosophical principles. In contrast to Greek philosophical methods, Hebrew methods involved few definitions and few fine theoretical descriptions. The Hebrew world was not interested in *defining* the good as much as in *doing* the good in specific everyday situations, which

---

Press, 1985), 64; and Richard J. Mouw, *The God Who Commands* (Notre Dame: University of Notre Dame Press, 1990), 10.

8. For an overview see William P. Brown, ed., *The Ten Commandments: The Reciprocity of Faithfulness* (Louisville: Westminster John Knox, 2004), 2–4; and Patrick D. Miller, *The Way of the Lord: Essays in Old Testament Theology* (Grand Rapids: Eerdmans, 2007), 3–16.

9. Commandments 8 (no stealing) and 9 (no false testimony) may be readily implied as well.

required wisdom. Wisdom was about *phronēsis*—practical wisdom for godly living.[10] The book of Proverbs distinguishes fools from wise persons not by differences in their intellect but by differences in their life decisions. The wise person manifests consistent obedience, in the fear of the Lord, whereas the fool practices consistent disobedience, in arrogance. James also highlights this in the New Testament: "Who is wise and understanding among you? Let him show it by his good life, by deeds done in the humility that comes from wisdom" (James 3:13). Biblical ethics is directed toward concrete conduct. This is why the largest part of biblical ethics is formulated in terms of specific commands.

Now back to the iceberg. As we suggested, commands (or prohibitions) are the tip of the iceberg that appears above the surface. They are presented as clear injunctions. But the Hebrew mind understood that the iceberg had much greater depth than a first glance might indicate. To continue our arctic metaphor, let us divide the iceberg into four overlapping sections. As we said, the upper visible portion consists of specific, culturally conditioned commandments and particular interdictions. For example, Leviticus 19:27 states, "Do not cut the hair at the sides of your head or clip off the edges of your beard." Many of these types of laws may seem irrelevant to us now, because of their cultural embeddedness. The second layer (still often visible above the water) includes more general commandments and norms. Often these are formulated as imperatives, including the Ten Commandments and the love commands of Christ. For the third layer of the iceberg, we descend below the surface and reach the values. Again, values do not tell us specifically *what* to do but *how* to value something. They do have an idealistic aspect, telling us how things are *supposed* to be. Values have a strong emotional dimension, highlighting the things we experience as good and important. Moving deeper down to the fourth layer of the iceberg, we discover worldviews and theological orientations (or lack thereof). Christian ethics, therefore, must serve to uncover, clarify, and discuss the visible *and* the submerged levels of the iceberg and reflect on how these various layers interconnect.

---

10. For more on *phronēsis*, we heartily recommend Daniel J. Treier, *Virtue and the Voice of God: Towards Theology as Wisdom* (Grand Rapids: Eerdmans, 2006).

The Density of the Iceberg

In the tradition of John Calvin, we will suggest a broad interpretation of the Ten Commandments.[11] The Ten Commandments are a summary of the entire revealed law, expressed in specific terms. The notion of divine accommodation is central to Calvin's theology here. God accommodated himself to human fallibility by giving clear laws by which to live. God's giving of the laws was an act of grace and promise. Although we are unable to completely obey his commandments, God revealed his will to us as a blessing and promise: "For God, while bestowing all things on us freely, crowns his goodness by not disdaining our imperfect obedience; forgiving its deficiencies, accepting it as if it were complete, and so bestowing on us the full amount of what the Law has promised."[12] The Ten Commandments are short apodictic statements directly revealed by God. They have a rich meaning that is broader than a superficial reading would acknowledge.[13] Philo of Alexandria called them "heads of law" (*kephalia*) or summaries, with the perfect number of ten.[14] Christian ethics transitions from these apodictic summaries to the world of godly values. Behind each commandment we can discover values. The canonical expression of these values is in the form of commandments. Conveniently and simply arranged, we can see the relationship between commandments/prohibitions and positively stated values as in the chart, opposite.

Old Testament scholar Christopher J. H. Wright makes an important contribution to ethical reflection on the law. He proposes a paradigmatic application of the Old Testament laws for social ethics today that remains faithful to their original framework. For example, we could apply the ethics of the Jubilee as a model or paradigm of "holistic concern for human need, theologically relevant to evangelistic endeavor as well as socio-economic

---

11. See John P. Burgess, "Reformed Explication of the Ten Commandments," in *The Ten Commandments: The Reciprocity of Faithfulness*, ed. William P. Brown (Louisville: Westminster John Knox, 2004.

12. Calvin, *Institutes* II.vii.4, http://www.ccel.org/ccel/calvin/institutes.iv.viii.html.

13. In this tradition, see Jochem Douma, *The Ten Commandments: Manual for the Christian Life* (Phillipsburg, NJ: P&R Publishing, 1996). This broader hermeneutical approach stands completely within the tradition of Calvin. Cf. Eric Fuchs, "Calvin, Jean: La philosophie morale de Calvin et le calvinisme," in *Dictionnaire d'éthique*, 1:230.

14. Philo, *De Decalogo* 6 and 21. See discussion in Brown, ed., *The Ten Commandments*, 6–9.

	Commandment/ Prohibition	Values
Commandment 1	No other gods before me	Give ultimate value to the one true God.
Commandment 2	No idols	The one true God is primary and exclusive in religious value.
Commandment 3	Do not misuse the name of the Lord	God's name is to be honored above all.
Commandment 4	Keep the Sabbath holy	God ordains time for rest and reflection.
Commandment 5	Honor your father and mother	Respect in family relationships is essential.
Commandment 6	No murder	Human life is to be respected.
Commandment 7	No adultery	Covenant relationships in marriage are vital.
Commandment 8	No stealing	The property of others is to be respected.
Commandment 9	No false testimony	Truthful communication is paramount in relationships.
Commandment 10	No coveting	Contentment with God's provision is crucial for holiness.

reform."[15] Wright submits that this approach recognizes God's purpose in using his people as examples to display to all nations God's redemptive character and moral obligations. Israel provides a concrete example showing the struggle of embodying God's values in the context of community, with both success and failure. This approach paradigmatically affirms God's ongoing kingdom work not only in Israel but also in the lives of all his people through all nations even today.[16] According to Wright

---

15. Christopher J. H. Wright, *Walking in the Ways of the Lord: The Ethical Authority of the Old Testament* (Leicester: Apollos, 1995), 32–33.

16. Ibid., 33–36. From this perspective Wright sees three different levels of interpretation complementing each other: paradigmatic, eschatological, and typological. He provides an interesting case study of the meaning of the Year of Jubilee. Christopher J. H. Wright, *Old Testament Ethics for the People of God* (Downers Grove, IL: InterVarsity Press, 2004),

even the specific order of the Ten Commandments reflects a scale of values. The arrangement of the commandments gives some insight into Israel's hierarchy of values. Roughly speaking, the order is God, family, life, sex, and property. Wright insightfully remarks, "It is sobering, looking at the order, that in modern society (in its debased Western form at least) we have almost exactly reversed that order of values."[17]

Wright points out three key elements of ethics in the creation triangle: God, humanity, and the earth. These are derived from Old Testament ethics, which is centered on God, Israel, and the land. The top of the triangle is the theological angle, for it should always be God who is at the apex of our ethical concern. The social angle (humanity) points to redemption, God's work of freeing humans from fallenness. The economic angle (the earth or land) recognizes the gift of God's faithful provision and the importance of using the resources of the land responsibly.[18] This "broad matrix of self-understanding" affirms the Creator as the God of Israel, the children of Israel as the elect in unique relation to God, and the land as the promised dwelling for his people. It is only within this covenantal relationship that many of the commandments make any sense. Wright's proposal fits nicely with our previous proposal of relating ethics to Christian anthropology, where we referred to three constituent relationships: with God, with others, and with creation (chapter 8). In salvation history, the church lies between the salvation plan for Israel and the eschatological renewal of all creation. So the church is responsible for being the renewed people of God, manifesting the kingdom of God through justice and care for the poor.

The Bible gives many specific commandments within particular contexts, which we may apply paradigmatically. We must interpret specific commandments in such a way that they are connected with their contextual worldview, while seeking application for today. For instance, consider the commandment in Deuteronomy 22:8: "When you build a new house, make a parapet around your roof so that you may not bring the guilt of bloodshed on your house if someone falls from the roof." In this case, the tension between human safety and economic interests is apparent. When a house was built in the ancient Middle East, building a balustrade was often

---

182–211.

17. Unfortunately, Wright does not fully explain what he specifically means by "values" and how they are different from principles or laws. Wright, *Old Testament Ethics*, 307.

18. Wright, *Walking in the Ways of the Lord*, 28–31. Wright emphasizes the importance of the land to Israel's covenant relationship with God, p. 30.

neglected. Just as contractors today often economize and compromise on the quality of their workmanship, so it was in the ancient world. Although this text may at first seem irrelevant to us, it clearly speaks to priorities: human life is more important than economic value. If something goes amiss because of poor safety measures, the employer is responsible. The general commandment "You shall not murder" becomes, in this context, "You shall do everything you can to protect your neighbor." So we see that a world of values lies beneath the tip of the iceberg.

The Messiah and the Revolution of Values

An Axiological Revolution

How does this approach to values help us better understand the role of the law in the New Testament? As we have stressed before, Jesus did not come to abolish the law but to fulfill it (Matthew 5:17–20). If Christian ethics neglects the law, it runs counter to Jesus' proclamation. This is not to say that the applied meaning of the law remains unchanged with the coming of Christ. But this is more than simply the cessation of ceremonial and civil laws. Jesus brings about a deep change in our attitudes toward the moral commandments through his life example and his message of grace and love. Certainly, the grace and love of God were fully present in the Old Testament, but Jesus' incarnated ethics illumines the message and sheds new light. When we keep our eyes on a tree and suddenly the sun emerges from behind the clouds, there is a fresh vitality brought to the green leaves and branches before us.

Jesus' ethics stands in sharp contrast to the Pharisaic ethics exclusively focused on particular injunctions and myriad human laws. Jesus called his people back to the underlying values and purposes behind the laws. The Sermon on the Mount, along with Jesus' many parables, stirred up an axiological revolution of values. Jesus taught that "you shall not murder" also means that we must have a deep respect for others, not violating them with our anger or insults (Matthew 5:21–22). Murder begins in the heart, when we disparage our neighbor. Likewise, adultery begins with an illicit lustful desire for a man or woman who is already committed to another (Matthew 5: 27–28). The parable of the unmerciful servant (Matthew 18:23–35) also illustrates this axiological revolution. The servant was forgiven a very large, unpayable debt, and yet he demanded that his fellow servant pay back a small debt. Jesus was emphasizing that those who have experienced God's radical forgiveness ought to forgive others freely.

In connection with the parable of the prodigal son (Luke 15:11–32), Richard Hays remarks, "To 'understand' these parables is to be changed by them, to have our vision of the world reshaped by them. To 'understand' them is to enter the process of reflecting about how our lives ought to change in response to the gospel—a gospel that unsettles what we 'know' about responsibility and ethics."[19] As we mentioned before, Hays speaks of the importance of metaphors. Through biblical metaphors we identify ourselves with the text. The time gap between Christians in the New Testament era and today can be bridged only by an "imaginative connection."[20] When we read the parable of the rich man and Lazarus, we are to identify ourselves with the rich man and make the connection using our imagination. Reading a text metaphorically, however, occurs through accurate listening, prayer, and life within a faith community. In this faith community, the Word takes shape, and the community itself becomes a metaphor of God embodied. The text shapes the community, and the community embodies the meaning of the text. Only within this relational framework can we really begin to understand the text.[21] What Hays describes with his metaphorical method is essentially a revolution of values brought about through a deeper understanding of the biblical message.

In Paul's life we also see this axiological revolution. He encountered Christ in full glory, was thrown from his horse, and was struck with blindness. The apostate Jews he had been persecuting were fully identified with the Messiah. By implication, Paul realized he had been persecuting the Messiah himself (Acts 9:4–5). This intense experience would change his life completely. His entire ethical framework would shift and begin again from identification with Christ: "I have been crucified with Christ and I no longer live, but Christ lives in me" (Galatians 2:20). Paul's values were rearranged and transformed: "What is more, I consider everything a loss compared to the surpassing greatness of knowing Christ Jesus my Lord, for whose sake I have lost all things" (Philippians 3:8). From then on his ethics would not focus so much on specific regulations as on unification with Christ and the guidance of the Holy Spirit. In a moral context, Paul consistently pointed out what God had done for us in Christ. There is

---

19. Richard B. Hays, *The Moral Vision of the New Testament: A Contemporary Introduction to New Testament Ethics* (San Francisco: HarperSanFrancisco, 1996), 301.
20. Ibid.
21. Ibid., 304.

virtually no distinction made by Paul between theology and ethics. The message is the story of God's work of transformation through which the believer is renewed into the image of Christ.[22] The Christian receives a completely new framework for values.

Sexual Immorality and Value Ethics

We would like to illustrate the relationship between value ethics and commandment ethics in Paul's letters with the passage about sexual morality in 1 Corinthians 6:12–20:[23]

> "Everything is permissible for me"—but not everything is beneficial. "Everything is permissible for me"—but I will not be mastered by anything. "Food for the stomach and the stomach for food"—but God will destroy them both. The body is not meant for sexual immorality, but for the Lord, and the Lord for the body. By his power God raised the Lord from the dead, and he will raise us also. Do you not know that your bodies are members of Christ himself? Shall I then take the members of Christ and unite them with a prostitute? Never! Do you not know that he who unites himself with a prostitute is one with her in body? For it is said, "The two will become one flesh." But he who unites himself with the Lord is one with him in spirit.
>
> Flee from sexual immorality. All other sins a man commits are outside his body, but he who sins sexually sins against his own body. Do you not know that your body is a temple of the Holy Spirit, who is in you, whom you have received from God? You are not your own; you were bought at a price. Therefore honor God with your body.

Paul was confronted with a serious moral problem in the Corinthian church. Some of the believers were visiting temple prostitutes. We might expect to read a powerful exhortation of judgment from the beginning of the letter. After all, the Old Testament prohibits adultery and sexual impurity. Paul, however, moved with caution, understanding that these Gentile

---

22. Ibid.
23. We will build on Gordon Fee's commentary. Gordon D. Fee, *The First Epistle to the Corinthians* (Grand Rapids: Eerdmans, 1987), 249–66.

Christians had not yet embraced Jewish morality or experienced a complete transformation of character. Some of this was due to an improper libertine dualism, separating body and spirit. These Corinthians believed that what was done in the body was morally neutral, or *adiaphora* (indifferent). So we find a seemingly strange quotation in 1 Corinthians 6:13: "'Food for the stomach and the stomach for food'—but God will destroy them both." This is no doubt a quotation from one of their own teachers. Paul refuted this dualistic thesis by drawing a distinction between eating food, which involves a part of the body, the stomach, and sexuality, which involves the entire body and spirit.

This is an example of Paul's use of value ethics. He provided arguments as to why the entire body has special value for those united with Christ. He sought to bring about an axiological revolution. The body has value because it belongs to the Lord in community as the body of Christ; so we honor God with our body. The Lord gives value to the body, so we must give it value. Paul provided a Trinitarian argument. The body is precious because God has a plan for it in the resurrection. God the Father will validate and fully redeem the body in the eschaton. We are part of the body of Christ Jesus, the temple of the Holy Spirit. Furthermore, our bodies are not simply our own to decide what is and is not appropriate, for they have been "bought at a price" (v. 20) and belong to God. Paul hit the heart of dualism by exposing a wrong-headed worldview and its accompanying dishonorable ethics. When the worldview adopts a more robust perspective on the value of the body, the principles behind sexual ethics also change.

The apostle Paul also gave a great example of how morality can be taught. He saw worldview, values, commandments, and virtues as one coherent whole. The Corinthians would discover the good if they learned to value things as God valued them. In the center of this passage, we do find a very clearly stated commandment: "Flee from sexual immorality" (v. 18). But this verse is not isolated from the discussion of renewed worldview and the valuation of corporeality and sexuality. We learn to experience our bodies as a part of Christ and as a temple of the Holy Spirit, understanding that Jesus bought our bodies with his sacrifice in our place—a timeless lesson in biblical values. Those who love God honor him with their bodies.

Purpose Ethics: Happy in God's Kingdom

The Relevance of Purpose Ethics

Besides values and commandments, Scripture also speaks of our purpose as human beings. We must remember that God's commandments are fully compatible with God's purposes for us as creatures created in his image. Sin not only transgresses his commandments, but also detracts from our original purpose of living vibrant, full lives with God. Christian ethics is concerned with restoring and enjoying this purposeful way of life. Purposes come close to values. In fact, values measure our specific purposes. If material property is one of our basic values (e.g., the purchase of houses, cars, clothes, barbecues, MP3 players), our purposes will fall in line with this value and give shape to its fulfillment.

When facing an ethical problem, it is not sufficient to consider only relevant commandments and values; we must also consider consequences. A one-sided principle ethics will deny or unconsciously push aside the consideration of consequences. Richard Hays refers to the powerful testimony of George Zabelka, priest-chaplain to the pilots who dropped the atomic bomb on Hiroshima and Nagasaki at the end of World War II (1945). The cleric initially considered the use of this bomb against Japan a justified action. He led a chapel service shortly before the calamitous action of that flight. But several years later, while visiting Japan, he became intensely aware of the devastating consequences of this horrific act. He became convinced that he was wrong in his perspective on just war.[24] It was one thing to defend a position from the books in the church and the academy, with eyes closed to the consequences; it was another to make decisions when aware of the outcome. We do not intend to blame or to exonerate Zabelka or to provide a defense of either pacifism or just war. Rather, we are stressing that a wise consideration of consequences will make us more fully conscious of our decisions.

Christian ethics must have an eye for short- and long-term consequences. At times we may make godly decisions with full awareness of the devastating consequences. But simply to ignore consequences is ethical negligence. It is also important to consider the "double effect" criterion. Besides the purpose of the action, and its understood or intended consequences, there is sometimes an accidental consequence. Unintended

---

24. Hays, *Moral Vision*, 318–19.

consequences must always be carefully considered and evaluated in view of the entire ethical decision. In Thomistic ethics, the principle of double effect is often used to explain the permissibility of an action that causes serious harm. In the extreme, this harm can even be the death of a human being, as a side effect of promoting some good end. In that case, this harm is considered to be a permissible side effect (or double effect) of bringing about a good result. However, it is important that only one of the effects is intended. This has to do with motives. For instance, Thomas argued that killing an attacker was justified, provided we did not intend to kill him.[25] A moral agent meets this criterion if he acts from honest motives, in pursuit of a good purpose, while under inevitable pressure. As you may guess, this principle of double effect is much debated in Christian ethics.[26]

Eudemonism in the Old Testament

It may seem strange to say that one important purpose in ethics is happiness. We are not speaking of a fleeting, hedonistic, pleasure-seeking happiness, but the enduring happiness and joy that can come from harmonious living with others in the kingdom of God. Biblical eudemonism is related to *shalom*, the peace, harmony, and completeness God desires for his people. Salvation history tells the story of God's blessing. Human beings were originally created happy, harmonious beings. The fall of humanity removed the blessing, causing chaos, shame, aggravation, hatred, and, consequently, unhappiness (lack of joy). Without God and his law, there was no blessing for humanity. Likewise, in the Torah, God promised to bless the land if his commands were obeyed, and he promised to curse it if they were disobeyed (Deuteronomy 11).

It is interesting how blessing is coupled with the fifth commandment: "Honor your father and your mother, so that you may live long in the land the LORD your God is giving you" (Exodus 20:12). Paul remarked that this is the first commandment to which a promise is attached (Ephesians 6:1–3). If children obey their parents, they will enjoy long life on earth. This is not an absolute promise with no exceptions, but a general proverbial rule. Parents are the channel through which God passes down values and norms. The blessing of long life is especially connected with practical

---

25. *Summa Theologica* II-II.64, 7.
26. See P. A. Woodward, *The Doctrine of Double Effect* (Notre Dame: University of Notre Dame Press, 2001).

wisdom. Through wisdom we can live a blessed life (Proverbs 3:16). The eudemonistic ethics found in much of biblical wisdom literature provides a refreshing accompaniment to the juridical framework of commandment ethics. Wisdom is about practical reflection on the laws of God, explaining the commandments and relating principles to tangible purposes. The disposition of the human heart comes to the fore. This link between virtuous living and harmonious happiness is characteristic of biblical eudemonistic ethics.

The book of Proverbs continually emphasizes natural consequences for poor choices. The man who indulges wayward women plunges into misery (Proverbs 2:15–19), and sluggards cause their own destruction (Proverbs 6:15). As the cosmos was created by the wisdom of God (Proverbs 8:22–31), so God's norms are linked with his created order in daily life. God gave a particular order to nature, so living in obedience to God, in accordance with that nature, generally provides earthly happiness. Wisdom is not some kind of philosophical theory. According to Bruce Waltke, *hokmâ* denotes "acting upon moral-spiritual knowledge out of internalization, thereby enabling its possessor to cope with enigma and adversity, to tear down strongholds, and so to promote the life of an individual and/or a community."[27] This type of wisdom is a divine gift that can be acquired only in humility, by those who value it above all other things of life (Proverbs 3:13–18; 8:11–12).

As we noted before, exceptions to eudemonistic "rules" exist, most noticeably in Job and Ecclesiastes. These books underscore the limitations of human understanding and wisdom.[28] Happiness cannot be determined because the unpredictable is always present. But the awareness that we cannot control our own lives is itself wisdom: "In his heart a man plans his course, but the LORD determines his steps" (Proverbs 16:9). The Bible calls us to plan and work hard but at the same time warns us that we cannot always determine our direction. No matter how well we prepare, blessings ultimately come from God in his way and in his time: "The horse is made ready for the day of battle, but victory rests with the LORD" (Proverbs 21:31).

---

27. Bruce K Waltke and Charles Yu, *An Old Testament Theology: An Exegetical, Canonical, and Thematic Approach* (Grand Rapids: Zondervan, 2007), 913.
28. For a classic work on this, see Gerhard von Rad, *Wisdom in Israel*, trans. J. D. Martin (London: SCM Press, 1972).

Jesus called the "weary and burdened" and promised them rest. He claimed that his "yoke is easy" and his "burden is light" (Matthew 11:28–30). Prior to these words, Jesus had said that salvation is hidden from the wise and the learned, but it is revealed to the simple (v. 25). The Son reveals salvation, and the New Covenant brings refreshment (Jeremiah 31:25). The heavy burden represents the commandment ethics practiced by the scribes. Jesus' burden is light because Jesus is gentle and humble in heart, full of grace and wisdom.[29] Jesus promised the full rest of shalom, peace, harmony, and completeness.

Christian eudemonism works in a congruent fashion with obedience to God. Jesus' burden is light, but he still demands that we follow him with heart and mind and soul. Summoning his disciples, he said, "For whoever wants to save his life will lose it, but whoever loses his life for me will find it" (Matthew 16:25). How then does a gracious God who wishes us ultimate happiness fit with the demands of radical discipleship? When the regenerated believer seeks Jesus and his kingdom, it causes an axiological revolution of basic values; and values and purposes, as we have noted, are closely connected. The true follower of Jesus attaches little value to properties and money, realizing that genuine treasures cannot be found on earth (Matthew 6:19–24), but only in service to the Creator.[30]

Character Ethics: A New Creation

The Inner Ethics of Jesus

In the New Testament, virtue ethics comes to the fore more clearly. With Jesus' emphasis on heart attitudes, a shift in accent from commandments to character takes place: "Blessed are the pure in heart, for they will see God" (Matthew 5:8). Evil begins in the human heart (Matthew 5:28; 15:19). For this reason, ethics begins with what we often call the "inner

---

29. Richard Hays points out that Jesus identified himself as wisdom personified (e.g., Proverbs 8 and several intertestamental texts). This perfect, divine wisdom provides the correct interpretation of the Torah. Hays, *Moral Vision*, 100.

30. This is not an "island"-style ethics in which the physical needs of people are ignored. On the contrary, a kingdom view becomes a source of inspiration for social involvement. The sharp contrast between present injustices in society and the biblical promise of shalom inspires the believer to share with others and to seek their happiness. Cf. George Eldon Ladd, *A Theology of the New Testament* (Grand Rapids: Eerdmans, 1993), 46, 64, 65.

self."[31] Disciples can be more righteous than the scribes (Matthew 5:20) by their authenticity and integrity of character. In the Sermon on the Mount, Jesus repudiates a legalistic, outward use of the law that neglects the intentions of the heart. We must not read the Sermon on the Mount with a wooden literalism, or we will miss the entire point of the passage. Loving our enemies is not a matter of simple duty—it is a matter of the heart. Conduct is a manifestation of character. A good tree bears good fruit, and a bad tree bears bad fruit (Matthew 7:15–20).

Like the Ten Commandments, the Sermon on the Mount should be read through the lens and in the context of deliverance. The Father has created a new people, redeemed from the bonds of sin and rescued from the "dominion of darkness" (Colossians 1:13) through the Son's atonement. The law is no longer written on tablets of stone, but on human hearts. The Beatitudes are for disciples of Jesus who adopt a dependent (i.e., "poor in spirit," Matthew 5:3) attitude, with gentleness and mercy. These are virtues of Christian character. So it is not merely an ethics of *doing* but of *being*. People are transformed because God rules in their hearts, and they become "salt and light" in the world. The source of such benevolence is always God's redemptive action, and from this redemptive action flow the tasks and works characteristic of a transformed person. In contrast to a world in rebellion against God, those who are pure in heart, as peacemakers, truly manifest the kingdom of God through virtuous habits.

Virtues in Paul

In Paul's letters we find several enumerations of godly virtues, but perhaps the most familiar is found in Galatians 5:13–26.[32] The virtuous life is described by Paul as living "by the Spirit" (v. 16), or keeping "in step with the Spirit" (v. 25). These expressions indicate continuity, a life habit— a virtue ethics. Typically in Paul's thought, the Spirit stands opposed to the desires of the flesh, the sinful human nature attempting to live apart

---

31. We are not advocating a Cartesian mind-body dualism; we are simply using this term for heuristic purposes.

32. See also Rom. 14:17; 15:4–5; 2 Cor. 6:4–10; Gal. 5:22–23; Eph. 4:2–3; Phil. 2:2–3; Col. 3:12–17. For an overview, see Glen H. Stassen and David P. Gushee, *Kingdom Ethics: Following Jesus in Contemporary Context* (Downers Grove, IL: InterVarsity Press, 2003), 50. In addition to these lists, the requirements for elders and deacons are also given as character qualities (1 Tim. 3:1–13).

from God. This opposition to the flesh is not by any means a repudiation of corporeality, but refers to a person who neglects to embrace Christ's redemption of the body. Those living according to the flesh are still trapped in the old age, under the law, in sin.[33]

Here, Paul also sums up the various effects of the Spirit's work in the lives of believers, describing the "fruit" of the Spirit. The list is not intended to be exhaustive but is given to provide a general direction.[34] It is interesting that Paul speaks of "acts" of the flesh and "fruit" of the Spirit. The former term emphasizes human activity, the latter the transforming action of the Holy Spirit. These virtues do not originate in the natural human being; they require the supernatural work of God.[35] Our capacity to live out these virtues as redeemed people stems from God's pouring his love into us through the Spirit (Romans 5:5). God's Spirit makes us free to serve others radically, in love (Galatians 5:13), within the context of community. The virtues are not primarily for strengthening the individual, but for serving others.[36]

A character or virtue ethics is not in itself the goal, but rather the result of the community of the people of God embodying God's values by remembering his faithfulness throughout salvation history.[37] In the community, God's redeeming and reconciling work is told and retold, lived and relived. The story of God's deliverance of his people from Egypt also becomes our story, as participants in the kingdom story of God. In the earliest church, in the book of Acts, this story is rehearsed over and over again. This "storying" community of God's people nurtures the godly virtues of believers.

---

33. See Gordon D. Fee, *God's Empowering Presence: The Holy Spirit in the Letters of Paul* (Peabody, MA: Hendrickson, 1994), 816–26; and Herman N. Ridderbos, *Paul: An Outline of His Theology*, (Grand Rapids: Eerdmans, 1997), 100–104.

34. Fee, *God's Empowering Presence*, 445.

35. Ibid., 445, 882, 444.

36. James McClendon speaks of the virtue of presence, of being with and for the other. God is there for us, so we must be there for the other. We do not withdraw emotionally and mentally, but we give ourselves up to the other as we are. James William McClendon, *Systematic Theology Vol. 1: Ethics* (Nashville: Abingdon, 1986), 106.

37. See Allen Verhey, *Remembering Jesus: Christian Community, Scripture, and the Moral Life* (Grand Rapids: Eerdmans, 2005), 15–28.

Virtues and Theosis

The virtues are, therefore, especially important for personal spiritual formation. In the second letter of Peter, we find an important list of virtues in the context of faith development. For the theology of the Eastern Orthodox Church, 2 Peter 1:3–8 is a key passage:

> His divine power has given us everything we need for life and godliness through our knowledge of him who called us by his own glory and goodness. Through these he has given us his very great and precious promises, so that through them you may participate in the divine nature and escape the corruption in the world caused by evil desires.
>
> For this very reason, make every effort to add to your faith goodness; and to goodness, knowledge; and to knowledge, self-control; and to self-control, perseverance; and to perseverance, godliness; and to godliness, brotherly kindness; and to brotherly kindness, love. For if you possess these qualities in increasing measure, they will keep you from being ineffective and unproductive in your knowledge of our Lord Jesus Christ.

The words "participate in the divine nature" are central to the Eastern Orthodox doctrine of *theosis*, or deification.[38] Theosis is about ultimate life purpose and the attainment of Christian perfection and sanctification. Humans were created in the image and likeness of God. Perfect harmony with God was lost at the fall of humanity. As a result, the image of God was marred and scarred. The image of God (*imago Dei*) itself, however, which is part of our structural humanness, remained. We must now strive for the restoration of the image of God through theosis. God became a human so that we might become like God. Christ, the new Adam, makes it possible for us to reach this completeness, through the process of sanctification.

The importance of theosis is expressed in Stanley Harakas' definition of Eastern Orthodox ethics: "growth to the likeness of God, the realization of theosis in character, motives, lifestyle, and social life." Theosis makes us

---

38. The concept of theosis dates from Athanasius (AD 296–373), and it was especially developed by Maximus the Confessor (AD 580–662). Cf. Daniel B. Clendenin, *Eastern Orthodox Christianity: A Western Perspective* (Grand Rapids: Baker Academic, 2003), 117–37; Vladimir Lossky, *The Mystical Theology of the Eastern Church* (Crestwood, NY: St. Vladimir's Seminary Press, 1976), 196–216.

fully human.[39] Orthodox theology puts a strong mystical, sacramental, and liturgical accent on the process of theosis.[40] Vigen Guroian emphasizes that in this passage of 2 Peter there is a connection between ethics and the sacraments. Peter speaks about entrance into "the eternal kingdom" (2 Peter 1:11). According to Guroian, "The sacraments are the doors to the eternal Kingdom." The Holy Spirit makes theosis possible through the sacraments.[41]

John Calvin opposed a fanatical and speculative interpretation of this passage that proposed that we could be merged into God himself. For Calvin, such a notion would have more to do with Platonic philosophy than with the teaching of the apostles.[42] Instead, theosis pertains to the Christian's goal of being conformed to the likeness of God and of receiving eternal life.

These qualities of transformation are deeply rooted in Patristic tradition. Participation in the divine nature is not so much a mystical reality as it is an ethical goal. The believer flees from sin and moves more and more toward God-likeness and moral perfection. This faith develops from within the community of faith, through Jesus Christ. We have become children of God through the Son (John 1:12).[43] The human being is to be restored

---

39. Stanley Samuel Harakas, *Toward a Transfigured Life: The Theoria of Eastern Orthodox Ethics* (Minneapolis: Light & Life, 1983), 229.

40. We see this especially in the monastic tradition of *hesychasm* (stillness). It is about transformation through continual contemplative prayer and beholding God. The culminating point of theosis, then, is beholding the divine light. The word *hesychia* literally means "rest" or "silence." It is a prayer method developed in the 14th century on Mount Athos. The most important theologian in this regard is Gregory Palamas (1296–1359).

41. Vigen Guroian, *Incarnate Love: Essays in Orthodox Ethics*, 2nd ed. (Notre Dame: University of Notre Dame Press, 2002), 64.

42. John Calvin, *Commentaries on the Catholic Epistles: Commentary on 2 Peter*, "2 Pet. 1:4." See http://www.ccel.org/ccel/calvin/calcom45.vii.ii.i.html.

43. We propose that this pertains primarily to God's moral character, not to his *substantia* but to his *qualitas*. Ceslas Spicq, *Les épitres de Saint Pierre* (Paris: Lecoffre, 1966), 212; Ceslas Spicq, *Théologie morale du Nouveau Testament* (Paris: Lecoffre, 1965), 94–95. We find this interpretation also in Wesley: "Ye may become partakers of the divine nature—being renewed in the image of God, and having communion with them, so as to dwell in God and God in you." John Wesley, *John Wesley's Notes on the Whole Bible: The New Testament, Notes on the Second Epistle General of St. Peter*, 1:4, http://www.ccel.org/ccel/wesley/notes.i.xxiii.ii.html. The aim in the Wesleyan tradition for moral perfection in love has a certain overlap with the Eastern tradition of theosis. Wesley himself was influenced by the Greek church fathers. See Theodore Runyon, *The New Creation: John Wesley's Theology Today* (Nashville: Abingdon, 1998), 80–81. There are other exegetical possibilities as well. Richard Bauckham

to the image of God. From this perspective, theosis is more about human-ization—becoming authentically human in the *imago Dei* and reflecting God's character—than it is about divinization.

The virtues mentioned in 2 Peter 1 reflect the character of God and are given to us through the Holy Spirit's work in our lives. God is loving, gracious, patient, faithful, and true (Exodus 34:6). Biblical virtue ethics is theocentric and is significantly different from Greek anthropocentric virtue ethics, where the human being acquires virtuous attributes by personal effort. When we live according to Christian virtues through the Spirit, we partake in the divine nature. This is not about ascent to become a "god," but about God's work in us. Faith is often considered the first virtue. It is through faith that we receive access to the divine power needed to live virtuously. Nonetheless, we still make a personal effort to acquire these virtues: "For this very reason, make every effort to add to your faith good-ness" (2 Peter 1:5). The Greek word translated "to add" (*epichorègeoo*) can also mean "to enrich." Faith sponsors the virtues. In this respect there is an unmistakable cooperation between God and us. God gives us all that is necessary for life and godliness, and it is our job to devote ourselves to living virtuously. This cooperation with God's work in our lives forms an inherent part of Christian virtue ethics. Virtues are trained qualities of character, habits that have become part of our nature. In Paul's words, we are created by God "in Christ Jesus to do good works, which God prepared in advance for us to do" (Ephesians 2:10).

The qualities mentioned in 2 Peter 1:5–7—faith, goodness, knowledge, self-control, perseverance, godliness, brotherly kindness, and love—are linked together. As we know from Paul in 1 Corinthians 13:13, we must always keep in mind that "the greatest of these is love."[44] Our ultimate life purpose is to carry the love of the triune God to all people. As the church father Ignatius wrote to the Ephesians, "For the beginning is faith, and the end is love. Now these two, being inseparably connected together, are of God, while all other things which are requisite for a holy life follow after

---

states that this verse pertains to the resurrection, the immortal life. See Richard Bauckham, *Jude, 2 Peter* (Waco, TX: Word Books, 1983), 173.

44. In the Wesleyan tradition, the highest goal of sanctifying grace is perfect love. E.g., Sermon 40, "Christian Perfectionism" on Phil. 3:12; Sermon 89, "The More Excellent Way" on 1 Cor. 12:31; Sermon 139, "On Love," on 1 Cor. 13:3. See John Wesley in *The Works of John Wesley*, vol. 7, ed. Thomas Jackson (Grand Rapids: Zondervan, 1958).

them."[45] Faith marks the beginning of our Christian life, and love binds it together with the virtues in "perfect unity" (Colossians 3:14).

45. Ignatius, *The Epistle of Ignatius to the Ephesians*, chap. 4, in *Ante-Nicene Fathers*, ed. Philip Schaff, vol. 1, *The Apostolic Fathers with Justin Martyr and Irenaeus*, ed. Alexander Roberts and James Donaldson, Christian Classics Ethereal Library, http://www.ccel.org/ccel/schaff/anf01.v.ii.xiv.html.

Chapter 11

Facing Moral Problems

Thinking Through the Matrix

We trust the preceding chapters have shown that the field of ethics is much broader than ethical problems themselves. Nevertheless, we will have done a disservice to the discipline if we simply dodge moral obstacles for the sake of sustained broader reflection. For it is often in the midst of a quandary where our ethics is truly put to the test. People often search for their deepest values, motives, and purposes in times of crisis. With this in mind, we will propose a hypothetical, though nonetheless relevant, case study in biomedical ethics, in order to provide a format for thinking through ethical dilemmas.

Case Study

Six years ago Elisabeth and James lost their only child, a four-year old daughter, in a tragic car accident. After several years of grieving, they are now trying, unsuccessfully, to conceive another child. After testing, and because of a complex combination of physiological factors, they are declared infertile. Elisabeth is thirty-five years old and James is thirty-seven. Time is short. They are offered the possibility of in vitro fertilization (IVF) as a last resort. Desiring to be well informed from physiological and spiritual points of view, they begin poring through the vast literature on this subject in books, articles, and Internet sites.[1] After prolonged reading and talking with trusted friends, pastors, and doctors, they are drowning in information overload. What should they do?

We make no pretensions of being able to solve this dilemma or to exhaust all possible ethical arguments for a particular solution here. We simply want to offer six "phases" to help us navigate through the turbulent sea of an ethical dilemma.[2] These are not miraculous formulas or frameworks into which everything must fit; they are simply useful aspects of ethical reflection that we believe should be considered throughout the decision-making process. Some of these may seem quite obvious and simple in formulation, but they are often difficult or neglected in practice.

Phase 1: Collect Relevant Information

How do we decide what information is and is not relevant? How do we decide what is a reliable source, with the sea of information instantly available to us today? Verifying the truth seems wildly difficult given the absence of checks and balances on the information highway. Both selecting and interpreting information are onerous tasks. Not all information is relevant for making a proper ethical judgment. It is often better to work with a few reliable sources than with a battery of dubious facts. Emotions often get the upper hand, and personal experiences easily become "right" interpretations. Our personal backgrounds, convictions, religious preferences, and cultures all bias our thought processes. The postmodern critique wisely warns us that neutrality is impossible. With this in mind, we still must strive—in the context of our community and with the help of our

---

1. The following literature may be helpful when considering such a dilemma: John F. Kilner, Paige C. Cunningham, and W. David Hager, eds., *The Reproduction Revolution: A Christian Appraisal of Sexuality, Reproductive Technologies, and the Family* (Grand Rapids, Eerdmans, 2000); Sandra Glahn and William Cutrer, *The Infertility Companion: Hope and Help for Couples Facing Infertility* (Grand Rapids: Zondervan, 2004). On the biotechnology revolution and the social debate, see Charles W. Colson and Nigel M. de S. Cameron, eds., *Human Dignity in the Biotech Century: A Christian Vision for Public Policy* (Downers Grove, IL: InterVarsity Press, 2004).

2. Scott B. Rae provides a step-by-step approach to ethical dilemmas, but our approach, as will be seen, is different. Rae limits ethical consideration to "principles" and later evaluates the consequences of each choice separately. We adopt an approach that draws from the insights of Erich Fuchs. See Scott B. Rae, *Moral Choices: An Introduction to Ethics* (Grand Rapids: Zondervan, 2000); Erich Fuchs, *Comment faire pour bien faire? Introduction à l'éthique* (Geneva: Labor et Fides, 1996).

community—to acknowledge our intellectual, emotional, and cultural biases and assumptions.[3]

In the case of Elisabeth and James, they must gain the knowledge necessary to understand the various procedures involved in IVF and embryo transfer.[4] This involves hormonal stimulation of follicle growth and extraction of mature eggs. Pre-embryos come into being through various techniques, and multiple implantations may be used in order to increase the chances of pregnancy. The embryologist judges the quality of the pre-embryos before implantation. If there are several good pre-embryos, the remainder may be frozen for later procedures. The ultimate success of IVF is based on much preliminary examination and the loss of many pre-embryos.

It is not easy to obtain a complete picture of the risks involved in these procedures. There is common agreement, however, that IVF increases the chance of miscarriage. Apart from biological factors, the psychosocial aspects of this treatment must also be considered. Understandably, couples face a great deal of stress during a program of assisted reproduction, and the process often requires several attempts to achieve any results.

Phase 2: Formulate the Particular Ethical Problem(s)

Ethical dilemmas often surface when facing difficult problems that demand quick decisions. This is why ethical reflection is vitally important, despite the urgency of making such decisions. Often an ethical dilemma does not hinge on one distinct moral obstacle, but on a cluster of problems. This becomes clear in our case study. Elisabeth and James clearly desire a child. They have experienced tremendous emotional grief over the loss

---

3. This is not to say that our backgrounds, cultures, and convictions necessarily bias us negatively. We would argue that these are equally used to shape our ethical decisions positively, especially as this pertains to the development of the Christian conscience. The main point we wish to emphasize here is the myth of neutrality with respect to ethical judgment and interpretation.

4. We are thinking of intra-uterine insemination (IUI); intra-cytoplasmatic spermatozoa injection (ICSI), a variation of in vitro fertilization (IVF) in which insemination occurs by means of injecting a good sperm through the wall of the egg (*zona pellucida*); gamete intrafallopian transfer (GIFT), where egg and sperm cells are placed into the fallopian tube laparoscopically; and zygote intrafallopian transfer (ZIFT) in which young pre-embryos, after fertilization in the IVF laboratory, are placed back into the fallopian tube laparoscopically.

of their daughter. Why must the suffering continue if there is potential for conceiving another child? Should they not use all means necessary to alleviate their sorrow? Psychologically, consideration must be given to the relationship between the grieving process of losing a child and the current grief of infertility. If they are able to conceive, will the new child be thought of as a replacement or accepted as a completely unique individual? None of these questions are easy, nor are the answers readily apparent.

Questions also arise because of the nature of assisted reproductive technology (ART) itself. Think about the issue of aggressive interference in the hormonal system necessary to create high follicle production. The artificial character of this treatment is sufficient in itself to require careful reflection. It is also important to consider the moral status of early embryos. Are these merely cellular organisms, or are they actual human persons in embryonic form? Do doctors and embryologists have the right to select between pre-embryos? There are myriad thorny questions that require thorough deliberation and consideration.

The questions become more complex when these issues are discussed in relation to a broader social context. In our particular case study, it is an intensely private matter between Elisabeth and James. In a pluralistic society, would others have the right or responsibility to impose their own values on Elisabeth and James? Is it not the moral task of any society to protect the weak against the selfish acts of the strong? As we can see, many questions arise when we probe the various layers of human concern involved in any particular ethical quandary.

Phase 3: Consider the Problem in View of the Matrix of Commandments, Values, Character, and Consequences

It is important to keep in mind the matrix of moral judgments involved in any given problem. We must gain insight into what role values play and which commandments are involved as well as the character of the persons involved and the possible consequences of various actions.[5] Elisabeth and James highly value family life, or, at minimum, they certainly value having children. But given their current options, the value of parenthood may be in conflict with the value of the life of early embryos. Does the commandment "You shall not murder" (Exodus 20:13) apply to embryos? If

---

5. Cf. Erich Fuchs, *Comment faire*, 53.

not, what are the reasons? Value judgments will be made. Also, what are the personal motives behind these judgments? Are there consequences or risks for the child? With the increased risk of miscarriage, who becomes responsible in such a case?

The relevance of social consequences is also difficult to grasp. The scenario with Elisabeth and James is described more in terms of personal than of social ethics. Nonetheless, there are social questions connected with the story. We must ask ourselves what kind of society we desire to live in and what life values we desire to pass along to the next generation. Although these questions are far from the minds of Elisabeth and James at this juncture, they are questions about the larger scheme of things that we must reflect on.

Phase 4: Consider Alternative Solutions

Some alternative solutions to moral dilemmas may be more expensive or less efficient but, in the long run, may create fewer ethical problems. After moral reflection, Elisabeth and James may choose to remain childless and refrain from employing medical intervention. Such a decision may increase their emotional pain for some time, but it may also reduce the ethical problems involved and, in this case, provide less financial strain. Another possibility would be an adjusted medical treatment. Elisabeth may be helped by intensive hormonal treatments. Or they may decide to inseminate only one egg, preventing the loss of additional embryos. Granted, the chances of success would significantly decrease, but the ethical conundrums would seem to decrease as well. Adoption is another alternative that deserves consideration, but it would have its own psychosocial factors to consider. Our intention is not to overwhelm the reader with a barrage of questions. We simply wish to accentuate the importance of thorough reflection in the four areas of commands, values, character (or virtues), and consequences, when it comes to ethical dilemmas.

Phase 5: Make a Decision

In one sense, this is not actually a part of the process of ethical decision making, but rather the culmination of the process. As obvious as it may seem, ultimately a choice must courageously be made, even though we have not exhausted all possible resources or gained comprehensive understanding of the issue. In fact, attaining exhaustive understanding is beyond our ability. We must make decisions while embracing our finite ways of being and thinking. With Qoheleth, we understand that life is an enigma; we cannot fathom what God does from beginning to end.[6] But our struggle for understanding must still continue. In the fear of the Lord, we responsibly seek God's direction, with the resources we have been given in the counsel of Scripture, the Holy Spirit, and the Christian community.[7] Moreover, decision making must always be done in the context of prayer. It is normal that we should present our difficulties, worries, requests, and dilemmas to God (Philippians 4:6). Prayer does not remove the hard work of the decision-making process, but the Holy Spirit must always be invited into the process.

Phase 6: Evaluate

After the decision is made, it is important to reflect earnestly on our decision, while observing the consequences.[8] Sometimes we may have the opportunity to adjust or reconsider our decision in view of unforeseen circumstances. Erich Fuchs suggests that we must "learn to learn" through this evaluation process. Only those who regularly practice this painstaking discipline will morally develop, and only the society that dares to evaluate itself is just. The virtue of humility is essential for thorough evaluation. We must always be willing to admit our mistakes in ethical decisions. Our motives are often ambiguous, so they require consistent evaluation. Along with humility, repentance and forgiveness are intrinsic virtues for a believer committed to making courageous choices in ethical dilemmas.

Moral Antinomies

How can we discern God's will in a given scenario if two command-ments appear to be in conflict? Think about medical grounds for the termi-nation of pregnancy when the lives of both mother and child are in danger. Should the physician intervene with an abortion in order to spare the life of the mother? The midwives of Egypt brought Hebrew children into the world in secrecy. Pharaoh called them to account, and they came up with

---

6. Ecclesiastes 3:10–13.

7. Erich Fuchs mentions the virtue of courage in making a decision. Fuchs, *Comment faire*, 53.

8. Fuchs, *Comment faire*, 55–66. We are not suggesting that all the consequences are made evident to us following any given decision. Sometimes only the immediate consequences are observed. Others will be concealed or only experienced much later.

the following excuse: "Hebrew women are not like Egyptian women; they are vigorous and give birth before the midwives arrive" (Exodus 1:19). God blessed them for what they did. Rahab hid the Israelite spies and lied to her own people (Joshua 2). Yet she is specifically praised in the New Testament for her brave deed: "Was not even Rahab the prostitute considered righteous for what she did when she gave lodging to the spies and sent them off in a different direction?" (James 2:25).

The brave lies of the Dutch Resistance saved the lives of thousands of Jewish people during the Second World War. German theologian, pastor, and ethicist Helmut Thielicke cites several horrible dilemmas from the Second World War in which suffering and guilt could not be avoided. Prisoners in concentration camps were sometimes forced to indicate within minutes which of their fellow prisoners were to be deemed "useless" and therefore killed. If this did not happen quickly enough, the SS unit would kill an even larger number of people. Sometimes prisoners committed suicide to prevent betraying their friends.[9] We recall the German industrialist Oskar Schindler, who made agreements with the SS in order to save the lives of many of the Jews who entered his employment.[10]

In a war-torn, troubled world where moral chaos often reigns, how do we respond to such moral antinomies? As Zygmunt Bauman puts it, "Human reality is messy and ambiguous."[11] But the grand mistake of modernism is the illusion that this messiness of humanity is simply temporary, until the rule of reason with its principled foundations takes precedence. The postmodern thorn in the side of modernity uncovers this illusion and reveals that this messiness is here to stay, with ambiguity regaining its lost respect.[12] But how can we respect ambiguity, as Christians seeking ethical answers? There have been various proposals. Some simply refuse the ambiguity altogether; others affirm the ambiguity but argue for making the best choice possible with the means available; others suggest that as technical rules do not lead us down the path of love, we must simply use Christ's love as the litmus test for all moral choices. These various proposals that have been advanced through the years are known in ethical discourse as situation ethics, absolutism, conflicting absolutism, and ethical hierarchicalism.

---

9. Helmut Thielicke, *Theological Ethics* (Grand Rapids: Eerdmans, 1979), 578–647.
10. See Thomas Fensch, *Oskar Schindler and His List* (Forest Dale, VT: Paul S. Eriksson, 1995).
11. Zygmunt Bauman, *Postmodern Ethics* (Oxford: Blackwell, 1993), 32.
12. Ibid., 32–33.

Situation Ethics

The theological problem of moral conflicts was made unmistakably evident in the liberation culture of the sixties, by *Situation Ethics,* the best-selling book of Joseph Fletcher (1905–1991).[13] Fletcher's work was a reaction against the rigid conservative legalism often displayed in Christianity with its various commandments and prohibitions. For Fletcher, commandment ethics constructs systems and functions like a straitjacket. He wished to liberate Christian ethics from this legalism, without ending up in antinomianism. Ethics always includes norms and values. But Fletcher proposed a middle road: a one-commandment ethic of love (*agape*). In each and every situation, we are obligated to apply love. According to Fletcher, there is no need for general ethics, which then needs to be applied to specific situations. The only reality is the moment of decision and the consideration of consequences that do or do not demonstrate Christian love. In this regard, situation ethics fit well with the sinking moral climate of the sixties.

The basic assumption is that love fulfills the law (Romans 13:8). Fletcher agreed with Augustine that we can reduce Christian ethics to one maxim, "Love with care and *then* what you will, do," assuming, of course, that we have the mind of Christ.[14] There is only one universal law; all others are relative principles that are contextually connected to this one commandment. As Fletcher put it, "We cannot milk universals from a universal!"[15] Fletcher removed the dialectic tension between law and love. In situation ethics, the twilight of the law disappears in the sun of love.

He illustrated this perspective with a story of a tragic moral conflict faced by a woman in a Russian prisoner-of-war camp in the Ukraine. A woman received a message that her husband and children had survived the war. She discovered that the Russians would release her if she was pregnant, because she would be a burden for the camp. In order to reunite with her husband and children, she attempted to get pregnant by having sexual relations with a man in the camp. In Fletcher's view, this act was not an

---

13. Joseph Fletcher, *Situation Ethics: The New Morality* (Philadelphia: Westminster Press, 1966).

14. Joseph Fletcher, *Situation Ethics: The New Morality*, 2nd ed. (Louisville: Westminster John Knox, 1997), 79.

15. Fletcher, *Situation Ethics* (1997), 27; see also Joseph Fletcher, "Three Approaches," in *From Christ to the World: Introductory Readings in Christian Ethics*, ed. Wayne G. Boulton, Thomas D. Kennedy, and Allen Verhey (Grand Rapids: Eerdmans, 1994), 208.

immoral deed because she sacrificed herself sexually out of love for her husband and children.[16]

The merit of situation ethics is, undoubtedly, its personalistic character. Love for the neighbor rightly receives a prominent place. Fletcher attempted to formulate a contemporary ethic in the climate of the 1960s without skirting difficult questions. He also effectively challenged the often-inhumane application of law ethics, without resorting to an overly simplistic subjectivism. But is an individual's perception of authentic love enough? Can Fletcher's situation ethics avoid an emotionally laden or capricious ethic? He presupposes the uniqueness of each situation, but is each situation truly *that* unique? In reality, there are significant similarities among the various ethical situations we encounter. Fletcher himself cited many telling examples.[17] His anecdotes stimulate our imaginations so that we think readily of analogous situations that we have faced.

Fletcher seems to have unnecessarily dissociated commandments and love. For the believer, obeying God's commands is an expression of love (1 John 2:3–5; 5:3). As Jochem Douma explains, "Love and commands are connected like yeast and dough; yeast must saturate the dough in order to get good bread."[18] Similarly, the apostle John cites Jesus as saying, "If you obey my commands, you will remain in my love" (John 15:10). Simply because legalism is usually absent in love does not imply that all laws themselves are inherently unloving. Parents impose many laws on their children, not out of selfish ambition but for loving protection. In the arena of social ethics, commitment to a simple love-commandment situationism presents enormous problems. How can we legislate criminal laws or basic traffic regulations with only one overarching law of love?

Absolutism

Christian absolutism stands diametrically opposed to situational ethics. For the absolutist, all of God's commands are perfect, just, absolute, and universal. God never requires us to sin against him or his law. So if we simply follow his commands, we will be doing the right thing. Ethical dilemmas are simply misperceptions due to lack of insight, lack of faith,

---

16. Fletcher, *Situation Ethics* (1997), 143.

17. Ibid., 82–83.

18. Jochem Douma, *Grondslagen christelijke ethiek* (Kampen, Neth.: Kok, 1999), 299; translation ours.

or a downright sinful perspective. There are no real ethical conflicts. God will always provide a way out of an apparent dilemma by providing the capacity to choose the good. "No temptation has seized you except what is common to man. And God is faithful; he will not let you be tempted beyond what you can bear. But when you are tempted, he will also provide a way out so that you can stand up under it" (1 Corinthians 10:13). Daniel, for example, kept all of God's commands, and he resisted all temptations to compromise. As we know, his faith and obedience to God protected him and his friends in the most extreme situations (e.g., Daniel 3). Augustine also argued along these lines, submitting that God did not bless Rahab on account of her lie, but because of the charity she demonstrated to the spies from Israel. If God allowed lying in order to suit a holy purpose, what would prevent stealing and adultery to be used for some other righteous cause?[19]

In moral philosophy, Kant's deontological ethics is a form of absolutism, since for him, moral duty is universal and timeless. Kant argued that no exception can be made to the rule of always speaking truthfully, even in order to protect the life of another. By lying to another we commit an injustice to all persons, because lying runs counter to the universal principle of righteousness.[20] This perspective is consistent with Kant's deontological ethics and his pietistic background. This view of the absoluteness of God's commands paves the way for an absolutist (and inflexible) ethics of reason.

Absolutism is common in more pietistic circles and in evangelicalism. One representative theologian of this perspective is John Murray (1898–1975) from Westminster Seminary.[21] His discourses are reminiscent of Augustine, emphasizing the commandments as consistent with God's intent in creating. The commandments are formulated in the negative because they are a response to the sinfulness of humanity. Ultimately, however, they are an expression of God's mercy. The Christian lives out of

---

19. Augustine, *Against Lying* (*Contra Mendacium*), 32, in vol. 3 of *Nicene and Post-Nicene Fathers,* ed. Philip Schaff, Christian Classics Ethereal Library, http://www.ccel.org/ccel/schaff/npnf103.v.vi.xxxiii.html.

20. Immanuel Kant, "On a Supposed Right to Lie Because of Philanthropic Concerns," in *Ethical Philosophy: Grounding for the Metaphysics of Morals and Metaphysical Principles of Virtue,* trans. James Wesley Ellington (Indianapolis: Hackett Publishing, 1995), 162–70; and Kant, *Ethical Philosophy,* 14–15. Also see Christine M. Korsgaard, "The Right to Lie: Kant on Dealing with Evil," in Stephen L. Darwall, ed., *Deontology* (Malden, MA: Blackwell, 2003), 212–31.

21. John Murray, *Principles of Conduct,* 2nd ed. (Grand Rapids: Eerdmans, 1991).

a deep respect for the law of God, without exceptions. But, according to Murray, God is sovereign. In a moral dilemma, God always provides a third alternative. If no solution arises, this is not the fault of God but springs from our own sinfulness.

Ultimately, absolutism leans on three propositions. First of all, God's character is immutable, so his commands are absolute. Second, rules are prior to results. Consequentialism is defeated by principle ethics in this perspective. Third, God's providence will always provide a way out of potentially sinful situations.[22]

The strength of this position is, without a doubt, its steadfast trust in God and its commitment to his commands, seeing God's commands as a merciful gift to help us along in the journey of life. Indeed, this should be our point of departure. But is the brokenness of the world underestimated by absolutism? Following absolutism, we might be inclined to approach the Bible as a handbook with answers to all imaginable dilemmas. There might be a tendency to make Christian ethics withdrawn and absent of influence on the social and political dimensions of everyday life. A full-orbed Christian ethic must take into account the matrix not only of commands and virtues but also of character and consequences.

An absolutist view of moral decision making often results in rigid legalism, in which the letter of the law becomes more important than the spirit of the law. This influences how particular ethical decisions are justified. We may convince ourselves that communicating a partial truth, rather than uttering a lie in a given situation, is justified according to the law. For instance, Augustine believed that Abraham was not lying to Pharaoh about his wife Sarah's being his sister in Genesis 20.[23] Sarah was indeed his half sister. Yet he told only half the truth, for she was both his wife *and* his sister. This raises the question, Is not a half-truth still a lie when the intention is to mislead or deceive?[24]

In the case of Rahab's lie, we are nowhere in Scripture presented with an evaluation of the morality of the particular lie itself, nor is the situation presented as a moral dilemma. The dilemma arises from our interpretation of the text and a desire to carry presuppositions from one text—"Do not

---

22. Norman L. Geisler, *Christian Ethics* (Grand Rapids: Baker, 1989). The third proposition would not apply to Kant's version of absolutism.

23. Augustine, *Against Lying* (*Contra Mendacium*), 23.

24. Cf. Norman L Geisler, *Christian Ethics*, 82, 90, 122.

lie" (Leviticus 19:11)—to another text—"In the same way, was not even Rahab the prostitute considered righteous for what she did when she gave lodging to the spies and sent them off in a different direction?" (James 2:25). In order to square the two texts, the absolutist must deny a justification of Rahab's deceitfulness by positing that only her deed of hiding the spies and her trust in God were to be praised.[25] The book of James, however, seems to praise her for the complete deed, which included both concealing and lying. We are not convinced that a sole appeal to absolutism, with its legalistic interpretive methodology, provides a satisfactory response to the rich complexities of such situations.

Conflicting Absolutism

The model of conflicting absolutism has roots in the Lutheran theology of the cross. In this model, the human being is simultaneously sinful and righteous. For this reason, we need the forgiveness of the cross over and over again. Eventually, we will receive total forgiveness and sanctification when we are dressed in white and cleansed by the blood of Christ (Revelation 3:5). Moral absolutes will continue in eschatological tension until the redemption of humanity and creation. A conflicting absolutist accepts the reality of the tragic in everyday life, acknowledging both the ambivalence of this world and the interim character of Christian ethics.[26]

This perspective experienced a serious revival during and after the Second World War. The devastation of war made people acutely aware of sin and guilt—a guilt that could be removed only by the cross of Christ. Lutheran theologians Helmut Thielicke and Dietrich Bonhoeffer were both deeply impacted by this dark period of history. Bonhoeffer was executed shortly before the end of the war for his involvement in a conspiracy to assassinate Hitler. He became a personification of the Christian tragedy in ethics. He understood that he was supposed to obey the civil government, yet he was keenly aware of its atrocities. Sometimes in extreme situations there is conflict between basic life necessities, and life becomes a matter of being or not being for others. Responsible action in extraordinary situations means that we leave behind the safe domain of laws and principles. In such rare cases, the *ultima ratio* lies beyond the laws of reason. But principles

---

25. Again, if hiding is also a nonpropositional deception, then we still have not escaped the dilemma.

26. Thielicke, *Theological Ethics*, 576.

are not annulled. In the drama of life, we must be deeply aware that in some cases a law has been violated and guilt is unavoidable.[27] According to Bonhoeffer a readiness to take guilt on ourselves is the essence of responsibility. Responsible action means both "willingness to become guilty" and freedom to act.[28] Jesus himself is our supreme example. He was not obsessed with his own goodness, but he came to earth out of love, to serve human beings in their brokenness.[29] He entered into human guilt, took the guilt of humankind on himself, and became for us the "sinless-guilty one."[30] All responsible conduct is rooted in this Jesus. Bonhoeffer shunned any form of self-righteousness, which is often characteristic of both absolutism and graded absolutism, which seem to place personal innocence above responsibility for other human beings. Such models are estranged from both the concreteness of human existence and the mystery of Jesus Christ.[31]

The conflicting absolutist model takes seriously the severity of ethical problems in the world, maintaining a commitment to the importance and legitimacy of God's commands and equally affirming complete dependence on Christ. For some, this model paints a picture of a chaotic world of paradox and dialectic, rather than of logic and coherence. What some see as a weakness, proponents of this model see as its strength. After all, our perspectives and knowledge are extremely limited. Our theological expression must be sensitive to mystery and make conscious use of the paradoxes of our existence.[32] In order truly to embrace God's magnificence, we must remain in touch with our own finitude. Yet conflicting absolutists must not resign themselves to the inevitability of sinful behavior. If so, moral dilemmas may not get the committed and honest reflection they deserve. It is essential to guard against a view of "cheap grace" (see Romans 6:1), neglecting the Christian's call to holiness (Matthew 5:48; 1 Thessalonians 5:23) through an ongoing process of sanctification.

---

27. Dietrich Bonhoeffer, *Ethics*, ed. Clifford Green, trans. Reinhard Krauss et al. (Minneapolis: Fortress, 2005), 272–73.

28. Ibid., 275.

29. Bonhoeffer cited Matthew 19:17; see *Ethics*, 240.

30. *Ethics*, 275.

31. Bonhoeffer disliked the pietistic attempt to save Protestantism as "religion." See Georg Huntemann, *The Other Bonhoeffer: An Evangelical Reassessment of Dietrich Bonhoeffer*, trans. Todd Huizinga (Grand Rapids: Baker, 1993), 100.

32. A superb example of this is in the writings of the religious philosopher Søren Kierkegaard.

Jesus faced this tragic world without sin, yet he understood the power and persuasive nature of sin: "For we do not have a high priest who is unable to sympathize with our weaknesses, but we have one who has been tempted in every way, just as we are—yet was without sin" (Hebrews 4:15). The key lies primarily in the expression "just as we are." But if Jesus avoided the tragic consequences of sinful compromise, was he indeed tempted "just as we are"? If he was always able to make the right choice, does this not lead us back to the absolutist model? Thielicke suggests that Christ, in the humility and accommodation of the incarnation, was guarded from all forms of compromise in a miraculous fashion. The "just as we are" was thus limited and not completely analogous with the general tragedy of humankind in sin. Christ was without sin; therefore, he transcended even his accommodation of becoming a man. For he was also the God who stood above all laws and willingly condescended to us.[33]

Ethical Hierarchicalism

The brokenness of the world around us, which is due to the effects of sin, compels us to come to a compromise when facing moral dilemmas. The model of ethical hierarchicalism helps us make the best compromise, even though the best may seem to us merely a lesser evil. However, because choices are required of us in the context of a fallen creation, guilt is not associated with these choices, assuming they are made in the context of biblical wisdom. In reaching the wisest compromise, then, God is obeyed. Jesus consistently made choices that had strong ethical implications for his day. He neglected to remain close to his parents at the Passover Feast in Jerusalem (Luke 2:41–52), and he apparently violated the Jewish Sabbath law (Mark 3:1–6). Jesus fully understood the idea of choosing the greater good in various contexts, and he did so without guilt.

There are nuanced understandings of this model. Norman Geisler at first suggested using the term *hierarchicalism* and later argued for the term *graded absolutism* or *ethical hierarchicalism*.[34] Geisler submits that all commands are absolute in their source and application. In this manner he clearly distinguishs his view from that of situation ethics with its one

---

33. Thielicke, *Theological Ethics*, 575.
34. He adjusted the nomenclature to prevent what he saw as a danger in a contextual approach of hierarchies in which norms become relative. See Geisler, *Christian Ethics*, 76, 116.

absolute command of love. In the hierarchical model there is a hierarchy of absolute commands. Although a higher command is of greater importance than a lower one, the absolute character of the lower command is not denied. Geisler provides this example: "Just as a magnet does not break the law of gravity in attracting a nail, killing in self-defense does not violate the law of respect and preservation of human beings."[35] But at this point we should ask, Should emphasis be placed on the absoluteness of commands or on the relevance of application of commands in particular life situations? Does it really make sense to describe absolute commands that, in given a scenario, will not and should not be followed in view of a higher absolute command?

The hierarchical model presupposes a gradation of lower and higher moral laws. Other models may not deny this presupposition, but in those models, the distinction is less fundamental. We find such divisions in Old Testament laws. For instance, a distinction is made between unintentional and deliberate sins (Leviticus 4:1–2; 5:15). It is obvious that not everything is regarded as equally evil. The punishment for theft is less severe than that for murder. Moral atrocities such as incest and bestiality receive the death penalty (Leviticus 20), but sexual relations before marriage only require the sinner to marry and pay a fine to the father of the girl (Exodus 22:16). When God shows the sins of Israel to Ezekiel in the temple vision, a gradation of sins is made (Ezekiel 8). When Pilate asks Jesus if he knows that Pilate has the power either to set Jesus free or to condemn him to the cross, Jesus replies, "You would have no power over me if it were not given to you from above. Therefore the one who handed me over to you is guilty of a greater sin" (John 19:11). Jesus also teaches that some matters of the law are more important than others (Matthew 22:36; 23:23). He is often concerned with bringing a right gradation to the hierarchy of moral demands (Matthew 10:37).

Yet in other contexts all sin appears to be equal. For instance, in the Sermon on the Mount, Jesus says, "But I tell you that anyone who looks at a woman lustfully has already committed adultery with her in his heart" (Matthew 5:28). Here Jesus is not speaking to the degree of the seriousness of individual sins; he is using hyperbole to make a clear point about the source of sin (the human heart). In a similar fashion, James writes, "For whoever keeps the whole law and yet stumbles at just one point is guilty of

---

35. Geisler, *Christian Ethics*, 129.

breaking all of it" (James 2:10). James resists a selective use of the law and emphasizes that the law is unified. In this context he stresses the primacy of love, or, more concretely, the primacy of mercy for the weak.[36] Again, it is essential to remember that commandments always represent values. We are required to obey the civil government, but if that same government attempts to force us to worship idols or murder innocent people, we are morally obliged to disobey the law (Romans 13:1–2; Titus 3:1; 1 Peter 2:13; cf. Daniel 3:16–18).[37]

When considering a hierarchy of moral laws and making compromises, the love commandment of Jesus must always be at the forefront (Matthew 22:37–40). We must have an enduring commitment to both God and neighbor.[38] For the sake of Jesus' love, we always desire to minimize evil in making choices for the good in a broken world. Rarely is the commandment of love for God in conflict with the commandment of love for the neighbor. But in such cases, we must obey God rather than other people (Acts 5:29).

Moral crises often leave us in a state of desperation for answers. Character ethics often meets principle ethics head-on. We are called to humility, maintaining a proper conscience before God, bringing everything to him in prayer within the wise counsel of Christian community (Proverbs 15:22). The heart of biblical righteousness is always located in God's grace and patient love. Jonah thought he completely understood what God would do to Nineveh, based on his own view of God's righteousness and judgment. But ultimately he failed to understand the wideness of God's grace and mercy. As Qoheleth the Teacher writes in Ecclesiastes, "Do not be overrighteous, neither be overwise—why destroy yourself?" (Ecclesiastes

---

36. L. Floor refers to the Jewish tradition in which refraining from care for the weak is equal to manslaughter (Sirach 34:24–27). See L. Floor, *Jakobus: brief van een broeder* (Kampen, Neth.: Centraal Boekhuis, 1992), 98.

37. The complex themes of civil disobedience and pacifism are certainly important to consider. See Richard B. Hays, *The Moral Vision of the New Testament: A Contemporary Introduction to New Testament Ethics* (San Francisco: HarperSanFrancisco, 1996); John Howard Yoder, *The Politics of Jesus: Vicit Agnus Noster*, 2nd ed. (Grand Rapids: Eerdmans, 1994), 193–211.

38. This central point in Wesley's doctrine of perfection is often misunderstood. It concerns God's gracious work in our lives, which makes us more and more dedicated to him. This is not about a complete angelic spotlessness where we are incapable of making mistakes. Theodore Runyon, *The New Creation: John Wesley's Theology Today* (Nashville: Abingdon, 1998), 91–101.

7:16). The ethical hierarchical model identifies itself with the tragic condition of humankind while also resisting the utopian legalism lurking behind absolutism.

Christian Freedom and Adiaphora

The term *adiaphora* (matters of indifference) is derived from Stoic philosophy and refers to things that belong neither to virtue nor to vice, but are rather neutral. Nowadays it is most commonly used for gray areas in the Christian life that Scripture does not address with a command or prohibition.[39] But is anything in itself truly *adiaphora*? The postmodern critique has wisely alerted us to the myth of pure neutrality. Our daily decisions can never be decontextualized; they are always situated. The design, make, and color of a particular automobile I purchase may be an *adiaphoron* and, as such, not subject to moral judgment. Such considerations may have only economic and aesthetic aspects. But if I choose a red car for the purpose of appearing powerful and chic, to impress my peers, then moral evaluation is certainly in order. If the decision is whether to purchase an automobile or to feed my family, this presents an entirely different set of values and circumstances for consideration. *Adiaphora*, then, may be used positively or negatively. Wealth and power, for example, can be used to destroy people or used to provide charitable aid and to make sound use of economic resources.

Martin Luther's associate Philip Melanchthon (1497–1560) also used the term *adiaphora* to deal with elements of faith having neither commands nor prohibitions in the Bible. For Melanchthon and his followers, *adiaphora* meant conceding to Roman Catholicism on matters of icons, liturgical differences, and church government. Other Lutheran theologians strongly disagreed, contending that nothing could be neutral for God.[40]

Regardless, we want to avoid the scrupulous extremism of asking whether God desires us to drink coffee or tea or to wear brown or blue socks for the day. Perhaps we should consider an alternative term: *diaphero*. This refers to that which is "superior" (Romans 2:18) and to discerning

---

39. See Carl F. H. Henry, *Christian Personal Ethics* (Grand Rapids: Eerdmans, 1957), 428.
40. Douma, *Grondslagen christelijke ethiek*, 279. Also see J. F. Johnson, "Adiaphora, Adiaphorists," *Evangelical Dictionary of Theology*, 2nd ed., ed. Walter A. Elwell (Grand Rapids, Baker Academic, 2001).

"what is best" (Philippians 1:10).[41] Although this word has the same stem as *adiaphora, diaphero* does not refer to neutrality but to the intentions of love and wisdom. Discerning that which is superior or best has everything to do with true Christian freedom. The principle of *diaphero* relates character ethics with value perception and the evaluation of consequences. Our habits of temperance and prudence are often exposed in little moments of our daily lives. Christian spirituality and ethics are completely merged. It is a matter of wisdom to discern how we use our Christian freedom in different situations.

In Scripture we find many freedoms with respect to eating and drinking (e.g., Romans 14; 1 Corinthians 8; 1 Timothy 4) and the celebration of religious festivals (Romans 14:5; Galatians 4:10; Colossians 2:16). In many cases this is about freedom with respect to various human rules. The apostle Paul often abandoned detailed legislation and Pharisaic casuistry. Richard Hays notes that we can find various elements of Paul's ethic in the popular Hellenistic wisdom and Judaism of the day, but these sources play no significant role in Paul's overall ethical reflection. Rather, Paul focused his ethics simply on two elements: the unity of the community, and the imitation of Christ. It is within this christological paradigm that the believer is to discern what is and is not important.[42] It is with Christ himself, rather than with a set of rules, that the most important framework for Christian ethical freedom comes.

Two important passages in Paul's first letter to the Corinthians are significant here: "'Everything is permissible for me'—but I will not be mastered by anything" (1 Corinthians 6:12) and "'Everything is permissible'—but not everything is beneficial. 'Everything is permissible'—but not everything is constructive" (1 Corinthians 10:23). Christian freedom is not simply neutral. We must always ask ourselves if our actions correspond with our deepest Christian values and spiritual development or whether they are the product of desires that seek to be our masters, instead of God. Once again, in these passages the love commandment becomes central.[43] The norm is love: "You, my brothers, were called to be free. But do not use

---

41. This term is proposed by the Dutch Reformed theologians Willem H. Velema and Jochem Douma. Willem H. Velema, *Oriëntatie in de christelijke ethiek* (The Hague: Boekencentrum, 1990), 115; Jochem Douma, *Responsible Conduct: Principles of Christian Ethics* (Phillipsburg, NJ: P & R Publishing, 2003), 172–73.

42. Hays, *Moral Vision*, 41.

43. Cf. Henry, *Christian Personal Ethics*, 429.

your freedom to indulge the sinful nature; rather, serve one another in love"
(Galatians 5:13).

Concluding Thoughts

It is obvious at this juncture that with our proposed matrix approach
we have not committed to one particular process for making ethical decisions. If you were looking for a book that would provide answers to all the
tough moral questions, perhaps you have come to our conclusion with
major disappointment. Yet answers or no answers, we firmly believe that
we must still courageously make ethical decisions in the mucky waters we
live in. Simply to postpone or defer all ethical decisions for lack of fully
determinate understanding would be a moral travesty.

Modernism's ethical structures created disappointment because they
forsook the human person in all its complexity for a machine of ethical
codes.[44] Postmodernism's critique and unveiling of this deception equally
disappoints the person who has been habitually trained and indoctrinated
into thinking that all answers must be given, obtained, mastered, and
practiced to the letter of the law. But simply to give in to the temptation of
despair is to take the postmodern revelation too far.

We did not write this book to create despair and frustration, but we
rather aspired to impart hope in the midst of the "unknowability" of the
enigma of life, in which we "cannot fathom what God has done from beginning to end" (Ecclesiastes 3:11). We believe the moral codes of modernity
created a false hope, a hope not in our loving Lord Jesus, but in idolatrous
structures of moral reason in the guise of Christianity. At the same time, we
have not denied a great appreciation for many who have preceded us in the
rigors of Christian ethical discourse and practice. We have attempted, with
all our limitations, to be as fair minded as possible.

Christian ethics is not found in rationalistic codes that ultimately
depersonalize it. Our modest goal has been to repersonalize ethics without
abandoning commandments, principles, virtues, or values. Christian ethics
requires a matrix of interconnections and possibilities to set it free from
such depersonalization. As Zygmunt Bauman aptly states, "To let morality
out of the stiff armor of the artificially constructed ethical codes (or abandoning the ambition to keep it there), means to *re-personalize* it." If we are

---

44. See Bauman, *Postmodern Ethics*, 33–34, 247–48.

to truly repersonalize Christian ethics, we must return "moral responsibility from the finishing line (to which it was exiled) to the starting point (where it is at home) of the ethical process"; that is, it must be "somehow rooted in the very way we humans are."[45] For Christ followers, this means that we must ultimately tie our ethics to a renewed image of God in the human person, within the context of the community of Christ. This is truly where all ethical hope lies.

45. Ibid., 34.

Bibliography

Afflerbach, Horst. *Handbuch christiche Ethik*. Wuppertal, Germany: Brockhaus, 2002.

Aiken, Henry David. *Reasons and Conduct: New Bearings in Moral Philosophy*. New York: Knopf, 1962.

Aristotle. *Nicomachean Ethics*, translated by Martin Ostwald. Indianapolis: Bobbs-Merrill, 1975.

Arrington, Robert L. *Western Ethics: An Historical Introduction*. Oxford: Blackwell, 1998.

Augustine. *The City of God*, edited by Philip Schaff, translated by Marcus Dods. Vol. 2 of *Nicene and Post-Nicene Fathers: First Series*. Peabody, MA: Hendrickson, 1994.

———. *Contra Mendacium*. In vol. 3 of *Nicene and Post-Nicene Fathers*, edited by Philip Schaff. Christian Classics Ethereal Library. http://www.ccel.org/ccel/schaff/npnf103.v.vi.xxxiii.html.

———. *Of the Morals of the Catholic Church*, translated by Richard Stothert. In vol. 4 of *Nicene and Post-Nicene Fathers*, edited by Philip Schaff. Revised and edited for New Advent by Kevin Knight. http://www.newadvent.org/fathers/1401.htm.

Barbour, Ian Graeme. *Ethics in an Age of Technology*. San Francisco: HarperSanFrancisco, 1993.

Barth, Karl, *Ethics*, edited by Dietrich Braun, translated by Geoffrey W. Bromiley. New York: Seabury Press, 1981.

Bauman, Zygmunt. *Postmodern Ethics*. Oxford: Blackwell, 1993.

Benson, Bruce Ellis. *Graven Ideologies: Nietzsche, Derrida and Marion on Modern Idolatry*. Downers Grove, IL: InterVarsity Press, 2002.

Bentham, Jeremy. *An Introduction to the Principles of Morals and Legislation*, edited by J. H. Burns and H. L. A. Hart. Oxford: Clarendon Press, 1996.

Bonhoeffer, Dietrich. *The Cost of Discipleship*. London: SCM Press, 2001.

———. *Discipleship*. Vol. 4 of *Dietrich Bonhoeffer Works*, translated by Barbara Green and Reinhard Krauss. Minneapolis: Fortress, 2001.

———. *Ethics*, translated by Neville Horton Smith. New York: Macmillan, 1965.

————. *Ethics*, edited by Clifford Green, translated by Reinhard Krauss et al. Minneapolis: Fortress, 2005.

Boyd, Craig A. *A Shared Morality: A Narrative Defense of Natural Law Ethics*. Grand Rapids: Brazos, 2007.

Brown, William P., ed. *The Ten Commandments: The Reciprocity of Faithfulness*. Louisville: Westminster John Knox, 2004.

Brunner, Emil. *The Divine Imperative: A Study in Christian Ethics*, Translated by Olive Wyon. London: Lutterworth Press, 1937.

————. *The Divine Imperative: A Study in Christian Ethics*, translated by Olive Wyon. Cambridge: Lutterworth Press, 2002.

Burgess, John P. "Reformed Explication of the Ten Commandments." Pages 78–99 in *The Ten Commandments: The Reciprocity of Faithfulness*, edited by William P. Brown. Louisville: Westminster John Knox, 2004.

Burggraeve, Roger. *Ethiek & passie: Over de radicaliteit van christelijk engagement*. Tielt, Belgium: Lannoo, 2000.

————. "'No One Can Save Oneself without Others': An Ethic of Liberation in the Footsteps of Emmanuel Levinas." Pages 13–65 in *The Awakening of the Other: A Provocative Dialogue with Emmanuel Levinas*, edited by Roger Burggraeve. Leuven, Belgium: Peeters, 2008.

Burridge, Richard A. *Imitating Jesus: An Inclusive Approach to New Testament Ethics*. Grand Rapids: Eerdmans, 2007.

Cahoone, Lawrence, ed. *From Modernism to Postmodernism*. Cambridge, MA: Blackwell, 1996.

Caputo, John D. *Against Ethics: Contributions to a Poetics of Obligation with Constant Reference to Deconstruction*. Bloomington and Indianapolis: Indiana University Press, 1993.

————. *Philosophy and Theology*. Nashville: Abingdon, 2006.

Childs, Brevard S. *Old Testament Theology in a Canonical Context*. Philadelphia: SCM Press, 1985.

Clendenin, Daniel B. *Eastern Orthodox Christianity: A Western Perspective*. Grand Rapids: Baker Academic, 2003.

Clines, D. J. A. "The Image of God in Man." *Tyndale Bulletin* 19 (1968): 53–103.

Colish, Marcia L. *The Stoic Tradition from Antiquity to the Early Middle Ages*. 2nd ed. Vol. 2. Leiden, The Netherlands: Brill, 1990.

Collins, Kenneth J. *The Theology of John Wesley: Holy Love and the Shape of Grace*. Nashville: Abingdon, 2007.

Critchley, Simon. *The Ethics of Deconstruction: Derrida and Levinas*. 2nd ed. Edinburgh: Edinburgh University Press, 1999.

Critchley, Simon, and Robert Bernasconi, eds. *The Cambridge Companion to Levinas*. Cambridge: Cambridge University Press, 2002.

Deeken, Alfons. *Process and Permanence in Ethics: Max Scheler's Moral Philosophy*. New York: Paulist Press, 1974.

Dooyeweerd, Herman. *A New Critique of Theoretical Thought*, translated by David H. Freeman, William S. Young, and H. De Jongste. Vols. 1–2. Jordan Station, Ontario: Paideia Press, 1984.

Douma, Jochem. *The Ten Commandments: Manual for the Christian Life*. Phillipsburg, NJ: P&R Publishing, 1996.

————. *Grondslagen christelijke ethiek*. Kampen, The Netherlands: Kok, 1999.

————. *Verantwoord handelen*. Kampen, The Netherlands: Kok, 2007.

Drummond, John J. and Lester E. Embree, eds. *Phenomenological Approaches to Moral Philosophy: A Handbook*. Dordrecht, The Netherlands: Kluwer Academic Publishers, 2002.

Fedler, Kyle D. *Exploring Christian Ethics: Biblical Foundations for Morality*. Louisville: Westminster John Knox, 2006.

Fee, Gordon D. *God's Empowering Presence: The Holy Spirit in the Letters of Paul*. Peabody, MA: Hendrickson, 1994.

Fensch, Thomas. *Oskar Schindler and His List*. Forest Dale, VT: Paul S. Eriksson, 1995.

Fischer, Johannes. *Theologische Ethik: Grundwissen und Orientierung*. Stuttgart: Kohlhammer, 2002.

Fletcher, Joseph. *Situation Ethics: The New Morality*. Philadelphia: Westminster Press, 1966.

————. *Situation Ethics: The New Morality*, 2nd ed. Louisville: Westminster John Knox, 1997.

————. "Three Approaches." In *From Christ to the World: Introductory Readings in Christian Ethics*, edited by Wayne G. Boulton, Thomas D. Kennedy, and Allen Verhey. Grand Rapids: Eerdmans, 1994.

Floor, L. *Jakobus: brief van een broeder*. Kampen, The Netherlands: Centraal Boekhuis, 1992.

Foucault, Michel. *The Order of Things: An Archaeology of the Human Sciences*. 2nd ed. London: Routledge, 2002.

————. *Power/Knowledge: Selected Interviews and Other Writings, 1972–1977*, edited by Colin Gordon, translated by Colin Gordon, Leo Marshall, John Mepham, and Kate Soper. New York: Pantheon Books, 1980.

Fuchs, Erich. *Comment faire pour bien faire? Introduction à l'éthique*. Geneva: Labor et Fides, 1996.

————. "Calvin, Jean: La philosophie morale de Calvin et le calvinisme." In vol. 1 of *Dictionnaire d'éthique et de philosophie morale,* 4th ed., edited by Monique Canto-Sperber,, 230. Paris: Presses Universitaire de France, Quadrige, 2004.

Fukuyama, Francis. *The End of History and the Last Man*. New York: Free Press, 1992.

————. *Our Posthuman Future: Consequences of the Biotechnology Revolution*. New York: Farrar, Straus and Giroux, 2002.

Fuller, Reginald H. "The Decalogue in the New Testament." *Interpretation* 43, no. 3 (1989): 243–255.

Geisler, Norman L. *Christian Ethics*. Grand Rapids: Baker, 1989.

Gerwen, Jef Van, Johan Verstraeten, and Luc Van Liedekerke. *Business en ethiek: spelregels voor het ethisch ondernemen*. Tielt, Belgium: Lannoo, 2002.

Gladwin, J. W. "Conscience." Pages 251–52 in *New Dictionary of Christian Ethics and Pastoral Theology*, edited by David John Atkinson, David Field, Arthur Frank Holmes, and Oliver O'Donovan. Downers Grove, IL: InterVarsity Press, 1995.

Glover, Jonathan. *Humanity: A Moral History of the Twentieth Century*. London: J. Cape, 1999.

Grabill, Stephen J. *Rediscovering the Natural Law in Reformed Theological Ethics*. Grand Rapids: Eerdmans, 2006.

Grenz, Stanley J., and John R. Franke. *Beyond Foundationalism: Shaping Theology in a Postmodern Context.* Louisville: Westminster John Knox, 2001.

————. *The Moral Quest: Foundations of Christian Ethics.* Downers Grove, IL: InterVarsity Press, 1997.

————. *The Social God and the Relational Self: A Trinitarian Theology of the Imago Dei.* Louisville: Westminster John Knox, 2001.

Guroian, Vigen. *Incarnate Love: Essays in Orthodox Ethics.* 2nd ed. Notre Dame: University of Notre Dame Press, 2002.

Gustafson, James. "Context vs. Principle: A Misplaced Debate in Christian Ethics." *Harvard Theological Review* 58 (1965): 171–202.

Halman, Loek, Ruud Luijkx, and Marga van Zundert. *Atlas of European Values.* Leiden, The Netherlands: Brill, 2005.

Harakas, Stanley Samuel. *Toward a Transfigured Life: The Theoria of Eastern Orthodox Ethics.* Minneapolis: Light & Life, 1983.

Hardin, Garrett. "Lifeboat Ethics: The Case against Helping the Poor." *Psychology Today* 8, no. 4. (1974): 38–43.

Häring, Bernard. *Das Heilige und das Gute.* Krailling vor München: Erich Wewel Verlag, 1950.

Hartmann, Nicolai. *Ethics.* 3 vols. Library of Conservative Thought. New Brunswick, NJ: Transaction Publishers, 2003.

Hauerwas, Stanley. *A Community of Character: Toward a Constructive Christian Social Ethic.* Notre Dame: University of Notre Dame Press, 1981.

Hauerwas, Stanley, and Samuel Wells, eds. *The Blackwell Companion to Christian Ethics.* Malden, MA: Blackwell, 2004.

Hays, Richard B. *The Moral Vision of the New Testament: A Contemporary Introduction to New Testament Ethics.* San Francisco: HarperSanFrancisco, 1996.

Henry, Carl F. H. *Christian Personal Ethics.* Grand Rapids: Eerdmans, 1957.

Hesselink, John. *Calvin's Concept of the Law.* Allison Park, PA: Pickwick Publications, 1992.

Hill, Thomas E. *The Blackwell Guide to Kant's Ethics.* Malden, MA: Wiley-Blackwell, 2009.

Hollinger, Dennis P. *Choosing the Good: Christian Ethics in a Complex World.* Grand Rapids: Baker Academic, 2002.

Huntemann, Georg. *The Other Bonhoeffer: An Evangelical Reassessment of Dietrich Bonhoeffer*, translated by Todd Huizinga. Grand Rapids: Baker, 1993.

Ignatius. *The Epistle of Ignatius to the Ephesians.* In *Ante-Nicene Fathers,* edited by Philip Schaff. Vol. 1, *The Apostolic Fathers with Justin Martyr and Irenaeus,* edited by Alexander Roberts and James Donaldson. Christian Classics Ethereal Library. http://www.ccel.org/ccel/schaff/anf01.v.ii.xiv.html.

Jochemsen, Henk, and Gerrit Glas. *Verantwoord medisch handelen.* Amsterdam: Buijten & Schipperheijn, 1997.

Johnson, J.F. "Adiaphora, Adiaphorists." In *Evangelical Dictionary of Theology,* 2nd ed, edited by Walter A. Elwell. Grand Rapids: Baker Academic, 2001.

Jonas, Hans. *Das Prinzip Verantwortung, Versuch einer Ethik für die technolgische Zivilisation.* Frankfurt: Insel, 1979.

————. *The Imperative of Responsibility.* Chicago: University of Chicago Press, 1984.

————. *The Phenomenon of Life.* Evanston: Northwestern University Press, 2001.

Kant, Immanuel. *Religion within the Limits of Reason Alone.* Chicago: Open Court, 1934.

———. *Religion within the Boundaries of Mere Reason*, edited by Allen Wood and George Di Giovanni, translated by Allen Wood. Cambridge: Cambridge University Press, 1999.

———. "On a Supposed Right to Lie Because of Philanthropic Concerns." Translated by James Wesley Ellington. In *Ethical Philosophy: Grounding for the Metaphysics of Morals and Metaphysical Principles of Virtue*. Indianapolis: Hackett Publishing, 1995.

———. *Critique of Practical Reason*, edited by Mary Gregor. Cambridge: Cambridge University Press, 1997.

———. *Groundwork for the Metaphysics of Morals*, edited by Thomas E. Hill Jr. and Arnulf Zweig, translated by Arnulf Zweig. Oxford: Oxford University Press, 2002.

Korsgaard, Christine M. "The Right to Lie: Kant on Dealing with Evil." Pages 212–31 in *Deontology*, edited by Stephen L. Darwall. Malden, MA: Blackwell, 2003.

Kuhn, Thomas S. *The Structure of Scientific Revolutions*. 2nd ed. Chicago: University of Chicago Press, 1970.

Kupczak, Jaroslaw. *Destined for Liberty: The Human Person in the Philosophy of Karol Wojtyla/John Paul II*. Washington, D.C.: Catholic University of America Press, 2000.

Levinas, Emmanuel. *Totality and Infinity: An Essay on Exteriority*, translated by Alphonso Lingis. Pittsburgh: Duquesne University Press, 1969.

———. *Otherwise Than Being, or Beyond Essence*, translated by Alphonso Lingis. The Hague: Martinus Nijhoff, 1981.

———. "Is Ontology Fundamental?" Pages 1–10 in *Emmanuel Levinas: Basic Philosophical Writings,* edited by Adriaan T. Peperzak, Simon Critchley, and Robert Bernasconi. Bloomington and Indianapolis: Indiana University Press, 1996.

MacIntyre, Alasdair C. *A Short History of Ethics: A History of Moral Philosophy from the Homeric Age to the Twentieth Century*. London: Routledge, 1998.

Maddox, Randy L. *Responsible Grace: John Wesley's Practical Theology*. Nashville: Kingswood Books, 1994.

Mardas, Nancy, George McLean, and Agnes B. Curry, eds. *Karol Wojtyla's Philosophical Legacy*. Washington, D.C.: Council for Research in Values and Philosophy, 2008.

McClendon, James William. *Systematic Theology Vol. 1: Ethics*. Nashville: Abingdon, 1986.

———. *Systematic Theology 1*, 2nd ed. Nashville: Abingdon, 2002.

Michener, Ronald T. *Engaging Deconstructive Theology*. Aldershot, UK: Ashgate, 2007.

———. "Kingdom of God and Postmodern Thought: Friends or Foes?" *Perichoresis* 6, no. 2 (2008): 219–239.

Miller, Patrick D. "The Place of the Decalogue in the Old Testament," *Interpretation* 43, no. 3 (1989): 229–242.

———. *The Way of the Lord: Essays in Old Testament Theology*. Grand Rapids: Eerdmans, 2007.

Moreland, J. P., and William Lane Craig. *Philosophical Foundations for a Christian Worldview*. Downers Grove, IL: InterVarsity Press, 2003.

Mounier, Emmanuel. *Personalism*. Notre Dame: University of Notre Dame Press, 1970.

Mouw, Richard J. "Alasdair MacIntyre on Reformation Ethics." *Journal of Religious Ethics* 13, no. 2 (1985): 243–258.

———. *The God Who Commands: A Study in Divine Command Ethics*. Notre Dame: University of Notre Dame Press, 1990.

Murray, John. *Principles of Conduct*. 2nd ed. Grand Rapids: Eerdmans, 1991.

Newlands, G. M. *Christ and Human Rights: The Transformative Engagement*. Aldershot, UK: Ashgate, 2006.

Nielsen, Kai. "God and the Basis of Morality." *Journal of Religious Ethics* 10, no. 2 (1982): 335–351.

Nietzsche, Friedrich Wilhelm. *The Will to Power: An Attempted Transvaluation of All Values*. New York: Gordon Press, 1974.

———. *On the Genealogy of Morals*. Arlington, VA: Richer Resources Publications, 2008.

Nullens, Patrick. "Leven volgens Gaia's normen?: de verhouding tussen God, mens en aarde en de implicaties voor ecologische ethiek." Ph.D. diss., Evangelische Theologische Faculteit, Leuven, Belgium, 1995.

O'Donovan, Oliver. *Resurrection and Moral Order: An Outline for Evangelical Ethics*. 2nd ed. Grand Rapids: Eerdmans, 1994.

Olthuis, James H. "Face-to-Face: Ethical Asymmetry or the Symmetry of Mutuality?" Pages 135–56 in *The Hermeneutics of Charity*, edited by James K. A. Smith and Henry Isaac Venema. Grand Rapids: Brazos, 2004.

Bahya ben Joseph ibn Pakuda. *Duties of the Heart*, translated by Yaakov Feldman. Northvale, NJ: Jason Aronson, 1996.

Pannenberg, Wolfhart. *Anthropology in Theological Perspective*, translated by Matthew J. O'Connell. London: Continuum, 2004.

Philo. *De Decalogo*, translated by F. H. Colson. In *Philo: In Ten Volumes (and Two Supplementary Volumes)*, edited by E. Capps, T. E. Page, and W. H. D. Rouse. 12 vols. Cambridge, MA: Harvard University Press, 1929.

Plato. "Euthyphro: Piety and Impiety." In vol. 3 of *The Works of Plato*, translated by B. Jowett. New York: Tudor Publishing, n.d.

Porter, Jean. "Virtue Ethics." In *The Cambridge Companion to Christian Ethics*, edited by Robin Gill, 96–111. New York: Cambridge University Press, 2001.

Postman, Neil. *Amusing Ourselves to Death*. New York: Viking Penguin, 1986.

Rae, Scott B. *Moral Choices: An Introduction to Ethics*. Grand Rapids: Zondervan, 2000.

Rae, Scott B., and Kenman L. Wong, eds. *Beyond Integrity: A Judeo-Christian Approach to Business Ethics*. Grand Rapids: Zondervan, 2004.

Rasmussen, Larry. "The Ethics of Responsible Action." Pages 206–25 in *The Cambridge Companion to Dietrich Bonhoeffer*, edited by John W. de Gruchy. Cambridge: Cambridge University Press, 1999.

Reuschling, Wendy Corbin. *Reviving Evangelical Ethics: The Promises and Pitfalls of Classic Models of Morality*. Grand Rapids: Brazos, 2008.

Rorty, Richard. "Human Rights, Rationality and Sentimentality." Pages 111–34 in *On Human Rights: The Oxford Amnesty Lectures*, edited by Stephen Shute and S. L. Hurley. New York: Basic Books, 1993.

Rothuizen, G. Th. *Wat is ethiek?* Kampen, The Netherlands: Kok, 1973.

Runyon, Theodore. *The New Creation: John Wesley's Theology Today*. Nashville: Abingdon, 1998.

Sayre, Patricia A. "Personalism." In *A Companion to Philosophy of Religion*, edited by Philip L. Quinn and Charles Taliaferro, 129–135. Cambridge, MA: Blackwell, 1999.

Scheler, Max. *On the Eternal in Man*. Hamden, CT: Archon Books, 1972.

———. *Formalism in Ethics and Non-Formal Ethics of Values: A New Attempt toward the Foundation of an Ethical Personalism*. Evanston, IL: Northwestern University Press, 1973.

———. "Ordo Amoris." In *Selected Philosophical Essays*, edited and translated by David R. Lachterman, 98–135. Northwestern University Studies in Phenomenology and Existential Philosophy. Evanston, IL: Northwestern University Press, 1973.

Schroeder, William R. "Continental Ethics." Pages 375–99 in *The Blackwell Guide to Ethical Theory*, edited by Hugh LaFollette. Malden, MA: Blackwell, 2000.

Schweid, Eleizer. "The Authority Principle in Biblical Morality." *Journal of Religious Ethics* 8, no. 2 (1980): 180–203.

Schweiker, William, ed. *The Blackwell Companion to Religious Ethics*. Malden, MA: Blackwell, 2005.

Smith, James K. A. *The Fall of Interpretation: Philosophical Foundations for a Creational Hermeneutic*. Downers Grove, IL: InterVarsity Press, 2000.

———. *Who's Afraid of Postmodernism? Taking Derrida, Lyotard, and Foucault to Church*. Grand Rapids: Baker Academic, 2006

Shildrik, Margrit, and Roxanne Mykitiuk, eds. *Ethics of the Body: Postconventional Challenges*. Cambridge, MA, and London: MIT Press, 2005.

Spader, Peter H. *Scheler's Ethical Personalism: Its Logic, Development, and Promise*. Perspectives in Continental Philosophy 25. New York: Fordham University Press, 2002.

Spicq, Ceslas. *Théologie morale du Nouveau Testament*. Paris: Lecoffre, 1965.

Stassen, Glen H., and David P. Gushee. *Kingdom Ethics: Following Jesus in Contemporary Context*. Downers Grove, IL: InterVarsity Press, 2003.

Taylor, Charles. *Sources of the Self: The Making of the Modern Identity*. Cambridge, MA: Harvard University Press, 1989.

Thielicke, Helmut, *Theological Ethics*. Grand Rapids: Eerdmans, 1979.

Thorsen, Donald A. D. *The Wesleyan Quadrilateral: Scripture, Tradition, Reason and Experience as a Model of Evangelical Theology*. Grand Rapids: Zondervan, 1990.

Tiessen, Terrance L. "Toward a Hermeneutic for Discerning Universal Moral Absolutes." *Journal of the Evangelical Theological Society* 36, no. 2 (June 1993): 189–207.

Todt, Heinz Eduard, Ernst-Albert Scharffenorth, and Glen Harold Stassen. *Authentic Faith: Bonhoeffer's Theological Ethics in Context*. Grand Rapids: Eerdmans, 2007.

Torrell, Jean Pierre. "Thomas d'Aquin: La philosophie morale de Thomas d'Aquin." In vol. 2 of *Dictionnaire d'éthique et de philosophie morale*, 4th ed., edited by Monique Canto-Sperber, 1947–54. Paris: Presses Universitaire de France, Quadrige, 2004.

Treier, Daniel J. *Virtue and the Voice of God: Towards Theology as Wisdom*. Grand Rapids: Eerdmans, 2006.

Vanhoozer, Kevin J. *First Theology: God, Scripture and Hermeneutics*. Downers Grove, IL: InterVarsity Press, 2002.

Velema, W. H. *Oriëntatie in de Christelijke Ethiek*. The Hague: Boekencentrum, 1990.

Verhey, Allen. *Remembering Jesus: Christian Community, Scripture, and the Moral Life*. Grand Rapids: Eerdmans, 2005.

Volf, Miroslav. *Exclusion and Embrace: A Theological Exploration of Identity, Otherness, and Reconciliation*. Nashville: Abingdon, 1996.

von Hildebrand, Dietrich. *Christian Ethics*. New York: D. McKay, 1953.

Wiker, Benjamin. *Moral Darwinism*. Downers Grove, IL: InterVarsity Press, 2002.

Willis, Robert E. *The Ethics of Karl Barth*. Leiden, The Netherlands: Brill, 1971.

Wolterstorff, Nicholas. *Justice: Rights and Wrongs*. Princeton: Princeton University Press, 2008.

Woodward, P. A. *The Doctrine of Double Effect*. Notre Dame: University of Notre Dame Press, 2001.

Wright, Christopher J. H. *Walking in the Ways of the Lord: The Ethical Authority of the Old Testament*. Leicester: Apollos, 1995.

———. *Old Testament Ethics for the People of God*. Downers Grove, IL: InterVarsity Press, 2004.

Yoder, John Howard. *The Politics of Jesus: Vicit Agnus Noster*. 2nd ed. Grand Rapids: Eerdmans, 1994.

Subject Index

Scripture Index